Tales Out of School

Tales Out of School

*Joseph Fernandez's
Crusade to Rescue
American Education*

Joseph A. Fernandez
with John Underwood

LITTLE, BROWN AND COMPANY
BOSTON   TORONTO   LONDON

3-94

First Edition

Library of Congress Cataloging-in-Publication Data

Fernandez, Joseph A.
    Tales out of school : Joseph Fernandez's crusade to rescue American
education / Joseph A. Fernandez with John Underwood.—1st ed.
        p.   cm.
    Includes index.
    ISBN 0-316-27918-8
    1. Education—United States—Aims and objectives. 2. Public
schools—United States. 3. Educational change—United States.
4. Fernandez, Joseph A. I. Underwood, John. II. Title.
LA217.2.F47   1993
370'.973—dc20   92-28731

10 9 8 7 6 5 4 3 2 1

MV-NY

*Published simultaneously in Canada
by Little, Brown & Company (Canada) Limited*

Printed in the United States of America

For all those teachers, parents
and school administrators who share
the dream and the vision . . .

And for Lily

Acknowledgments

IT WOULD BE AN EXERCISE in futility for the authors to try to name everyone who has lent a hand in the gathering of thoughts and information for this book, or to point out all those very special people who had an impact on the subject as he made his way to recognition as an educator. Many appear in the text anyway, and they already know how much they mean to both of us. By the same token, it would be a sure sign of ingratitude if we didn't risk naming a few who helped make a difference in the two main theaters of operations covered in the text: in Miami, those soldiers of the system who contributed so much to change — Angie Welty, Connie Kostyra, Barry Craig, Pat Tornillo, Joe Tekerman, Russ Wheatley, Gerry Dreyfuss, Tom Cerra, Frank Petruizello, Jim Fleming, Alex Bromir, Gavin O'Brien, and Tom Young; and the school board members who championed the cause — Holmes Braddock, Bill Turner, Mickey Krop, Bob Renick, Janet McAliley, and Betsy Kaplan. And in New York: Stan Litow, Robert Wagner, Jr., Mayor David Dinkins, Governor Mario Cuomo, Sandra Feldman, Jim Vlasto, Joe Saccente, Burt Sacks, Felix Rohatyn, Reuben Mark, Charlie Hughes, Askia Davis, Iggy Leung, Dick Beattie, Robin Wilner, Lynne Savage, Jill Blair, and Doris Gonzalez-Light. Please attach no significance to the order they are named. None was intended.

—Joseph Fernandez and John Underwood

Tales Out of School

PART I

YOU NEED TO KNOW three things if you want to make any sense whatsoever out of the mess of education in America. To do something about it, which is in my department, you need to know a lot more, but it helps to start with three things:

1. The vast majority of those who call for change really mean that what they'd like is for schools to be the way they were when *they* were in school, when a "crisis in discipline" meant an epidemic of speaking out of turn, and when teachers complained about "substance abuse" they were talking about bubble gum. Forget that image. The schools we so fondly remember can be found now only in books. They cannot be brought back any more than you can put smoke back into a cigar.

2. By all rights, education should be an easy sell because you never find anyone who is "against" it. No advocacy groups clamor for its overthrow, no politicians or columnists protest its irrelevance. Unlike nuclear power, or abortion rights, or the graduated income tax, education has no enemies. The trouble, therefore, can only be with those who are "for" it. In education, I've found, you can easily mistake the actions of those who are for it as being against it.

3. There isn't anything wrong with the schools of America that can't be cured. There is certainly a lot wrong, but none of it is terminal, and most of it comes from external influences. When Leona the high school graduate can't find Texas on a map, and Leon the college basketball star reads at the third-grade level and wouldn't know the square root of nine from a six-pack of beer, everybody says the schools

have failed. The schools haven't failed. We've failed the schools. But we can also save them. There are ways.

As those points pretty much set the table for what follows — the events and discoveries, and inevitable controversies, of what now seems like several lifetimes in the combat zones of education — it might be good to expand on them a little before going further, beginning with the problem we have accepting the fact that our schools can never again be what they were (Point 1). That they are no longer sanctuaries from the "real" world (I doubt they ever were) but now more than ever reflect the hard realities of the communities that surround them.

How hard are the realities? This hard:

The California Department of Education compared the complaints of its teachers in the 1940s with those through the '80s. In the '40s, the "major" offenses in California schools were, in order: (1) talking, (2) chewing gum, (3) making noise, (4) running in the halls, (5) getting out of turn in line, (6) wearing improper clothes, and (7) not putting refuse in the wastebaskets.

And today: (1) drug abuse, (2) alcohol abuse, (3) pregnancy, (4) suicide, (5) rape, (6) robbery, (7) assault, (8) burglary, (9) arson, (10) bombings, (11) murder, (12) absenteeism, (13) vandalism, (14) extortion, (15) gang warfare, (16) abortion, and (17) venereal disease.

The worst-case scenario has been a way of life now for decades: school yards ravaged by violence and drugs, and sometimes by deadly gunfire. Teachers disillusioned and dispirited, and sometimes emotionally and physically scarred, getting out at the first opportunity. Students so tuned out to traditional constraints that no taboo is too sacred to violate. A recent survey of one inner-city high school in Chicago revealed that one-third — *one out of three* — of its female students were pregnant.

Only a fool could mistake the implications. Society's failings not only affect but *infect* our schools. In heartfelt efforts to do something about it, we have overwhelmed our classrooms with sociological indoctrination. The scholastic consequences have been disastrous. You wonder about low achievement figures and abysmal test scores? You wonder why administrators like me push for a longer school day and a longer school year? That's one reason: the growing burden on teachers and principals to get everything in.

With traditional core studies squeezed from all sides, school curricula now run the gamut from safe driving to safe sex. Teachers unravel the mysteries of everything from "race relations" and "conflict resolution" to table manners. California started "relaxation" therapy during class hours for stressed-out elementary schoolers some time ago and other states followed suit, even including courses in yoga. President Bush was right when he said that we expect our teachers to be social workers, psychologists, and family counselors. We expect too much.

A friend of mine was talking with a second-grade teacher at an urban school in the East. The teacher had been on the job for twenty-three years, she said, and every year it seemed she had to deal with new mandates for "health" and "social" instruction. My friend asked her how much actual meat-and-potatoes academics she thought she was giving her students (the kinds of basics that, when neglected, make for all those shocking test scores).

"About five hours," she said.

"That's not so bad," my friend said. "Five hours a day should be more than enough."

"No, not five hours a day," replied the teacher. "Five hours a *week*."

"How can that be?" he asked.

"Listen," said the teacher, "before we can educate 'em, we have to domesticate 'em."

An exaggeration? I wouldn't be so sure.

Understand that I'm not saying our schools should retreat from these issues. To the contrary. Once that door was opened, it could never be closed again. We *have* to take them on. Society demands it. The schools may be the only place left where they'll get a proper airing, in a context that will do the most good.

But the therapy doesn't come without cost or consequence. In Miami we had to put together a program on gun awareness for elementary school kids. There had been a series of tragic accidents — little kids finding guns in the house, being curious, getting killed. There had also been the *un*accidental killings, altogether enough to make us see the need in a gun-obsessed society for some strong indoctrination on the ultimate peril of firearms.

What does "put together a program" mean? It means that people have to be trained. It means developing a curriculum (nobody writes one for nothing). It means doing research on it, then evaluating it, then implementing it. All that costs. And wherever you put in something new, something else gets nudged aside. The school day is locked in. If you order a "gun awareness" program for kindergarten through sixth grade, something has to go. But what?

Well, you can't take out the "substance abuse" programs, because you've got to instruct kids early on the horrors of drug use. You can't drop "sex education" classes, or the other "safety" programs, or any of the aids to social adjustment. Those things have to be taught early. So what goes? Pieces of this go. Bits of that. Some geography. Maybe some history. Some science.

And when the consequences result, you get bashed from the other side. "Our kids can't name the seven seas! Our kids never heard of Waterloo!" It's true. They can't and haven't. But you have to make a determination: is it more important to know about Napoleon, or to be prepared to get through the sociological mine fields we now call "childhood" in America? Because in far too many cases, we simply can't teach them both.

Talk to any elementary school teachers or administrators today and they'll tell you that their curriculum is so cluttered they can't possibly make it do all that is required of it. And it's not that the cluttering items aren't important. That's not the argument. They're very important.

But it's time we recognized such burdens (among all the other burdens) for what they are, and how they contribute to the widespread failure to understand what really happened to our schools, and why *all* "alien" influences must be addressed. I have taken a lot of heat in New York City since late 1991 when we introduced a "condom availability" plan in response to the AIDS plague and its deadly effect on our teenagers. After conferring with health and social agencies, and much soul searching, we announced our intention to make condoms available to high school students — and unleashed a fire storm of protest. The charge was made that we no longer taught "values and morals" in the public schools (because of church-state prohibitions), but instead had opted for a policy of amoral accommodation.

Which, incidentally, was nonsense. Schools *can* teach character issues — and they should, and they do. I don't know of any public school system in the country that doesn't have a strong values-clarification curriculum, whether it's rooted in religious teachings or not. Our socio-family programs preach abstinence when it comes to teenage sex and celibacy before marriage.

The schools have been dealing with those issues since the 1950s. Where had these people been? More important, where were their eyes and hearts? In New York, at this pivotal moment in time, we are faced with some frightening realities: that as many as 80 percent of our teenagers are sexually active and that 10 percent of the nation's full-blown AIDS cases reported among adolescents live in New York City. We acted on that basis. A life-or-death matter.

But the larger issue was missed again, as it is missed almost every time. The teaching of values isn't the problem. The problem is poverty. The problem is dysfunctional families. The problem is drugs, and crime, and violence, and truancy, and broken dreams, and hopelessness, and despair. The problem is that two-thirds of the black children of America are born out of wedlock and that more than half grow up with only one parent, often below poverty level, and in an environment ravaged by crime and drugs. The problem is that the ills and sins of the society are visited on the schools of America. My first year as chancellor of the New York City school system, some three thousand crack babies were among our sixty thousand kindergartners.

If we expect to provide the answers for the salvation of our grieving schools under such duress, we must wake up to their agony and throw the full weight of all our genius and resources into their deliverance.

Point 2, however, would argue that the leadership we have counted on for this reclamation has been more a liability than an asset, that the real enemies of education are those who are "for" it — and who in many cases make their living from it.

A full decade after the grim evaluations in *A Nation at Risk*, produced by a commission created by then Secretary of Education Terrel Bell, we are still paralyzed by our inability to prioritize the need. This failure to act is as bewildering as it is tragic. If you were to ask me how we could justify having spent the nation into huge deficits without fixing our schools, I'd say it simply makes no sense and is impossible to justify. If you were to ask me how we could have slipped so far academically without having a national emergency declared and acted on with something more salutary than encouraging words or more tangible than the fiscal equivalent of Band-Aids, I'd say it was time to quit examining the patient and start reevaluating the doctors.

The federal government is "for" education. We are told that all the time. President Bush, a caring man, declared himself the "education President" and pushed a package of national goals to be reached by the year 2000. They are goals worth shooting for — campuses rid of drugs and violence, a high school graduation rate of 90 percent, learning acceleration that would restore us to first place in the world in science and mathematics, illiteracy eliminated in the adult population, and so forth.

But it won't happen. It won't happen unless we commit to making war on the problems of the schools the way we made war on Iraq. It won't happen until we commit to bailing out our schools the way we committed to bailing out the profligate savings and loan industry. That kind of commitment is not even in the talking stages.

I was in Washington for a meeting of the Council of Great City Schools, one of those active, enlightened organizations whose efforts are inspiring reform even as they go unnoticed in the press. The main speaker at lunch at the L'Enfant Plaza Hotel was an undersecretary of education, Ted Sanders, who was there to reaffirm the administration's loyalty to the cause.

When he opened up the floor for questions, I asked Mr. Sanders how much the federal government was spending on education for the year. I already knew the answer, but I wanted to hear him say it.

"Eight billion dollars," he said.

I asked how much the distinguished new secretary of education, Lamar Alexander, had requested for the 1992 budget.

"Nine billion."

Nine billion dollars. A lot of money — until you realize how far it has to stretch (to the *eighty-four thousand* public schools, K-through-12, in America) and that the federal budget is $1.45 *trillion*.

In other words, the administration was allocating *less than one percent* of the taxpayers' money to their embattled schools. What does that tell us about priorities? The Persian Gulf war cost the United States an estimated $45 billion, not counting the parades. The price tag for resolving the savings and loan debacle will surpass $160 billion. The Pentagon's proposed budget for 1992 was $290 billion — or about thirty times what was to be spent on schools.

And at this writing the Russian leadership, trying to hold together its newly minted democracy, is rattling the cup for a massive infusion of dollars and trade credits. And a huge relief fund is being considered for the newly independent Baltic states. And Israel wants $10 billion in loan guarantees for the resettlement of Soviet Jews. And on and on and on, ad nauseam.

The question is as obvious as its answer: is the good health of its schools as important to the United States as the independence of Kuwait or the economy of the "new" Russia? Of course it is. Who, in fact, would dare argue otherwise? Yet when it comes to funding and enacting the necessary legislation that would open avenues for bold new programs and incentives, the same kind of commitment doesn't apply. You don't have to be for or against any of these expenditures to see the irony and appreciate the inconsistency.

State and local governments, through property and sales taxes, have always supplied the bulk of school funding, of course, and I'm not proposing we change that. But one percent of the federal budget for education is not just tightfisted and shortsighted to the extreme, it's downright cynical. Imagine what it would mean to divert just one percent more — from so many dubious causes and back from so many other shores — to the needs of our children. Imagine what a budgetary boost that would mean: *double* what our schools are getting now.

Educators agree that the key to saving all those "at-risk" kids in all those inner-city wastelands is to get to them early, as preschoolers, with programs that will nurture them physically, socially, and mentally. The federally funded Head Start program, which allows for some poor kids who would traditionally start in kindergartens at age five to start at age three or four, was initiated to help in this way.

President Bush set as one of his goals that every child will come to school "healthy and ready to learn." That means getting them into school early, giving them breakfast, giving them lunch. We do that in New York. The only reason we don't give them dinner is we're not open that late. I think we should be, but we're not. Nonetheless, for five days a week, they're in school, getting two nutritious meals a day, getting their inoculations, getting profiles done for special needs, and the like. It sounds good, and it is. To a point.

But the hard truth is that we're still way short of the mark. America spends the least of any industrialized country in the world on our prekindergarten and kindergarten children. We spend less than France, less than Germany, less than Japan, less than Italy, less than England, less than all of them.

In 1991, only 40 percent of the three- to five-year-olds from lower-income families were enrolled in preschool in America. That's unconscionable. In New York, we represent 70 percent of all the poor kids in the state, but only 43 percent of our at-risk kids are in preschool programs. Head Start, for all its good intentions, reaches only a quarter of the children who are qualified for it. That's unconscionable, too.

And yet, from political left to political right, you hear the same tired cliché whenever the subject of additional funding rears its head: "I'm the education President, but the solution for our schools isn't to pump a lot of money into the system."

Well, what *is* the solution? Could Congress have rescued the S & Ls without money? Could George Bush have conducted the war against

Iraq without money? If money isn't a major ingredient in the solution for our schools, what is?

"Choice" isn't the solution. That's the buzzword out of Washington these days: give parents the right to choose which school their kids attend, the idea being that if you make schools more competitive, the competition will make them better. I'm not totally opposed to that. In fact, as you'll see, I'm in favor of trying almost anything to turn our schools around. There are some great ideas out there.

But I wonder how far we'd have gotten trying to push "schools of choice" in the '60s and '70s without being called segregationist? Or even racist? Because I *am* opposed to choice if it means more of the same shrunken horizons for inner-city kids, and that's the way it usually works. The people who take advantage of choice are not the ones who need it most. In Miami or New York or anywhere else, parents who have the wherewithal will avail themselves of "choosing." Parents who don't, won't. If they're faced with finding transportation (and paying for it) to get their kids out of the ghetto school in Harlem to a better school in Queens, nine times out of ten they'll stay in Harlem.

I'm opposed to choice, too, when it means treating public schools as the schools of last resort. The plan usually calls for allowing tax dollars, in the form of tuition vouchers, to follow students even to parochial and private schools. On the surface that seems fair enough — giving parents an option as to where their school tax money will be spent.

But it is *not* fair. Private and parochial schools don't have to take the same kids we do, which is one reason why their academic performance is said to surpass that of the public schools. They can screen out — or kick out — the low-achiever, or the misfit, or the socially or religiously "inappropriate," or even the physically or mentally impaired: the many "special education" children who require extraordinary expenditures.

In short, they can be selective, and that amounts to selective flight when choice becomes a reality. And for that reason I'm against it. Especially when it means using our public school dollars to fund it. They're dollars we can't afford to lose.

And what happens to the schools (and the children) that are left behind when flight takes over? The kids who have given them real diversity are gone, and they are left to die on the vine of a dwindling enrollment. Which, of course, is the underlying motive: to put "bad" schools out of business. Some schools may well need to be closed down, but that's hardly practical as a policy when we're already in a national crisis over classroom space and under constant pressure for construction funding. No, we shouldn't be closing schools, we should be *improving* schools.

Revealingly enough, for all the damage it could do, the government's investment in "choice" would factor out to little more than a token. I suspect that's one reason it gets so much encouragement from politicians — a high-profile change with little federal money involved. The plan basically calls for the states to underwrite it, with the feds providing various incentives but chipping in only $230 million. As *Time* magazine noted, you couldn't buy a baseball franchise in the National League these days for that little.

In June 1992, Whittle Communications, with great national fanfare, announced a plan to build a thousand private "schools for profit" across the country. Choice with a capitalistic twist. Whittle called it the Edison Project and predicted that once the idea took off, an explosion of construction would lead to a huge network of like schools to challenge the public school system — and return 15 percent to investors. Individual tuition would be set at $5,500 per pupil, but scholarships would be available for inner-city youth and costs would be defrayed by having parents do "volunteer" work and students perform janitorial services.

Whittle was said to be putting $2.6 billion into the project. Benno C. Schmidt, Jr., a renowned fund-raiser, resigned as president of Yale University to head it up. I applauded the effort, as I would any attempt to create new educational opportunities, and said that I would lead the cheers if the thousand schools got built, did well, and made lots of money for their investors.

But there are several key questions to ask about such a plan, including what the paying customers (the parents and their children) might have to say about being required to do grunt work so that shareholders could maximize their profits. I'm very much for getting parents and kids involved in helping their schools, but not as slave labor. The most obvious question public school advocates would have, however, is the one that asks how Whittle will manage when it discovers that $5,500 per pupil will not even come close to covering the expense for building, equipping, and operating a modern education center, much less make up the difference in revenues lost when scholarships are handed out.

The obvious answer is the one to fear most about privatizing a school system: that what Whittle expects is for the voucher plan to kick in, allowing parents to divert tax dollars to those schools. Which means that not only would public schools suffer but their tax dollars would be used to make money for private investors. Capitalism run amok. And in the end just one more scheme to use "choice" as a weapon against the public school system.

Which makes the Whittle plan no more a solution for American education than the so-called "beacon" schools the Department of Education plans to earmark for special private financial assistance (i.e., no federal money) in each congressional district. To make a grand display of what would happen when a school is given a transfusion of resources from all sides is to prove only what we already know. The school would get better. No mystery to it.

The real question is, what will happen to the thousands of schools that *don't* get that special treatment? That answer is also clear: they'll continue to suffer.

No, the solution isn't "choice," or closing bad schools, or spotting a few "beacon" schools around the country to remind us of our shortcomings. The solution is to revitalize *all* schools.

That being said, my gut feeling is that we won't be getting that total commitment from the federal government any time soon. Short of a taxpayer revolt, one that would lead to legislation requiring a budget overhaul to give schools new priority status, it won't happen. And to that I would say, OK, we'll keep plugging away with the tools at our disposal, finding other ways to cope. We've been doing it for years.

Having government tightly wound in school business is not always a blessing, anyway. I shudder to count the times I've had to go to Albany or Tallahassee, or to petition Washington for mandate relief on funded programs that came with so many strings attached that it was almost impossible to make them work. Joe Tekerman, my executive assistant in Miami and a close friend from our teaching days, figured it out one time that the money we spent doing the required audit trailing of federal commodity subsidies (eggs, butter, ground meat, etc.) could have provided lunch for every kid in Dade County every day for a year. Instead, it was spent on red tape: cashiers, monitors, etc.

Like the sweets we learn to live with and feel we can't live without, federal assistance has become an important dietary supplement in school budgets. But by no means is it a consistent nutritive. About 9.4 percent of New York City's $7 billion school budget is covered by federal funds, due in part to our large concentrations of poor kids. Relatively speaking, that's a lot. In Miami, the federal contribution is a drop in the bucket: less than one percent (actually .67 of one percent, minus the food subsidies) of Dade County's $1.6 billion school operational budget for 1991–92. Federal aid is based on meeting eligibility requirements, of course, and considering the alternative (no help at all), I'm sure we'd all say it's worth the hassle.

But the hassle doesn't end when the red tape runs out. Where the feds really fail is in those areas where they don't meet their *own* responsibilities. Miami especially could argue that position because it is hurt badly by the government's insane immigration policy (really no policy at all) that allows vulnerable areas to be overrun by refugees and immigrants, putting a strain on school revenues and services that makes a travesty of the whole realm of federal assistance.

The areas hardest hit are well known. In the late 1980s California researchers found that 90 percent of the state's six hundred thousand non-English-speaking students came from outside the United States. New York City, long a melting pot, is presently coping with a massive influx from eastern Europe and Asia. Other areas feeling similar pinches might surprise you. Boston initially had the largest influx of Haitians. Dallas, even though well inland, gets more than two thousand immigrant students every year. Lowell, Massachusetts, has a fast-growing Cambodian population.

But in Miami — where, remember, federal money covers less than one percent of the budget — the nonpolicy achieves a level of havoc all its own. One of every four Dade County students (or about 26 percent) was born outside the United States. Miami has 54 percent of all the Cuban-American families that reside in the United States, the result of the ongoing exodus from communist Cuba. It is the favored destination for Haitian and Nicaraguan political refugees. The total influx amounts to about four thousand school-age children a year. At one point when I was there, we were having to accommodate twenty-five Nicaraguan refugee children every day — the equivalent of a classroom a day! — at an unreimbursed cost of $694 per student.

School systems that have to absorb such shocks wind up not only overcrowded but having to provide all manner of support services for children who come in at the bottom of the economic ladder and require specific, and sometimes uncommon, bilingual instruction. Imagine the difficulty of finding Cambodian teachers in Lowell. Miami has it particularly tough with its Haitian refugees. The Haitian poor don't even speak French — they speak a creole that is virtually an unwritten language. The curriculum for Haitian refugee children had to be written from scratch. We had to produce our own materials to teach them, and hope to find enough bilingual teachers who could handle the patois.

A good bilingual program will get immigrant or refugee kids main-streamed (i.e., able to cope in regular classrooms) within two or three years. The ideal model emphasizes teaching them English quickly, usually with two English classes each day, and the rest of their academics — math, social studies, etc. — in their native tongue. As their English improves, they are gradually moved into regular classes. Even in good order it is a painstaking process: costly, time-consuming, and often frustrating for all parties.

But the turmoil caused by uncontrolled immigration makes it far worse because it damages the chances of *every* school kid, creating a nightmare condition of overcrowded classrooms and underfunded programs. And when it includes a shortage of good bilingual teachers, unless the kids are extremely bright they won't survive. Our dropout rates of Hispanic kids are far greater now than of any other ethnic group. Imagine yourself in a Moscow classroom, surrounded by people speaking words you don't know and can't even pronounce. Even in the best of circumstances academic performance is limited. How anyone can possibly expect math and reading scores to get better, or even hold their own, in such a crucible is beyond reason.

Washington's course of action, then, would seem to be clear: "We made these lousy rules, we'll pay." Or, "We'll spread the debt around so that all American taxpayers will take their fair share of this burden." But Washington doesn't say that. It says, "We made these rules, now *you* pay."

In time, the failure has a domino effect on the whole system. For example, in 1989, Dade County taxpayers voted in an unprecedented $980 million bond referendum for building new schools and renovating old ones in an effort to relieve the overcrowding that was largely due to the immigration problem. They basically put their homes up for collateral, because it was to be done through property taxes over the next five years.

But under the immigration siege, the demands on school dollars only got worse. We were able to get some federal mandate relief while I was there (some prominent Republicans live in Miami, including Jeb Bush, the President's son), and some funding — about $10 million — came through in October 1990, but it was like taking a sponge to a flood. Miami now finds that it will not be providing what it was supposed to provide with its bond money.

The last I saw, enrollment in Dade was up again, to 302,000. And funding from the state was down by $174 million, putting the system in such peril that Superintendent Octavio Visiedo, one of my former cabinet members, had to face teacher layoffs, larger classroom numbers, curtailed busing, diminished services, and the possibility of long delays in constructing all those schools Miami so badly needs.

But this is not a book about the failures and inadequacies of the federal government. I suppose we all have one of those in us, and though it might be tempting, it would hardly serve a purpose. It's a peculiar madness anyway, this bias toward funding education in the United States. You look at the polls and they all say the same thing — that the public is willing to pay to get education back on track. That it's willing to support making American schools first-class — not just to bring them back to parity with those of our free world competitors, but back in line with our own historic respect for the redeeming power of education.

So, obviously, it is a matter of finding the trigger. Which *is* what this book is about, and brings us to:

Point 3: that there is nothing wrong with education in America that can't be fixed.

I take this one more personally than the others, out of the conviction born of experience that tells me that it's true. We *can* restore our schools to greatness, and given a united support (where it was never united before) from government and business and the community at large, we can even do it quickly. No, not overnight, but in good time — meaning at a pace swift enough to make you aware that it's happening.

This is not just theory with me. What I have learned about reforming education has come from doing it — in the classroom, in the school, in the system. And *not* doing it, too, because experience also tells me that, Lord, it ain't easy. But I would hasten to ask: what is, that's worth anything anymore?

I have been in education for almost all my adult life. Most of that time was spent not only making waves (it becomes a habit) but also making allies — getting the uncommitted to commit — in the search for answers. I have run the fourth-largest school system in America — Dade County, Florida, which is Greater Miami — and am now running the largest, New York City, with almost a million students and a thousand schools. (I don't expect to be running it much longer because you can't separate politics and education in America, and the politics in New York are almost certain to bring me down sooner or later. I say that without rancor — I've enjoyed the ride, bumps and all — but rather with a resignation for the way things are. If you make waves in New York, you learn not to lean back in your chair.)

We made great strides in Miami to turn that system around, pioneering a whole realm of take-a-chance reforms and a plan of action now well known in education circles as School-Based Management, Shared Decision Making, a strategy for change that gives greater power to teachers, principals, and parents — the people who know best why Johnny can't read — in the running of their schools.

We also confirmed in a substantive way a strong belief of mine: that when properly informed and duly motivated, the public will respond to school needs even at great cost. The $980 million bond issue Miami voters inflicted on themselves for new school construction in 1989 was the greatest single act of public self-sacrifice on behalf of schools in the nation's history. The secret was no secret: we presented the need, targeted the voters we had to win over, and went to work. It can be done anywhere.

In New York, we have waged a three-year assault on the bureaucracy of a school system that was described by the *Daily News* as "a nightmare" and a "sick joke" before I took the job. Supporters, from editorial boards of the major dailies to union leaders, have characterized our efforts as a "renaissance" (and critics, "the handiwork of a dictator," meaning me) as we streamlined operations, routed out the deadwood, and fired a variety of rogues and miscreants.

We eliminated building tenure for principals — a practice, unique to New York City, that rewarded incompetence with permanent job location — and brought down the odious Board of Examiners, a ninety-two-year-old certifying body that was rife with patronage and served mainly to get in the way of progress and affirmative action in the crucial hiring of teachers.

Even under the hammer of oppressive budget cuts ($750 million worth in two years), we spread the wings of School-Based Management and invigorated the system with an appetite for reform. And in less time than I thought possible, math scores rose to the highest level in six years. Reading scores went up, attendance went up — the elementary schools to 90 percent, the highest in twenty-five years. The dropout rate went down — from 24 to 17.2 percent. It had never been that low.

But the nature of reform is that no matter how well you're doing, for every two steps forward there'll be the inevitable step back. The negative influence is usually some implacable governing agency hardened to change (a school board, for example), but sometimes it's an all-encompassing calamity that for the moment is just too tough to overcome (like drastic budget cuts), or one so provocative (like the condom debacle) that it diverts attention from other things. In any case you have to be careful not to be beguiled by a false spring.

New York's reading and math scores tumbled again in 1991–92 when the budget cuts hit home. I was afraid they would. You can't "retire" forty-five hundred experienced teachers (replacing them with two thousand inexperienced teachers) . . . and pension off 207 principals . . . and increase class sizes to unwieldy proportions . . . and cut mentoring services to the bone . . . and reduce supplies and provide fewer up-to-date texts . . . and expect academic performance to go unscathed. The green young teacher who can barely handle twenty-five kids in a normal classroom load will be a basket case trying to deal with thirty-five or forty.

The setback was a painful object lesson for New York, even as it reaffirmed education's first law of dynamics: you can't do it with mirrors. My consolation was that our School-Based Management schools scored better across the board than the others. We checked the forty or so that had been operating for the full two years under SBM and found they outperformed non-SBM schools in their districts every time.

But with all our trials and triumphs, I have no doubt that if response could have been measured on the Richter scale, the biggest impact we made in terms of public awareness had nothing to do with academics at all but with our pushing the plan to make condoms available to our high school students. Even as it won school board approval, albeit on a split vote, naysayers and headline jockeys had a field day.

The Catholic church (*my* church) led the charge. "King Condom Fernandez" was depicted in words and cartoons as the tempter at the schoolhouse door, passing out prophylactics like they were party favors. Every open session of the school board became an exercise in bullying and finger waving. A rabbi got up at one meeting and said that we had taken "the first step on the road to sterilization." A group of blacks called it "a white man's plot" to reduce the black population.

The controversy did not die, and it will probably follow me to *my* grave. It will certainly follow me out of town when I leave because it became the focus of my troubles with the board, the power I must answer to (and whose blessing I need most to be effective) in the city. I have no doubt that this board is "for" education. But, collectively and individually, it is so politicized, and its actions so nettlesome, that on more than one occasion I have openly challenged its character and threatened to quit. At one point I was so obviously riled by time-wasting intrusions and demands — some board members were micro-managing us to death — that the new chairman, H. Carl McCall, felt the need to hustle us out of town for a weekend retreat to clear the air.

This is not the same board that hired me. It may well be the one that fires me.

And that would not be untypical of what happens with crusades in education. Keep forever in mind that we are in this mess *not* because there is no mood for reclaiming our schools (everybody now beats the drum for that) but because too many of those in a position to act wear the colors but don't fight the fight. There is a dark side to the moon that shines so brightly for change, and to ignore it is to ignore the mess itself. People, not policies, make the political indifference, the bureaucratic intransigence. People who are "for" education. Like Pogo, we have met the enemy, and he is us.

To show you how it works, let me take you through one example of what can happen when the same good idea is nurtured in two different nurseries. In Miami, where I was always trying to stir things up, proba-bly the most far-reaching (and far-out) plan we came up with was something we called satellite schools. Schools *at the workplace*, with the buildings and maintenance costs provided by the sponsoring corporate entity (or entities), and the teachers, curriculum, and supplies — and control — provided by the school board. A significant new bonding between schools and the business community.

Satellite schools offered a two-tiered benefit: a way to help relieve the burden on classroom space without having to pay for it, and a hedge against the growing crisis America has with latchkey kids and after-school child care. In New York City, where the problem is acute, six out of ten schoolchildren come from one-parent homes. Usually the one parent works — and lives in dread of not being there in an emergency or of having the kids, even five- and six-year-olds, coping alone after school.

Employers tell me, and studies bear them out, that there's a period of time during the workday when productivity falls off dramatically and that it coincides with the time kids are getting out of school. This is particularly true for women, and with their numbers in the work force burgeoning, that means the problem is not going to go away. It's going to get worse. Child-care centers are a fast-growing national disgrace. Books have been written about the indifferent supervision and neglect, the filthy, overcrowded facilities, and the unqualified (and sometimes menacing) personnel. Prospects are that 30 million American kids will be affected by 1995.

I'll get to the development of the idea later, but we wound up successfully planting three satellite schools in Miami before I left. The feedback from the first, at the south Dade headquarters of American Bankers Insurance, read like a benediction. The absentee rate for both children *and* parents dropped sharply, and tardiness was practically unheard of. Parents with children in the school and the day-care center proved to be four times more likely to stay on the job. The company's turnover rate was 17.6 percent overall, but only 4.1 percent among those parents. A clear-cut victory for innovation.

As a result, part of my well-publicized reform package for New York when I took the job was satellite schools. I tried for twenty months to get one started, hoping to at least demonstrate the possibilities. But even when we had the potential classroom donors, it was like pulling teeth to get the various agencies to work together to make it happen. You wouldn't believe the excuses we got: "It's on the seventh floor . . . There aren't enough windows . . . It's this, it's that."

I finally put my executive director of funded programs, Burt Sacks, on it, and we got a commitment from Kingsborough City College to offer space as part of a Family College Program we had created to get young adults off welfare and into (or back into) college. Our plan was to put in a pre-K-through-2 "super-start" facility, integrating it with special ed kids and financing our end with Chapter I (federal) dollars. Kingsborough donated a single-story classroom building and we tailored it to the kids' needs (smaller desks and toilets, etc.).

Then our various school agencies descended on the site, causing another series of delays, after which they managed to produce a totally unacceptable game plan. They said it would take "at least a year" to get through all the red tape and that improvements would cost "as much as $500,000." After I stopped screaming, I told Sacks to put it up for private bids. We made adjustments and got the repair costs down — to $60,000.

Time slogged along. It wasn't until February 1992 that we finally got the satellite opened, to bells and whistles. Dignitaries on hand for the ceremonies included a representative from the Department of Education who called it "a model for the future." The future should have been in place a lot quicker. Nothing in education should be that painstaking.

The point is that you have to have cooperation, strong alliances, and a synthesis of goals and programs to make reforms happen, and it's a never-ending struggle. Even now, while enjoying good relations with the two most powerful political figures in the state, I have to deal with my own mixed feelings about how *they* will perform when the needs of education hit their desks. I remind myself not to be overly optimistic.

Governor Mario Cuomo is "for" education and has been a major ally in some of our efforts, but he can be as oblique as any other politician when it comes to confronting an issue. I fully expect to take him and the legislature to court over the state's refusal to grant New York City schools their fair share of state funding. It's not even close. We're entitled to 37 percent based on enrollment; we get 34 percent. In a multibillion-dollar budget, three percentage points is a multimillion-dollar disadvantage. To be exact: $485 million.

At last count, per-pupil expenditures were lower in New York City than any other place in the state. By comparison, our 1991–92 school budget figured out to $5,100 a year per pupil. Westchester County's was $7,950. You don't have to look far to see the consequences of such inequity. In some schools in the city, kids read out of social studies books that are more than twenty years old, still list Richard Nixon as President, and describe the civil rights movement of the '70s as a current event. Teachers use up valuable classroom time writing updates on the blackboard.

When I broached the subject with Cuomo, I got one of the most engaging, most thoughtful non-answers I have ever heard. He is a strong-willed governor and a great public speaker, and when you're with him one-on-one you can't help but be impressed with his communication skills. No matter what subject you might be on, he can move you to one he'd prefer, like baseball, and make you think it was your idea. He's also the only man over fifty I ever met who remembers his junior high school fight song and isn't ashamed to sing it for you. He's certainly not tuned out to education's needs. His wife is involved in the mentoring programs around the state.

But I doubt you'll ever hear Mario Cuomo referred to as "the education governor," and that's too bad. He may have missed a great opportunity. He has a fine education commissioner in Tom Sobol, and some topflight superintendents and union heads around the state ready to do his bidding, and he could forge an alliance that would make a mark the whole country could look to. It just doesn't appear to be one of his priorities. He tends to distance himself on such things. As an example, at a governors' meeting in Mobile, I was the only superintendent asked to make a presentation on behalf of the Council of Great City Schools. All the high-profile governors were there. All except Cuomo.

Mayor David Dinkins is "for" education and is an eminently likable man, and for the most part we get along. His support of the condom plan was pivotal. But the uphill battle he must wage on New York City's myriad problems is enough to daunt the most willing public servant, and with the infrastructure crumbling and the quality of life going down with it, he is a man on the edge. The money crunch has crippled the city. Public services have been cut. Garbage lines the sidewalks. The parks are opened less. The streets go uncleaned, the bridges unrepaired. A proposal to save electricity by turning off every third streetlight got a citywide laugh. Who could tell the difference?

My heart goes out to Dinkins. He didn't create this situation, he inherited it. But every problem in New York is tackled on the basis of the quick fix. When the polls said crime was the number one problem, the city rushed to hire five thousand cops — a quick fix. Crime didn't lose much headway. And how will five thousand cops on the street stop the crack epidemic? The AIDS epidemic? The spirit-killing malaise in the poverty areas?

It doesn't take an educator's eyes to see that solutions for so many of these things, *including* crime, are directly tied to education. An overwhelming share of the mayhem committed in New York City is now the work of teenagers. Close to five hundred children under sixteen were shot in 1991. Boys and girls carry guns and knives, extort money and property, mug each other, *kill* each other. What are we doing to turn *them* around? And is there a correlation between their violence and their dysfunction — a connection to be made with the fact that so many of them are unemployable and well on the way to becoming sociopaths? You bet there is.

What makes it tough for Dinkins and me to get along in this tinderbox is the fact that education cannot be treated as a quick-fix item. Most of the problems we have are with the mayor's deputies and budget director, who run scared all the time. There is a notable lack of long-range planning. And even in the short haul, education doesn't get its due. No hue and cry was made to save it from the city's crippling budget cuts of '91 and '92, and although by New York law we are entitled to 25 percent of the city's funding, we get 23 — again, a huge differential in actual dollars — and aren't even sure what that represents, because the two sides can't agree on the way it factors out.

Our budget includes funding from the state as well as the city. With our student numbers way up, the state had to increase its contribution (again, by law), but Dinkins's people went the other way, taking the position that state money was "budget relief," and instead of giving us our rightful share actually gave us less. We calculated that to be in compliance the city owed us $300 million. The city said $32 million.

The true number probably lies somewhere in between, but I'm sure we'll have to sue (under a statute known as Stavisky-Goodman) to get it. Meanwhile, Dinkins's people have developed a siege mentality. They are convinced that I'm after the mayor's job, a breathtaking misconception that got started when ex-mayor Ed Koch made comments in mid-1991 about Joe Fernandez being "an excellent candidate for mayor of New York." Koch knows better, but Koch is Koch. His opinions abhor a vacuum. From his new pulpit as a columnist for the New York *Post*, Koch loves to rattle the establishment.

I have insisted all along that I have no ambition outside education. None. But the press — and Dinkins's lieutenants, who are more paranoid about it than he is — won't let it die. The *Times* ran a box-score comparison of our management styles, salaries, etc., with a story about our "rocky relationship" over the budget cuts in May 1992, and said that aides of Dinkins still think I want to be mayor. I joke about it and play along at meetings with editorial boards, but it's more distracting than it is flattering. Besides, the chancellorship pays more.

I am reminded by old friends and new critics that I tend to be less than patient under these circumstances — under *any* circumstances where progress is being blunted by bureaucracy or indifference. I plead guilty. I am *very* impatient when people who are directly involved do not appreciate the magnitude of our task. If somebody's rear end is paused between me and where we have to go, I'm going to kick it. We're out of time in America when it comes to education. Anything that holds us back is the enemy. The dam isn't leaking, it's tumbling down.

So I push. I push very hard. I believe that education needs catalysts in seats of authority like the one I'm in, leaders who are willing to work harder than anyone else to make schools better, to try things, to take the risks, to raise hell with the status quo. When I hit the ground running in New York, it surprised a lot of people, especially when the heads that were about to roll began to squeal in protest. Some were appalled, more (according to the papers) were delighted. But I don't believe you can do these things quietly, and when the bandwagon starts moving, it can be a very exciting place to be.

The host on a PBS television show said to me recently, "Some of your critics charge that you act too much like a CEO. That you approach education like it was a business." Guilty again. The connection is valid. The New York City school system is the twelfth-largest corporation in America, with an operating budget of $6.9 billion, a capital budget of $4.3 billion, and a work force of over 125,000. If you took inventory of the property investment we have, it would be in the hundreds of billions. The school systems of every other major urban center in the country are much the same — massive undertakings, laden with economic responsibility. If that means we have to look at ourselves more as businesses to make them work, so be it.

The difference is that we're not just in *any* business. We're in the business of preparing lives for the future of America. And we're at a point in history where a hard-headed marketing approach may well be needed to get this business off the deck. Not just in New York City. Everywhere.

The good news — and one of the reasons I keep trucking through the turmoil — is that progress *does* happen when you tie the mission of schools in to the communities they serve and the businesses whose work force they supply. Corporations, businesses, and civic enterprises *are* responsive (if only for selfish reasons) when the truth is driven home: that they are directly affected by the quality of our graduates.

It doesn't take a master of deductive reasoning to fathom that America's failures in the classroom have weakened us in the marketplace, and that the reverse has to be made true. Any step in that direction is a right one.

People thought I was joking when I proposed to warranty our high school graduates in New York City — to put a "limited guarantee" on every kid we send into the work force. Nobody had done such a thing before. But I was dead serious. One of the criticisms we get in New York is that employers have to wade through thirty-four interviews to find one qualified applicant. (The average nationwide is seventeen to one.) Part of the problem is that pre-employment drug tests eliminate a lot of our kids, but mainly it's a matter of academic shortcomings that can be corrected if addressed.

Under a pilot program we started with Nynex Corporation (a division of AT&T) in 1990 and then opened up to others in September 1991, we pledged that if a graduate is deficient in any basic skill — if he doesn't read or write well enough or compute well enough to handle the job — we'll take him back for more training. The employer keeps him on the payroll, we work with him at night or after hours until he is brought up to speed. Both sides profit: the company gets a better-qualified worker, the worker doesn't lose out to somebody from Westport.

If there were such a thing as the Joe Fernandez Hit List for Improving Schools, community involvement would rank right up there. I think it's imperative that we find more ways to get free enterprise keyed into the process. We've already found more than a few. In Miami, when we had to form a political action group to get the bond referendum passed, the Chamber of Commerce provided $450,000 to do the publicity, the circulars, the newspaper ads, the TV time. In New York, Booz Allen, the consulting firm, did a $1 million study for us on our transportation and purchasing services, pro bono. The Academy of Finance gave us an office building for a special Chancellor's School. IBM supplied twenty-five middle-level managers to instruct and serve as mentors at my School-Based Management schools — not just for one day a month or an hour a week, but for as much as half their working time.

You don't read about those things because they don't make headlines, but they typify the kind of potential that's out there. Americans are a wonderfully generous people. In 1990 alone, during an economic down cycle, personal philanthropy in this country totaled $92 billion. I'm on my people all the time to explore every possibility, tap every source: foundations, health organizations, community-based organizations, corporations, mom-and-pop stores, everybody. I have a standing rule with my staff: if there's a foundation grant or a donation or a service out there to be had, we go for it. If I learn of one we *haven't* gone for, I want to know why. In writing.

The purpose of engaging all this support is quite to the point. Once upon a time American education was the envy of the free world. Now, from almost any perspective, it's in such a shambles that in the last decade of the twentieth century it is probably our most discredited institution, with a present image of failure that makes its friends loath to speak of it kindly and its champions confused as to what a clear course of reform should be. But reformation is exactly what is needed: an explosion of workable ideas to expedite a renewal, with businesses and government willing to join in bold new initiatives.

We should be primed now to try almost anything that will improve the chances of our children, that will get them better prepared for school, make their studies more enriching, their environment safer and more conducive to learning. We are limited only by our imagination.

And we should be for almost anything that will improve the working conditions and the incentive of teachers, and give them more standing. "Professionalization," we called it in Miami: raising the sights and the stature of teachers, in some cases as a concomitant of School-Based Management.

Great strides were made. My salary when I started teaching in Dade County in 1963 was $4,500 a year. Raises inched along in $100 increments. With a growing family, I had to work two and three outside jobs to make ends meet. Now Dade teachers start at $26,500 a year, the average salary is up to $38,500, and when a job opens up, instead of attracting two qualified applicants, eleven rush in to apply. You have no idea how much that kind of competition improves the quality of teaching.

You talk now to the people in Miami, even the ones who didn't like my style, and they'll tell you that during my superintendency something new and invigorating was going on all the time, everywhere you looked. We became the most "national" school system in the country. Our schools drew delegations from all over, some from other countries, looking to see how we did things. Teachers and principals said it was like riding a buzzsaw, but they felt alive again. If you get that kind of impetus from the first chair, real change can happen quickly.

Along this line, it has been pointed out — not always generously — that the one idea I push hardest, School-Based Management, is a major contradiction to the way I do things. I can understand the confusion. Joe Fernandez thrives on being in control. SBM would share the decision-making process with teachers and parents at the point of attack — at the schools themselves. Why would he want to relinquish control where the most good can be done?

As we'll see, it's a lot more complicated than that, but I don't have trouble with it. Because underlying the passion I bring to the process is an obsession to make education better, and I have no illusions about being the only one who has the answers. I have a big ego, but when it comes to that, I have no ego at all. I'd like to see a *thousand* superintendents out there forcing the action, getting more people involved, creating mini-revolutions in every school district of America. When I was a teacher, I had a new idea every week; I was always trying to find ways to improve the system. Every good teacher and every good principal has ideas. They need to be encouraged, not stifled. New York is just beginning to see how it can work.

Being misinterpreted goes with the territory, of course. So do the mistakes you make. I've made some lulus. When you go against the establishment, preaching a gospel that says the institutions need changing, not just the people, you are not always going to get the highest approval rating.

But I believe we are put on this earth for a reason, and mine, despite a most unlikely beginning, was to be in education. And when I say I know it can be fixed, I speak not just as a true believer, but with an appreciation for my own experience.

I know firsthand what education can do to save a life. I don't have to ask the experts or read books about it. I've been there.

I know about tough neighborhoods. I grew up in Harlem.

I know about families struggling. My mother worked most of her adult life at Columbia University — as a maid. My dad drove buses and cabs, worked as a deliveryman, washed windows.

I know about racism and prejudice. In some areas of this country, being Puerto Rican is as tough as being black.

I know about dropouts. I was one.

I know about gangs. I was in a few. I still have the scars.

I know about the folly of drugs. I used them.

I know what scratching for an education is like when you finally come to realize its importance. I got my high school diploma in the Air Force. It was my salvation.

I know what it's like to teach in the meanest conditions, to battle the inertia and apathy and the capacity for violence that marks big-city education and makes it so frightening. I also know the joy you feel in turning those things around.

It's ironic the way it all worked out. David Dinkins wonders now if I have an ambition to be the mayor of New York City. God knows, I didn't even want to be the chancellor of its schools. I kept saying "no" until I heard myself say "yes," but it wasn't my ambition. The only real ambition I ever had was to be the principal of the first high school I taught at, and I didn't make it.

In fact, my wife, Lily, and I wound up in Florida only because our first son had chronic croup and needed perpetual summer, and when we piled into the station wagon we borrowed from my father and headed south, it was because we hadn't saved enough money to get us to Arizona, our first choice.

That's what I mean about being here for a reason. If everything had turned out the way *I* had intended, I might be growing old teaching geometry in Tucson today.

PART II

I F THE TREE always grew as the twig was bent, I wouldn't have made it as an educator. I might not have made it, period, but teaching most certainly would not have been a prospect. I'm afraid that an almost perverse indifference, not to say disdain, for the profession is a given in the inner city and is something administrations in every metropolitan school system should be working overtime to change. In my old neighborhood just being educated was a reach, and teaching was something you looked on more with suspicion than respect, like riding a bull.

I remember going back to 126th Street after Lily and I were married, to a little gathering of neighbors in the third-floor walk-up apartment where I did most of my growing up. We were sitting around talking about moving to Florida and I said, "I'm going to be a teacher."

My buddies from childhood, who hadn't forgotten our calling as devout truants, looked at me like I was foaming at the mouth.

"A *teacher?*"

They saw me as a bus driver, or a cop — especially a cop — or anything with a nice, safe connection to government. Jobs without exotic training (i.e., college). Jobs "with steady paychecks."

A steady paycheck is an elusive thing for many hardworking people in this country. My parents, Joe and Angela, knew the value of it as well as anyone. I don't know how many jobs my father had during the depression, or until he wound up years later cleaning out airplanes for Pan American, but usually it was two or three at a time. When I was

born, he was working part-time helping build Sing Sing prison, for
$20 and a bag of rice every two weeks. My mother delivered me on
December 13, 1935, in the ground-floor apartment on East 111th
Street where they lived then because a hospital bill was a luxury and
she didn't have anybody to stay with my six-year-old sister, Angie.
She hired a doctor for $10 to attend her and cradled her newborn in
Angie's doll carriage.

My dad did anything and everything to make a buck. He ironed
sheets and mended shirts at the Commodore Hotel on 42nd Street. He
washed windows on skyscrapers, worked as a deliveryman for a handkerchief factory, drove cabs, drove trolleys, drove buses. My mother
worked, too, when she could, as a seamstress in a nearby tent factory,
then for some time as a maid at Columbia University — where (small
ironic twist) I wound up going to college, and where (second ironic
twist) I was awarded the Medal for Distinguished Service thirty-two
years later.

So my parents had developed a very pragmatic view of life and
didn't see the point in raising children to be less so. Or more so, for
that matter. By practical definition, a higher calling was one that provided a faster way to make ends meet. Once, when I was in the eighth
grade at Annunciation Boys School — I must have been thirteen or
fourteen years old — a priest came to our school to recruit for one of
the religious orders. He showed this film of the seminary in upstate
New York, a beautiful place, like a summer camp, with guys sitting
around studying in well-appointed dorms or out playing ball on a
wide expanse of grass and trees. I thought, Boy, that's for me. The
only grass and trees I knew about were over on Riverside Drive.

So I signed the card. I think even then I wanted some structure in
my life, something to tie to, and I thought, OK, I'll be a priest. Then I
forgot about it until one day I was in the street playing stickball and
my mother called me from the upstairs window. "Joe! Get up here!"

I walked in, and there was this priest from one of the Dominican
orders, sitting in the living room with my mom and dad. It was a
weekend, so they were both home. My dad said, "What's this? You
wanna be a priest?"

My mother said, "He's too young, and that's that." And it was. Latino males in Spanish Harlem were counted on to pitch in as they grew
up, not run off to a seminary. But I doubt they'd have been so adamant had they known the paths I'd be taking in the next four or five
years.

Life in Harlem is undoubtedly a lot meaner now, but I don't know that the attitude toward school has changed any. There was no premium on education. School wasn't something you gave a lot of thought to, just somewhere you had to go. And I *didn't* go, very often, once I was old enough to sample the alternatives. Sports were more important. Gangs — in my circle, the Riffs — were more important. Girls were more important. And drugs, eventually, were more important.

Before I dropped out of Commerce High, a public school that was my last stop before the U.S. Air Force, my routine was to kiss my mother good-bye in the morning, ostensibly heading off to school, then join any available Riffs and any girls we could coerce, ride the IRT to Columbus Circle, and spend the day downtown. We didn't even check into school. We'd pool our money to get one guy into the Paramount Theater, where Sinatra started and there was a stage show with the movie, and he'd let the rest of us in through the fire door. I was into drugs by then, and we'd do some of that, too. Or just hang around 42nd Street, the way kids today hang around malls. Then in the afternoon we'd go home and tell all about our day in school.

I got kicked out of Bishop DuBois High before that for skipping class. I could do the work, I was actually a good student when I tried, it just wasn't important to me. Among various efforts to stave off scholarship, I once smeared calamine lotion on my face and blamed three weeks of truancy on a bad case of poison ivy, ostensibly contracted in the deep woods of Spanish Harlem. That was the last straw for Father Buckley, the principal. Father Buckley liked me, I think because I brought a sense of humor to my misbehavior, but he was no fool. This time he wasn't even mildly amused. "Get out," he said, refusing my request for clemency. "And don't come back." I said, "Aww, Father."

What makes that kind of attitude? A lot of things, but more than anything else an environment that can put you at cross-purposes with your own best interests very early in life. It was classic tenement living, which implies struggle, with people piled together in those wretched warrens, reverting to a kind of survival mentality. It was always volatile. I remember going into the streets of Harlem after the riots in the late '40s, when I was just a little kid, and seeing National Guard soldiers on the roofs and signs on the stores: "Negro-owned. Don't break."

In our area there was actually a rich ethnic mix: Spanish (Puerto Ricans), Irish, blacks, some Greeks, a few Italians, one Indian family. It didn't become predominantly black and Spanish until later. It was the lower class, but most families had both parents at home, which had to make a difference compared with today, and everybody knew everybody else within a four- or five-block area. You looked to each other for things. It was like having your own little town.

I didn't have a bad home life. I had two caring parents and a loving sister, my best buddy as a child, and there was always food on the table. We didn't have television to remind us how deprived we were, not until I was older. I got a new pair of shoes once a year, and every Easter my mother took me down to a cut-rate clothing store on 14th Street and bought me a suit with two pairs of pants. We never got an allowance, but we didn't think about it, because everybody was in the same boat. We didn't have an automobile, but nobody did, except Johnny Thornton's family, and it was more a conversation piece than a car: a '29 Dodge. I didn't learn to drive until I was twenty-one and in the service.

We didn't *need* to be reminded that we were "P-Rs." *West Side Story* was our reality, and biases against one group or another were worn like badges. I must have been self-conscious about it, maybe even a little ashamed, because I never learned to speak Spanish, except for a few halting phrases. I never really tried, which I know now was stupid. My mom told me later she resented that, but not enough to make it an issue.

My mom and dad were first-generation Puerto Ricans, although both had some French blood mixed with the Spanish. One of my mother's sisters was blond and blue-eyed, another was a redhead. Neither side of the family was without culture. My dad's parents were musicians in the philharmonic in San Juan. But when they were killed in a car accident, it left him, at age fourteen, the oldest of seven children. He weighed the options — and ran off and joined the merchant marine.

That's how he met my mother. She'd gone to college for two years, and one summer took a passenger ship to New York, the same ship my dad was working. They dated, and when she emigrated to New York with some of her family, he came, too, and they got married. The only thing she insisted on was that he quit the merchant marine.

Mom was the disciplinarian of the family, but only because she had to be, with Dad gone so much. When you see her now, short and slightly built, you don't appreciate the steel she had in her. When she said, "Be home by three," I was home by three. At least early on. The final word, however, was my dad's, in the best Latin tradition. The ultimate threat in my house was "I'm gonna tell your father." She didn't have to say it twice.

Dad was a big, handsome guy who in my eyes could have doubled for Clark Gable. Acted the part, too. A man's man *and* a ladies' man. Very popular, very politically oriented, very active in the community. Even as a kid I could see the effect that had. He belonged to the Abraham Lincoln Club, which was left of center (a supporter of the Loyalist side during the Spanish Civil War), and later the connection got me in some hot water with the Air Force. But for a kid it was fun. When they had parades, he'd take me, and I'd march along with him, holding his hand and one edge of the Puerto Rican flag.

He was very loving, my father. I think I get that from him, the affection I have for my four kids. Mom worshiped him. Literally waited on him hand-and-foot. She'd always hold dinner for him. He'd come home from work and shower, and she'd be ready with clean clothes and something to drink. He'd dress and go to the candy store up the street to play cards, and when he finally came back to eat, it was usually with a friend or two. Our kitchen was always a gathering place, for *everybody's* friends, which I loved.

Discipline in those days wasn't a big deal because I wasn't a problem, at least until I got older, and because I had a healthy fear of my old man. One time I threw a skate at my sister and broke a kitchen window. The break was in the shape of a cat, and Angie blackmailed me for months to keep me in line. "If you don't straighten up, I'm telling Dad about the cat."

I was rolling dice one night in a hallway of another building, out later than I was supposed to be, and I felt this big tug on my shoulder. I said, "Get the hell away, can't you see I'm busy?" I didn't even look up. My father's voice boomed in my ear, with no hint of tolerance in it: "Get upstairs!" I can still feel the chill up my spine. But he didn't hit me or anything. He never did. My mom would pinch my ear, but they never used a strap or a belt, or a hand or a fist. Correction, sure. Lots of it. But nothing physical.

Actually, the third-floor walk-up on 126th Street was our fourth home in the area. In the eternal search for more space, we moved to Moylan Place when I was eight or nine. It was a one-bedroom, but it had another room we could convert and a big kitchen with an old-fashioned icebox. It was my job to empty the tray and haul in the ice when the delivery truck came around. When we moved to LaSalle Street, a block away, my mother's sister's kids, Al and Hugo Moralez, came to live with us. I shared a room with them, but there was no hall, and therefore no privacy, because the three rooms we used for bedrooms (one had been the dining room) opened into one another and you had to walk through one to get to the other.

Luxury was achieved when we moved to 556 West 126th Street — an apartment with a hall! It was what was known as a railroad flat, and the hall wall had a big bow in it, but it ran the length of the unit, making bedroom doors meaningful. We also had our first refrigerator, with a tiny little freezer, and the place was big enough for my folks to take in a boarder, a man from Spain named Manuel, and so close to the elevated Broadway line that you could feel the vibrations. There were shops nearby, too, including a poultry store where they sold live chickens. I had friends on every floor, mostly Irish and Jewish, and I didn't think you could ask for anything more.

I see it now, long-abandoned and covered with obscene graffiti, the paint peeled down to nothing, the brick walls crumbling, and the neighborhood grim and beaten-looking, and I am reminded how quickly some horizons fade. And why I hate cockroaches so much. We didn't have rats in Apartment 33, at least not often, but we had thundering herds of cockroaches. You'd come home late, or wake up at night and go for water or to the bathroom, and you'd snap on a light, and squadrons of them would scurry across the floors and counters. You could *hear* them scurrying. I realize now that it was a pretty shabby place, 556 West 126th.

But as I said, we kids didn't see ourselves as poor. It was life, that's all, and you lived it without much expectation. My parents were disappointed when I dropped out of school later, but education was never pushed in our house. We didn't read much at all, except for the comic books my dad liked. On weekends he'd have us listen to the classical music that was part of his heritage or the "Battle of the Crooners" — Sinatra vs. Crosby — on radio. My dad could play the trumpet and bragged that all his brothers and sisters played musical instruments. He took me to Puerto Rico to see them when I was seventeen. It was the first time he'd been back in all those years. The "natural musicians," I was pleased to see, had all done well in life. One brother became a judge, another a doctor, one an educator.

Most of my memories of school coincide with my early blindness to its importance, which is to say, they are few. I have great voids where experiences (and enlightenment) should be. I was in public school from kindergarten through fourth grade, but all I remember about kindergarten is being taken there and crying, and I remember nothing about the first grade except that I must have been perceived as a bright kid because I was allowed to skip the second grade.

Ah, but I *do* remember my third-grade teacher, because in the manner of good teachers everywhere, she reached us in a special way, and in the manner of impressionable little boys, I fell in love with her. Until I got to college, of all my teachers only three stick in my memory: Sister Veritas, my eighth-grade teacher at Annunciation Boys School, who looked like she was eight feet tall and favored me with errands to run; Brother Norwood, my math teacher at Bishop DuBois High, who made the subject come alive for the first time . . . and Mrs. Brown, my third-grade teacher at PS 125 in Harlem. In my child's eyes Mrs. Brown was beautiful in every way. Now, of course, I would say she had those wonderful motivational skills that seem to come naturally for dedicated teachers.

She was always finding ways to open the world to us. She took our whole class to the Bronx Zoo one day. Another time she took a group of us to her apartment in Washington Heights (I was awed by the greenery), where she fixed us lunch and baked homemade cookies. I must have been close to nirvana that year because I won the good citizenship medal from the Daughters of the American Revolution. For a perennial class cut-up, and a Puerto Rican to boot, that was something.

My main problem with school was that I never had a problem with it. Not academically in those crucial early years. I knew I could get by, so I never studied. If I had homework, I'd do it on the steps of the school before class. My son Keith was that way, an A student all the way through college by absorbing what he needed during class. But I also resisted *going* to class, even in elementary school. When we were still at Moylan Place, I'd skip eight or ten days a semester by hiding under the steps, then slipping away. It's a wonder I have any memories of school at all.

What I *do* remember, in detail, is the neighborhood. The neighborhood mattered, even as poor as it was and the troubles and bad habits it fostered. My best friends were two tough Irish Catholics: Johnny Thornton, who lived right below me, and Gene McCann, who was on the floor above. Geney's a customs officer in Newark now, and Johnny wound up with a job I had in the bookstore at Columbia University when I was going to college, and they'll tell you that even as a kid I liked to run things.

We were all athletic, played all the sports, but I'd have to be the catcher in baseball and call the plays in football. In school and out, I'd always be creating some minor havoc, usually getting my buddies to go along. I learned early, though, that you have to be careful with that kind of influence. Once, we talked the superintendent of our building into giving us a little room downstairs on the alley side to start a club. We whitewashed the walls, brought in an old couch somebody gave us, and fixed it up pretty good. Then one day I found a big wooden desk in a junk heap.

To get the desk to the clubhouse meant going around through the alley where the janitor from another building kept his Doberman, a notoriously hostile animal. No one was particularly anxious to do that, but I convinced my buddies that we could get the desk past the dog if we kept our cool. I'd read somewhere, in a Ray-O-Vac ad in a comic book I think, that if a dog attacked you, all you had to do was freeze and it wouldn't bite. So we were carrying this desk and we made the turn into the alley, and here comes the Doberman. My three buddies stood their ground, stark still. Didn't move a muscle. And every one of them got bitten. I didn't, because I ran like hell.

Like my father, I was never lazy, never afraid of work. As a kid I took all kinds of jobs for spending money: hawking sodas at Van Cortlandt Park, shining shoes, setting pins in a bowling alley on 125th Street, sweeping the floor and cleaning the glasses in a bar. One summer I worked a couple weeks as a messenger at 110 Livingston Street in Brooklyn — the building that houses the New York City Board of Education. Another small ironic twist. I cleaned the floors in a nearby candy store a few times, too, but I think they hired me for protection more than anything else.

The older I got the more sensitive I became to the perils of inner-city living. When you're little, it's mostly a matter of having bigger kids pick on you, and you learn about strength in numbers. You learn not to go certain places by yourself. After a while you become street smart. You find you can move around pretty freely, but you know where and when to do it. You know *never* to go into some neighborhoods at night.

Gangs were prevalent, but I didn't get involved until I was in my teens and ranging farther from home. A lot of our movement was tied to sports, because when you played ball, you'd go to the different athletic clubs and neighborhoods. Sports were more club-oriented than gang-oriented, but they made you venture out. Sports, and girls. I probably left the neighborhood more than any of my buddies, for both reasons.

When I started dating Lily, she lived on 145th Street, and that was Dragon territory. I had to walk through two or three different turfs to get there, but I knew how to do it. I eventually joined the Dragons, too, as a convenience. It made the coming and going easier. All gangs — the Saints, the Dukes, the Dragons, etc. — had their own style and makeup. The difference with the Riffs was that we were an ethnic hodgepodge — Puerto Ricans, Irish, Greeks, Jews, blacks. Like Our Gang.

My memories of teenage life along Amsterdam Avenue are colored more by turf wars than sock hops, but the wars weren't as deadly as they are today. When we fought, it was usually with fists, maybe a few bats or sticks, rarely knives or guns. The zip guns we had were famous for their malfunctions. The barrels were made from radio antennas. I tried one once and it backfired and I never tried it again. I preferred fists. There I thought I was tough enough. I was a skinny kid — 145 pounds when I went into the service — but I was tall and wiry. You couldn't get me down.

I won more battles than I lost, but I took some lumps. One New Year's eve, my friend Bobby Duran and I were coming back from a party, a block away from the neighborhood, when two older guys came up to us. I knew one of them, and I nodded. Without saying a word, the other guy whacked me on the side of the face. I went down, more shocked than hurt. They took off. When I got home and looked in the mirror, I had a black eye. And a grudge.

That summer we were down at Riverside Park, playing softball, and I spotted the guy who hit me. So did Bobby. The guy saw us, too, and took off before we could get to him. I never saw him again, which was fortunate for one of us.

As the neighborhood began to change, it got meaner. Right or wrong, gangs are like family and you think of your fellow members as blood whether they're good guys or not. Guys who hadn't grown up with you were not to be trusted. The fighting began breaking down along ethnic lines. Before, it hadn't mattered. We had black friends in the neighborhood. Sonny Finley, the guy who'd catch my passes and make me look good in football, was a Riff. Bobo Bermudez was black, too, and a kid we called "Long Arms," because his arms almost touched the ground.

But as most of the whites — the Irish, the Italians, the Jews — pulled out, blacks new to the neighborhoods hung out with blacks, Puerto Ricans with Puerto Ricans. I still had black friends, and we'd go up into Harlem to some of the hangouts, but you knew better than to go around the Apollo Club or the Baby Grand late at night. When drugs started getting more popular, the violence escalated, both in frequency and magnitude. Heroin became a big thing, and with that gang activity increased. You joined to survive. They still didn't have the firepower they have today, but it was just a matter of time. The arms race was on.

One night a few of us went to a party on 116th Street, at an apartment on the sixth or seventh floor. The local gang found out we were there, and when we heard they were coming after us, we took off down the stairs and out into the street, going like mad, leaping over things. But they were many and we were few, and they caught us right outside the Nemo Theater. Had us surrounded, our backs against the ticket booths. Most of them had sticks, but there were some knives and a few zip guns.

Thank God, at that critical moment the movie broke, and people started streaming out. With all those witnesses, the rumble was over before it started.

I remember one incident that truly scared me. I hit a kid with a rock one day, hard enough, I thought, to kill him. We were squared off for a gang fight on Riverside Drive, and he threw a Pepsi-Cola sign at me. I ducked, but it boomeranged and came back and cracked me on the nose. The blood gushed out, it was a bad cut, and I went wild. I grabbed a rock and hit him in the head, and *he* started gushing. That ended the fight. They took us both to the hospital for stitches. I don't know about him, but my face still carries the evidence.

You ask, what role did school play in all this? None. In such an environment, the way the system worked then (and in too many cases works now), school was irrelevant, except for the purely academic. An island in the stream, but not of it. You weren't taught to make the connections between education and solution. There weren't any "conflict resolution" courses. When I got into narcotics, and face-to-face with my own dissolution, there weren't any "drug awareness" programs to mark the way out. The public school might just as well have been on Mars for all it meant to a neighborhood kid's survival problems.

The one thing you gain under such conditions, if you make it through, is a certain toughness — not just an I'm-not-going-to-take-any-crap attitude, but a better feel for knowing you can get by. The things I face now seem like nothing compared to what I remember as the way it was, so fear is less a factor in my thinking. Even the worst things I have to deal with in the New York school system don't really faze me. Something happens, and everyone runs around like the sky is falling, but I always see it as transitory. "This will pass . . . keep going . . . there's something better ahead."

It's hard to be a teenager in any inner city in America today, of course, with the poverty and the dope, the violence, the twisted sense of values that emerges when the realities hit home. We were poor and didn't know it. Today, a third of our kids in New York City are from families on welfare, and with communications what they are, and the increased mobility, they know it, and it hurts all the more. Television shows them the gap between the haves and have-nots, and in their confusion as to what that means they learn to covet *things*, to *need* things, for status. In the inner cities of America, kids kill other kids for a cheap watch, or a jacket, or a pair of basketball shoes.

In Spanish Harlem we had knifings and an occasional killing, but killing wasn't the common occurrence it is today. During my first ten months as chancellor, we averaged a school kid murdered every other day — stabbed on subways, shot in school yards or on street corners — and often for no more reason than a dirty look. Today we have a "security officer" — a cop — in every school, more than one when necessary. Some high schools have fifteen or sixteen cops working the halls and grounds.

The inside reflects the outside. Kids walk over bodies to get to school in some places in New York — over derelicts sleeping in the street or people drunk or drugged out. I passed a corner the other day and saw a drug deal going down right across the street from an elementary school. The *Daily News* ran a series of articles focusing on what kids see from their school windows. From one view overlooking a park, they photographed fights, and drug taking, and people fornicating. Teachers pull the shades to keep the images out, but kids aren't stupid. Not only do such things affect their thinking about life, they diminish their respect for the law. It's double jeopardy.

Of course, when you're from what we euphemistically call "the streets," you tend to see things differently anyway. You're always anticipating, always sensitive to the risk. I never lost that. Lily has, but I haven't. She has always been more trusting. At times, in certain places or situations, I'll say, "Watch your purse, be alert." It's like a sixth sense, and you don't learn it in school.

Where my parents dropped the ball was in not emphasizing education at all, except as an extension of church. But with my father driving a bus all day and a taxi at night and my mom working, as with so many families today, the routine demands of life just got in the way. Angie got her high school diploma and later, when she was married, went to college, but she was engaged and preparing to leave the nest when I reached high school and wasn't around to prod me. Not that it would have mattered. I was already too far gone.

It's one of the *large* ironies of my life that I find myself today preaching the absolute need to stay in school. Across the country, we have a 27 percent dropout rate, compared with, say, Japan's 6 percent, and I'm looking for ways to change that all the time. But in what had to be the most crucial time of my life, I had to drop out to save myself.

My mother had switched me to Catholic school beginning in the fifth grade, I'm sure for the discipline. I'd been a regular churchgoer, not entirely by choice, and at Annunciation Boys School we got not only a heavy dose of religious training but also the regimentation parochial schools are famous for. In that environment, school *is* church, and vice versa.

I value my Catholicism today, and the teaching I got and the orderliness it brought to my life, but I have to say that as I grew into adolescence, much of the sin the sisters railed about sounded pretty good to me. The added discipline had little effect. For me, school was a place to have fun, and not just at the expense of my fellow students.

I was always in trouble. Not for doing anything really bad, but for joking around, making mischief, getting other kids to do things. Practical jokes, mainly. At Annunciation, I had a healthy respect for Sister Veritas (*my* health; she scared me to death), and I was so good around her that she'd pick me for the job whenever serious errands had to be run downtown or somewhere. But the others were fair game.

The sisters' candy wagon, for example, was one of my targets. They'd come around after lunch with stuff they got wholesale but sold for a profit (I knew it worked that way because Sister Veritas had me pick up a supply one time), and they'd have the candy lined up in neat configurations, the Hershey bars facing one way, the Tootsie Rolls another. When they turned away, I'd mix everything up. They'd go nuts. One teacher, Brother Willie, wore thick bifocals and had a hearing aid, and during study period, I'd be in the third row, singing from the side of my mouth — da-da, ta-ta-ta, da-da — just loud enough for him to hear but not know where it was coming from. He'd jerk his head around and stalk up and down the aisles trying to figure it out.

I'd do anything for a laugh. Most Catholic schools have dress codes, and we had to wear shirts and ties, with a jacket or a sweater. I got some scissors one day and started grabbing ties and snipping off the ends. It became a fad, and before long I had a reputation. After chapel one morning I sneaked in and turned all the crucifixes upside down. When everybody came in for prayers at the end of the day, the guys started giggling. When the sisters saw it, I was the one they blamed. They couldn't prove it, but anything like that happened, it was "Get Fernandez!" I was a marked man.

Hotfoot humor notwithstanding, I got through Annunciation without calamity and moved on to Bishop DuBois High School, a couple stops farther away on the bus line, and a school I could have learned to love if I'd been there long enough. It was a converted old mansion, big enough for only about three hundred kids, which meant that as an athlete you could play on all the teams (they were desperate for bodies), which I did: baseball, track, basketball.

But by then I was skipping school regularly, and it finally caught up with me when Father Buckley, seeing through the layers of calamine lotion, kicked me out for good in the tenth grade. That's one advantage private schools have always had, the ability to expel you for almost any reason. Catholic schools claim they don't do it, but, of course, they do, and they have the threat of it working all the time. That, together with the fact that you're there because your parents want you to be, and are paying for the privilege, makes for a strong bond between school and home. Kids in public schools usually don't have that bond. By comparison, the chronic troublemakers in public schools practically have to commit a capital crime to get expelled.

I doubt that I appreciated it at the time, but I got a lot from my Catholic school experience. As an adult I've always been very well organized, very responsive to detail, very regimented, so the structure and the discipline must have had an effect. If the public school in the inner city was an island, the parochial school was a fortress — no more relevant to what was going on in the streets, perhaps, but good for creating a distraction-free environment for learning.

I don't agree with all of it, but there's much to say for the way the Catholics run their schools. Dress codes, for example, can be a good thing, particularly now when kids put so much emphasis on clothes (those accursed labels), accentuating the gulf between rich and poor. The advantaged kid can't flaunt it when he's wearing the same thing, at the same cost, you are.

Uniforms are also good for fostering esprit de corps, with the sense of belonging. I also think that when you come to school dressed in a shirt and tie and a neat pair of pants instead of a tank top and faded jeans, you inspire more respect all around. By showing it, you're apt to get it. It makes a statement. I've never been to a school where having uniforms made things worse, and it always seemed to make things better.

We allowed uniforms to be required at some schools in Miami, especially at SBM schools, where they had the power to vote them in. In New York we have more than a hundred schools where uniforms were approved as a matter of "choice." The central board sets minimal guidelines for dress for the thirty-two local boards in the five boroughs: no shorts or see-through blouses, no shoes with metal cleats that can damage furniture, no ornaments or symbols that might be inciteful (like a KKK badge or a swastika), no radios, no beepers, no hats, and so forth. Some things you can't restrict, like length of hair. The courts found that to be an infringement on personal rights.

But the individual school can go beyond the board's rules on other things, like uniforms, when it has community support. Frank Mickens, the popular black principal at Boys & Girls High, has a rule against decorative gold teeth. He gets away with it because the parents support him. Other schools would have a riot on their hands.

The truth is, today's Catholic and private schools can't be fairly compared with public schools. It's apples and oranges. The Catholics say they do a better job with less expenditure, and maybe they do, but they don't have the overhead we have, and don't pay their lay teachers what we do, and don't pay the clergy on their staffs hardly anything. They don't have the broad array of curricula that we do, either. If you go strictly by test scores, they are doing a better job. But how much of that is traceable to their stricter enrollment policies? And the parental involvement? And the much broader latitude they're given for disciplining?

I've never been a believer in corporal punishment for school children. I think violence begets violence. The fear of it is one thing, but the application of it is another. And the unevenness. You grow up with it in parochial schools. When I was in school, nuns slapped you in the face if they thought you were impertinent. One nun used to pull my ear so hard it felt like it was being separated from my head. At Bishop DuBois, the priests and brothers were not shy about hitting kids. I liked my Latin teacher, Father Kowski, but he was a brute. If you made a mistake conjugating a verb, he'd whack your hand with a ruler. If you pulled back, the punishment was doubled. Every day he'd beat the hell out of your hands.

We can't do any of that in public schools, and I wouldn't want us to. And I have to think Catholic schools aren't as tough as they used to be, either, what with the inclusion of so many lay teachers (who could never be as tough as the nuns *I* remember) and a general softening of standards. For me, it didn't seem to matter either way, because I liked being on the edge, testing the limits. I was always playing with fire.

I was well into the "testing" stage with the most compelling fire of all, drugs, when I moved from Bishop DuBois to Commerce High. Everything I was doing that could be considered wrong came to a head there. Commerce was downtown, on 59th Street near Columbus Circle, and I talked Gene McCann into going with me. It was another world, a predominantly black inner-city public school that for whites amounted to survival of the fittest. Literally. We soon got into a test of strength with a gang of blacks that was shaking people down for money in the hallways. When they hit on one of my buddies, I rounded up some guys and confronted the ones who did it, and we took *their* money. And it went back and forth.

The way it was escalating, any day I expected the worst — a stabbing or shooting, a homicide. Fortunately, and ironically, we weren't there enough to make it happen. We were skipping school more than ever, going to 42nd Street, or sometimes not even going downtown at all, but heading out 125th Street to the Jersey ferry docks to swim in the Hudson River. By then we were using drugs on a regular basis. I wasn't addicted, I thought I was too smart for that, but I was certainly flirting with the prospect.

Drug use is a progressive thing, of course, despite what advocates of legalization say. Most people start with drinking. It wasn't unusual for some of us to get drunk on Saturday night. But that never appealed to me. Too sloppy. And it made you sick. Pot was the next step up, and that *did* appeal to me. It was cheap. You could buy a "bomb," a real thick joint, for a dollar, and pass it around.

But after a while, you didn't pass it around. You smoked it all yourself. And then that wasn't enough, so you started snorting heroin. Then shooting it. Always going for a little bigger thrill, a little longer high.

They have proof now that marijuana was never as harmless as people thought, that it does permanent damage physically and mentally. But for me, in the ignorance of the day, it was just a kick. Drugs don't affect everybody the same way. With pot, you lose all sense of time. Events seem to stretch out. I remember smoking a joint on the roof of the building on 126th Street and walking down the stairs — *drifting* down the stairs — and it seemed like it took two hours. Heroin gives you a prolonged high. Everything is pronounced. You notice things you hadn't seen at all when you were sober. You're not violent or anything, just high. You get violent only when you're hooked and don't have it. With me, when I came down, I'd get hungry.

I thought of myself as a moderate weekend user, but soon enough it wasn't uncommon to get high on Friday night, Saturday night, and Sunday night. I was never hooked. I never *had* to have it. But the fascinating thing was that nobody knew we were doing it, or if they knew, they weren't saying. My parents didn't know. The schools were deaf, dumb, and blind to the problem in those days. They didn't even talk about drugs in sociology class or "effective living" courses. If a friend or family member was involved, it was swept under the rug. Even at Commerce, where you could see drug deals going down in the hallways, no real concern was voiced about it. You didn't hear of any action being taken.

The thinking about drugs has changed a lot, of course. Even the most benighted individual has heard the dire statistics, so obviously there's a greater awareness. But there's also a much more virulent strain of narcotics on the street now. We didn't have crack cocaine to tempt us. Heroin, yes, and heroin is making a comeback, sad to say, but as bad as it is, it doesn't have the violent effect crack has. By every evaluation, crack is deadly. A quick hit, a quick euphoric high, a fast comedown, and then the intense craving for more.

And although the awareness is there, and in some areas usage is down — a 17 percent decline among teenagers in 1991, a significant victory for education, I think — we still have a whole generation of people who are using drugs regularly. Heroin now is into the thirty-five- and forty-year-old groups, people who followed my generation. Drugs are still *the* major problem in the poorest neighborhoods, and so-called smart people still think it's cool. Everybody has read the stories. We've had scandals on Wall Street. They busted a guy who was second in command in the U.S. Attorney General's office in Washington. The *mayor* of Washington got caught in a drug raid and left the office in disgrace.

You have to know how incredibly dumb that is. If you don't, you know it when the tragedies accumulate around you. When the grim scorecard *tells* you how dumb it is. I look back now and find myself amazed by how clearly you can draw the line between those who didn't fool around with drugs and those who did, and see the success in life on one side and the failure and heartbreak on the other.

In our neighborhood, the tragic stories wrapped together like snakes in a sack. One of the first to go down in our group was a Puerto Rican boy, dead in his teens of an overdose. The only Indian in the group became an addict. A guy we called "Skinny," for obvious reasons, went to jail for killing the attendant of a toll station that he tried to rob for drug money. They scuffled and a gun went off.

It was like a killer virus, the drug influence, infecting one life with another. The sister of a good friend of mine was one of the few girls in the neighborhood who used drugs. She married another user, and when they had a baby it was born physically impaired. Her husband became a heroin addict and died of an overdose, and she wound up a prostitute and living with Skinny's younger brother — who got stabbed to death in a bar fight over drugs. Then *she* died of an overdose. The grief caused by drugs still haunts that family.

My closest friends, Johnny Thornton and Gene McCann, turned out well, pretty much able to steer clear of the influence. Geney stuck it out at Commerce, got a second high school diploma at Bishop Du-Bois, and now has a nice home in Jersey and two beautiful daughters.

Lily Pons, my wife-to-be from 145th Street, would have nothing to do with narcotics. She was my first long-term commitment, the only girl I talked future with, but because of my stubbornness about drugs early on, we were an on-again, off-again romance. One of Lily's best friends had a brother who was an addict, but Lily's brother Billy didn't use anything and wound up a colonel in the Air Force. If you knew the players, you could almost predict the outcome.

Sometimes you get fooled, though. A few years ago, Lily and I were sitting in a restaurant in Little Havana, and I noticed this man two tables down who looked just like Skinny, except he had no hair. He caught my eye and came over. "Joe Fernandez?" Sure enough, it was him. We talked. He said he'd straightened himself out ("I broke the habit") and become a reborn Christian in a Spanish church. But it was an awkward reunion. The neighborhood closeness was long gone. We exchanged phone numbers, but I haven't heard from him since.

The thing I find to be consistent with every drug user I've known is what any counselor would tell you is crucial: that when you're into it you *never* think it's a habit. You *always* think you can control it. "I'm just going to do it tonight." "I'm just going to do it now and then, or on weekends." The next thing you know, you're hooked, or you've overdosed. And as the police blotters show, the bitter consequences are no respecter of persons.

One of the first people I had to fire in New York was a high school principal who was a cokehead. Parents and teachers had become suspicious; his attendance record indicated something was wrong, and the school was in chaos. Complaints poured in. I directed his superintendent to fire him, and when she didn't, I fired her and ordered the local board to replace him. They did, soon enough; it was an open-and-shut case. But the principal couldn't see it at all. He even sued us, unsuccessfully, to try to get back into the system.

My own feelings about the drug solution are tempered by the times, I suppose. I'm against legalization, but with the peril in the streets and the lives that are ruined every day in America, we have to find a way to take the profit out if we're going to get a quick response. The crime rate is way up because of the big money involved in drugs — the *cost* of drugs. And an addict will do anything for a fix — hurt anybody, rob anybody. Steal his sister's radio. Hock his father's watch.

But when they talk legalization, I think about people like the ex-principal and I *know* I wouldn't want my teachers using drugs. Some do already, I realize, but I wouldn't want it to be "all right." Or, for that matter, for it to be OK for airplane or harbor pilots, or truck drivers, or doctors, or lawyers, or anybody else who has the well-being of others in their hands. And I certainly wouldn't want students in my classrooms to be on drugs. So it's a dilemma. And given the results so far, I think it's obvious that education remains the best solution.

All the nation's schools now require substance abuse programs, from first grade on, and school-related incidents are going down. It's one area where federal involvement has been positive. Much of the program is founded on scare tactics, which some object to, but I find not a bad way to present it. But again, we're only part of the community. When the kids leave the school yard and encounter dealers in the streets, and see busts and shoot-outs in the neighborhood, and go home to find their mothers and fathers using crack, it's tough to make them see the total picture.

The beginning of my own fateful turnabout came in one night of horror on 135th Street when I was still enrolled at Commerce High. Jimmy Conn (not his name) had become my closest friend during that time, partly because of the experimenting we were doing with heroin.

Jimmy was a Scotch-Irish kid from a poor family, with no father at home. Actually, he lived outside the neighborhood, up in the 130s, but we were very close, to the point of swapping clothes to wear.

This particular night we were at somebody's house and got tied into some really potent heroin. I got sick almost immediately, a scary new kind of sickness. I remember saying to Jimmy, "Something's wrong. We gotta get outta here."

By the time we got downstairs to the street, we were both reeling. I can barely remember my friends walking us up and down the sidewalk, trying to keep us from fading out. They probably saved our lives. I was half in and half out for hours. Jimmy came to first. When I finally did, I was scared enough to realize it was time to make a change.

I dropped out of Commerce the following week and enrolled at Textile High, down in Hell's Kitchen, where I didn't know anybody. I could tell immediately it wasn't going to work. I was there only a week and dropped out again.

Then John Coleman, a counselor for the New York State Guidance Service, suggested I try to get into a private school. John was somebody to turn to. I had been a regular at his Manhattanville Neighborhood Center, which was nearby and a great place for teenagers: four stories tall, with pool tables downstairs, Ping-Pong rooms, a basketball court, a big area for dances. The whole idea was to keep kids off the street, so John kept it open until 10 o'clock at night, and he and I talked a lot. The guys didn't do drugs there, but sometimes they would shoot up across the street in the park. I think John knew. He was no dummy.

Anyway, he kept telling me that someday, somehow, I'd make it to college, the odds be damned. "You can do the work," he'd say. "You'll be making a big mistake if you don't try."

When I quit Commerce, he arranged for me to take a battery of tests. The results confirmed that I had academic ability and an aptitude for mathematics. John got me enrolled at Rhodes, a private school in a five-story mansion in the East Seventies. It was small, with small classes — actually too small for comfort. In just a couple of weeks I knew I wasn't going to last.

Meanwhile, John had given me a bunch of college catalogues, I guess for inspiration, and even though I knew I didn't have a prayer at that point, I got excited about the possibility of a career in engineering or electronics — not only a way out, but a way to make some money. I had no illusions, however. No long-range plans. I just knew I couldn't keep doing what I was doing. It was as much a case of running from something as to it.

I don't know whether I came up with the idea independently, or through John Coleman's leading comments, or Lily's pleas to "get a life," but I turned in the one direction that I felt could make it happen.

I left Rhodes in May, and in June I went into the Air Force.

Jimmy Conn went with me to join, but he couldn't pass the physical. He had track marks on his arms from the needles.

As last chances go for making it in life, the best move I could have made was going into the service. As it turned out, I was not yet out of the woods with drugs, but I was on my way to being an educated man. My emancipation.

PART III

SOMEWHERE AMONG OUR MEMORABILIA Lily has a token we had made at a novelty store in Times Square to commemorate our "going steady" as teenagers. The date is stamped on it: November 17, 1951. I was a month shy of my sixteenth birthday, and if we were going steady, I was going nowhere. Just another smart guy from the neighborhood making all the dumb turns. But at least I knew enough to see it. And I knew when I dropped out of Commerce High a year later that if we — if *I* — were to have any future at all, I had to break the pattern.

I made the decision to join the Air Force with only Lily's knowledge and was adamant about sticking to it no matter what anyone said. Lily said she understood, but I think she picked up on the fact that I had made up my mind, so I really didn't know how she felt. About the only promise we made at that point was to write. My parents, on the other hand, tried to talk me out of it. My mother thought I was "too young" and "too skinny." My father thought I was too hard-headed, but he had made a similar hard-headed decision himself at fourteen and softened when I said I was going whether they signed the papers or not. They relented.

I took the required sixteen weeks of basic training at Sampson Air Force Base in upstate New York, right outside Geneva on Lake Seneca. And I don't know if it was the charged atmosphere or a changed attitude, but I thrived on it. The routine — the discipline, the rigorous physical regimen — was more of a tonic than a test. At the end I took a battery of examinations to help determine what I could do for the Air

Force for the next four years, and given its stated need for radio technicians, I signed to study communications. I was earmarked for advanced training at Scott Air Force Base in Belleville, Illinois, just southeast of East St. Louis.

Then I went home on leave and did an absolutely insane thing.

I hadn't used drugs for sixteen weeks. But I also hadn't come to any final conclusions about how much that mattered. When you're young and indestructible, you are easy prey to the age-old lure of "it can't happen to me." It is a self-deception that every school drug-awareness program now hammers on.

Jimmy Conn and I were at my parents' place (they were out), and he had come onto some "expensive" heroin. We shot up in the kitchen and started to leave. Before I could get downstairs, I suddenly felt myself losing control — that terrifying downward spiral toward unconsciousness. Jimmy saw it. He got me down the street to a little diner just past the place where they sold "fresh-killed chickens," appropriate enough for someone too stupid to realize how close he was to the chopping block, and started pumping coffee into me. He and a couple of other buddies took turns walking me up and down the street.

Again, I don't know how close I was to overdosing. You never know. I finally revived, unharmed, but this was strike two, and it scared me enough to make me swear to myself never to shoot up again.

I still wasn't convinced I had to give up all drugs, all the time, however. At Scott, I was back into an environment that made it convenient not to. I was into jazz then, and in keeping with the times you could sit around enjoying music and the dope of your choice in just about every joint in East St. Louis. There was plenty of it on the base, too, and when the opportunity came for a little after-hours smoking or snorting, as often as not, I took it.

But sometimes you grow up in spite of yourself. In school at Scott, I rediscovered the pleasure of learning, together with the sobering realization that I had a *lot* to learn if I was going to qualify for something better in life.

In no time I got my high school equivalency certificate. I signed up for just about every course I could fit into my schedule, even if it was only remotely related to communications or electronics. I took an extension course in math, where I'd always had success. Before I dropped out of school, I had advanced through trigonometry: algebra 1 in the eighth grade, geometry in the ninth, algebra 2 in the tenth, and trig in the eleventh. I'd also made good enough grades in biology and chemistry to feel I could cut it in the sciences as well.

So I jumped at anything I could to expand my expertise. Later, in Japan, I even took a writing course at Sofia University, a branch of Tokyo University. The desire to teach hadn't hit me yet, but I made up my mind I wasn't going to get to the end of my enlistment, like so many men I served with, and find myself qualified to do nothing except reenlist.

If I was gung-ho at Scott, it was because it was clear that it paid dividends, sometimes unusual ones. Every recruit hears the line "Don't buck the system, and *never* volunteer." I volunteered for anything I thought could do me good, a habit that carried over nicely into my teaching career. You'd be surprised how many good things happen to you when you're willing to outwork the other guy.

One day there was a notice up at headquarters: "Wanted: Typist." I applied. I told the company clerk I'd taken typing in high school, which I hadn't, but I could use two fingers as well as anybody and what they needed wasn't a typist so much as a guy who wouldn't get bored to death typing up KP and duty rosters. That was the part that returned the dividend. By typing those rosters, I never, ever pulled KP. I left my name off all the lists.

By this time Lily and I were talking full commitment. She came out to Scott for a week when I got time off, and we decided to make wedding plans for my first extended leave home. It turned out to be a two-and-a-half-year wait. Most of my class at Scott was ticketed for overseas duty, in my case to a base in Spain. That appealed to me. What was left of the Korean War was in the other direction, and I thought, well, Mom will be pleased on both counts. I'd be out of harm's way, and I'd finally learn to speak Spanish.

Then at the last minute I got summoned into the Office of Special Investigations for one of those taps on the shoulder that change everything. Instead of going to Spain, I was ordered back to Sampson to spend the next two months with a group of fellow witnesses ordered to testify in the court-martial of a thief who had been operating there when we were in basic training. The thief was our commanding officer.

His name was Major Seavers, and he had evidently been working the same scheme for years. First, he offered to keep new recruits' money in the company safe during their sixteen weeks of basic training. (As he put it, they would have no use for it anyway "except to lose with at cards.") Then, when they were finished and preparing to leave for assignment elsewhere, he called them in, announced the safe had been burgled, and with a pained look on his face and a wad of bills in his hand, offered to cover some of their losses with his "own money." He said he "felt guilty" about what happened.

None of our group took him up on his offer; we thought old Major Seavers was as much a victim as we were. But he had reason to feel guilty, all right. I'd given him only thirty or forty bucks to hold, so I wasn't much of a loser, but some guys had entrusted him with hundreds. His overall take must have been well into the thousands of dollars, because he made the same offer to each new class. When the OSI doped it out, a number of us were ordered to Sampson for his trial — and conviction.

My class went on to Spain, and a couple of months later I was sent to Japan. Not a bad alternative, actually, but it cost me my one chance to be bilingual. I didn't have a prayer of learning Japanese.

Ask any American service veteran and he'll tell you Japan was easy time in the '50s. Mine would have passed routinely — studying at Sofia University and heading up a crew maintaining classified communications equipment at a multiplex center outside Tokyo — except for two incidents. I'm still not exactly sure what happened in either, or if they were somehow related.

We were working firemen's shifts, twelve hours on and two days off, manning this huge multiplex at Higashi Fuchu. It was good duty. Our barracks were like hotels — two men to each apartment, each with his own bedroom, bath, and private closet. I had a black roommate from New Jersey who liked music, and we'd pass like ships in the night. I'd work my shift, then usually zip into Tokyo, and when I got back he'd go.

One night I was in bed, just getting to sleep after my shift, when I was jostled awake by a tug on my arm and a flashlight in my face. Two guys from the OSI got me up, strip-searched me, and tore my room apart. I asked what they were looking for, but they wouldn't tell me until one of them finally pulled the spindle off my 45 record player. Out dropped two small bags of heroin.

To this day I don't know for sure how they got there, because they weren't mine. I was taken in and questioned, then released without charge. My roommate never returned. I didn't see him again until after the service, in Jersey. He said he hadn't put the stuff in there, either, but they'd transferred him and he wound up getting busted in rank.

I didn't even get a reprimand. I didn't lose rank or anything.

But some time later, I was called in by the first sergeant and told I was being transferred to Korea.

I said, "What for? I'm scheduled to go home in six months."

"No, you're going to Korea for a year."

It was a shock, because had I finished my second year in Japan as scheduled, I would have qualified for returning stateside and being let out in six months, a half year early. By going to Korea, I had to serve the full time, meaning six more months there and the last six in the states.

But why? Did it have something to do with the raid on my apartment? I tried for weeks to get an answer. Finally, a friend at headquarters, a technical sergeant, checked it out. He told me I hadn't passed a security check. I was cleared to handle "classified" material, but the new cryptographic equipment required "top secret" clearance.

"You didn't qualify for top secret."

"Why not?"

"Because of your dad."

"My *dad?* What did *he* do?"

"He was in the Abraham Lincoln Brigade."

Ah, yes. The flag-wielding, super-patriotic Abraham Lincoln Club, made up of men who had fought in, or sympathized with the Loyalists during the Spanish Civil War. I had to laugh, it was so ridiculous. My father the radical. But there was nothing I could do. It was part of the lingering legacy of the McCarthy hearings, when anyone resembling a "Communist sympathizer" was apt to remain a threat to the republic until his third or fourth incarnation. Well, thanks, Dad.

But as I said, I think you're put on this earth for a reason, and going to Korea turned out to be another step in the right direction. Korea gave me my first chance to teach.

Except for some skirmishes in the mountains, the war was virtually over when I got there. The two sides were into the lull that accompanied the peace talks. I was stationed at a Korean Air Force base called K-13, about two hours from Seoul up near the 38th parallel, the same base Ted Williams had flown out of when he got shot down during the heavy fighting.

It was a far cry from Japan, utilitarian to the extreme. The base and the countryside were uniformly bleak. But morale wasn't that bad. It was one of those bittersweet things you later call "an experience." We lived in Quonset huts, and my main job was to train ROK (Republic of

Korea) personnel in the use of our electronic equipment. They were regular Korean Army officers, training to be pilots, and we taught them everything. What made it interesting was that most of them didn't know much English, so I had to teach them to handle the American terms for the equipment and the technical procedures.

I had one other job, and it almost got me killed. For three months at a clip, a five-man team from K-13, including one Korean houseboy, had to man a "Homer" site up in the mountains, about three hours away by a mostly bombed-out mountain road. A Homer is a beacon that sends out a steady coded signal to help allied pilots determine where they are in the flight patterns. The site was nothing more than a little Quonset hut with an outdoor shower and privy, each a test of will in the Korean winter. Our only responsibilities were to turn on the spare generator and check the code signal on the beacon every six hours to make sure they were working.

You could do both jobs in three minutes, so dividing it up among the four of us meant each one had a once-a-day, three-minute chore. Which meant the three months were mainly spent fighting the cold and the boredom. For the first time in my life I became an avid reader. We sat around the Quonset hut, reading, playing cards, drinking coffee. Sometimes we went outside with our carbines and shot at bottles and tin cans. We used to hope the homing device would break so we would have to fix it, just for something to do.

The Korean houseboy was our one luxury. He not only did the chores and most of the cooking, but would also forage around the mountain shooting pheasant for the pot. We ate well and ignored the no-drinking rule.

The one other downside was the rats. They were as big as cats. In fact, whenever a crew took cats up there to kill the rats, the cats would disappear. Some Koreans eat cat, so it could have been poachers, but I always blamed the rats. One of the guys on my team hated those rats more than anything. If he saw one at night, he'd grab his carbine and shoot at it, right through the walls of the Quonset hut.

On my last trip up, we had to negotiate the mountain road in a snowstorm, in the dark, while pulling our water supply in a big trailer behind our Jeep. I was driving, right into the teeth of the storm, when the Jeep hit a crater in the road and started to skid.

I was able to brake to a stop, but the trailer jackknifed and slid off the road. It was a four-wheeler, very heavy, and when we realized it was still moving and threatening to pull the Jeep with it over the cliff, we all jumped out. The back wheels of the trailer were over the edge before the whole rig finally stabilized. We couldn't see very well, but it was obviously a sheer drop. The trailer teetered on the brink, making ominous groaning noises.

Under the circumstances, we abandoned the Jeep and trudged up to the Homer site on foot. There we radioed the base to send a tow truck.

I don't know what the odds are that someone would actually get pulled off a road and down a mountainside by a trailer, but whatever they are, I'm sure they'd be small next to what they'd be for doing it twice. But several years later, with Lily and three of our kids, I was towing a U-Haul through the mountains of Virginia in another snow-storm and almost did it again.

I'll get to how that happened later, but I think it's safe to say I should have only a very probationary license to pull trailers around the coun-tryside.

My rank was up to staff sergeant when the Air Force shipped me home in January 1956, to serve my last six months at Mitchell AFB in Hempstead, Long Island. My life was now as close to being well or-dered as it had ever been. I had put the insanity of drug use behind me forever, something Lily would have insisted on anyway for us to get married, which we did, in May, in the Catholic church in her parish. We set up housekeeping in a tiny apartment in the attic of an Italian family in Elmont, New York, right near the Belmont race track (no temptation at a sergeant's salary). Lily commuted into New York City for her secretarial job with Metropolitan Life, and I drove to the base for the night shift at the bachelor officers quarters, the BOQ.

My job was a no-brainer. I just had to be there in case some officer checked in after hours. Since that mostly happened when the privileged few flew in for a big event, like the World Series, I'd spend most of my time in a lounge chair reading or watching TV, and foraging into the leftovers from the officers' frequent parties. My only "action" occurred one night when I was sitting there with my feet propped up doing exactly that, having a drink and eating dip. Without the customary warning call from operations, and with no personal aide announcing the arrival of a dignitary, I suddenly heard this impatient "Hrrumph, Hrrumph," and in walked a little fat guy with a big cigar in the side of his mouth and a uniform that drooped with medals.

"I'm General LeMay," he said. "You're supposed to have a room for me?"

It was Curtis LeMay, commanding general of the United States Air Force. I took care of him without further embarrassment, and no fanfare, so maybe "action" isn't the right word. "Thrill," however, would apply — the thrill of spending a few minutes with an all-time military superstar and war hero. I remembered it if he didn't.

With my service time running out, I was given the usual pitch to reenlist. In those days, they'd offer you a bonus, a ninety-day leave, and an extra stripe if you extended. That or let you go to officer candidate school (OCS). My brother-in-law Billy opted for OCS and wound up a full colonel. But I was only slightly tempted. I was really thinking college, although I had no program, just the desire, and the belief that I was somehow on the right track.

The weekends usually found me on duty at the BOQ, so Lily and I saw each other only coming and going. Lily never complained. If you want to know how a thirty-six-year marriage holds together, talk to Lily. She was determined to keep us going no matter how much she sacrificed of her own interests and desires. With her in the city during the day, I took another math course at Hofstra University, not far from the base. Then, anticipating my discharge, we moved in with my folks on 126th Street and *I* did the commuting, out to the base in the '52 Chevy Lily's dad gave us as a wedding gift.

Upon release, I enrolled at Columbia University under the GI Bill of Rights. Given my druthers, I'd have preferred a small school where I could have gotten more personal attention. Columbia in every respect is a monolith. But I'd found a job in the bookstore at the College of Physicians and Surgeons in Washington Heights, Columbia's medical school campus, and with that and the tuition exemption, Lily and I were in pretty good shape. We found an apartment of our own on West End Avenue and, after some preliminary sparring with the landlady, moved in.

The landlady said, "Oh, 'Fernandez.' You're not Puerto Rican, are you?" She wasn't smiling.

I said, "No. We're Venezuelan." I wasn't even sure where Venezuela was.

It was really nothing more than a second-story tenement efficiency, but it was within walking distance of the university, and Lily, daughter of a carpenter and a natural with a hammer and a paintbrush, converted it into a little Eden. Everything was falling into place.

For sheer anxiety, however, those first few weeks at Columbia were the toughest of my life. It hit me that here I was, a high school dropout, with a dubious dedication that went all the way back to grade school, trying to cut it as a full-time student at one of the nation's most prestigious institutions. Columbia University, for crying out loud. The *Ivy* League!

To make it worse, I was there on a trial basis. Under Columbia's rules, you couldn't officially matriculate until after your first year. You had to maintain a B average through then, and if you didn't, you'd be done before you started. Whatever course credits you accumulated wouldn't count.

My uncertainty was heightened by the imposing size of everything: a big school, with big classes, some accommodating two hundred or more students at a time in lecture halls. I decided that first semester would be my litmus test. If I could make my grades, if I could hold my own with others who were much more qualified, I knew I'd be OK. In such a crucible, everything gets magnified: the highs seem very high, the lows seem very low.

I can pinpoint the day — actually, the very moment — I knew I was going to make it. That first year, I took only general studies courses and lucked into one of those extraordinary professors whose ability makes you rise above your own. I was studying math only as part of my liberal arts curriculum, not as the education major I eventually made it, and I signed on for a college algebra course taught by Dr. Sidney Meyer Levy.

Dr. Levy was a little Jewish man with a large reputation that included helping pioneer the School Mathematics Study Group (SMSG), which later became known as "the new math." In the classroom he was an absolute maestro, playing his students like an orchestra. When exposed to such genius, you can hardly wait for the next session.

There were a couple hundred students in his college algebra class, some of them ex-GIs like me, and the whole basis for grades was three tests. You sank or swam on those scores alone. There could be nothing personal about it. In fact, I doubt that Dr. Levy knew any of us at all, since the lecture hall was so crowded and he never took attendance.

After the first test, he took the next class period to hash over the results. He was going through our mistakes when he suddenly stopped and said, "Who is Joseph Fernandez?"

I almost didn't answer. I thought, Oh, man. I'm in trouble.

But I raised my hand, and he said, "A perfect paper!"

He almost shouted it. The only perfect paper in the class.

I practically floated through the course from there. My next two grades were almost as good, and at the end of the semester Dr. Levy asked me if I'd ever thought about making a career out of mathematics, maybe even teaching. I said I hadn't really considered it, but I would.

The next semester he was teaching "finite numbers," and I signed up for that, too, and did well again. I was beginning to think he might be right. Math was clearly my long suit. And I'd enjoyed teaching the ROK troops. Maybe teaching would be fun. But new success can be a heady thing. With my sights now raised, I began thinking I might just continue on into engineering. Or even expand into the sciences and be a doctor. Imagine that.

For the next two years, I took a full class load at Columbia and worked a number of part-time jobs to supplement Lily's income. I worked in the medical bookstores at both campuses, I worked in the zoology department taking care of the animals they experimented on, I worked in the post office during Christmas rush. In the summer, I loaded freight on the docks. I even delivered milk, albeit much slower than the company's wishes. A milkman had to be able to carry four bottles in each hand, and I could never do it, so my route always took me longer. Instead of finishing by 7 or 8 A.M. with the others, I'd be out until 11 o'clock, defeating the whole purpose of an early-morning job. I barely made it to my classes.

Then came another of those life-changing nudges.

Our first child, Keith, who had been born in 1957, had serious respiratory problems. He contracted one scary case of croup after another and was obviously struggling. The doctors said he might outgrow it but recommended a warmer climate. They suggested Arizona or Florida.

Florida was closer. I made arrangements to transfer from Columbia, and we withdrew the $800 we had saved, and Lily screwed up all her courage for the first real move of her life. I borrowed my father's old Plymouth station wagon to serve as a moving van and we loaded up and headed for Miami. My cousin, Al Morales, was part owner of a men's clothing store there, and he promised me a job. The job never panned out, but after a week in a motel on Brickell Avenue, we were invited to stay with Al's mother-in-law, who lived alone in a house near Tamiami Trail in what is now Little Havana.

I enrolled at the University of Miami, again on the GI Bill, and started scouting out jobs that would fit around my class schedule. The hard realities of my situation — the late start, the limited resources, and being married with a family — would eventually curb any real hope of going on into engineering or medicine, but at the time I was moving too fast to worry about it.

I got an afternoon job as a recreation director at an elementary school, where the progressive Dade County Parks and Recreation Department had set up a facility as part of a huge expansion program. I could make it to the playground from the university right about the time school let out at 3, and most days I stayed until 6 or 7, coaching the kids. I liked being outdoors, I liked sports, so it was a natural. I also got my first taste of the joy of teaching kids. As it turned out, I wound up teaching many of them high school math a few years later.

On weekends I worked for a magazine distributor, traveling up and down the east coast from Marathon on the Florida Keys up through Dade County and into Broward County, monitoring the racks at grocery stores and pharmacies to make sure the company's products were properly displayed. It was another no-brainer, but quite profitable by our meager standards. Including gas mileage allowances, I could take home as much as a hundred bucks a weekend.

Meanwhile, Lily got a secretarial job with one of the deans at the University of Miami medical school, Dr. John Finnerty, and by pooling our resources we were able to buy a little three-bedroom, one-bath house on the west side of town in a Mackle Brothers development called Miller Heights. I borrowed $1,500 from my folks, which represented most of their savings, for the down payment and secured a 4.5 percent GI loan for the remaining $10,000, which factored out to about $67 a month in payments. The house had tiny rooms that we thought were huge, and it sat on a 75-by-100-foot lot that by suburban Miami standards is a postage stamp but to us looked like the King Ranch. It even had fruit trees in the backyard. We loved it.

For a while we got by on one car, being close enough to the university for either of us to drop the other off. My dad had made a gift of the Plymouth. He said Harlem was no place to raise a large automobile anyway. We had left him a little '59 Ford Anglia I'd gotten in trade for the Chevy, but a year later, he and Mom came to visit in the Anglia and left that with us, too. Thus by the perennial generosity of loving parents, we had fulfilled the suburbanite's dream: to be a two-car family.

Eventually, Dad got Pan American to transfer him to Miami. He had to take the midnight-to-eight shift cleaning planes, but he did it so that he and Mom could be near us. They never returned to New York to live after that. My sister Angie, my main source of encouragement as a boy, joined us, too, for a while when her own marriage broke up. Her ex-husband made it big in electronics — drove a Rolls-Royce, flew his own airplane — but that was after the split. She never got to enjoy any of his success, which seemed unfair. But later she married a good man named Dick Jones, who's now a vice president for Belden Wire and Cable in Ohio.

I did well enough in my classes at Miami to prompt a meeting with Dean Finnerty about the prospects of going on to medical school. He went over my transcript and found I lacked only two science courses to qualify for premed. He said he'd help find financial assistance if I decided to go for it. And for a long while I thought I might. I actually didn't declare as a mathematics major until my senior year, when I made the dean's list.

By then I knew I couldn't abide another five or six years of schooling. Time and trials take their toll on goals, even hidden ones. I had started college at the ripe old age of twenty-one, and by having to piecemeal it through jobs and moves and family obligations, I didn't get my bachelor's degree until I was twenty-seven. And by the time I got my master's six years later, Lily and I had four great kids: Kevin following Keith by five years, Kristin four years after that, and Kami bringing up the rear four years later. They were all grown and I was pushing fifty when I got my doctorate.

But I have to admit it. Even when I started teaching, that little flame stayed alive in my mind — fed, I'm sure, by ego as much as anything else. I enjoyed teaching, from the very beginning; I knew I would be good at it. And I was at the point where I just couldn't wait any longer to make it in "the real world." But I was a long time giving up that private dream of the Dead End Kid ascendant: "Joe Fernandez, Engineer." "Joe Fernandez, Doctor."

Look at it another way, from the larger perspective. Horatio Alger deserves to be kept alive in America, especially for kids in places like Spanish Harlem. If a panel of experts had been given my school record through my seventeenth birthday and asked to predict my future, none of them would have said I had one. Not in anything but the least demanding, least rewarding jobs.

In many countries, in fact, I wouldn't have. In America, we have something special going for us called free, compulsory education, and we are required to make it available to the least of our brethren. There's a lot of talk today about modifying that holy legacy. Some administrators say school isn't for everybody, that we should give up sooner on the "uneducable," those who slow us down and try our patience (or worse) in the classroom. They argue that we would be better off being a little less zealous about their reclamation and a little more realistic about their chances.

After all, look at all the skimming that goes on in the other industrialized nations. England has one of the largest dropout rates in the world. A country that prides itself on producing the Truly Educated Man loses something like 60 percent of its students in the winnowing-out process. And it's intentional. When you are fourteen in England, you take a test that determines whether you continue in school or go into the work force, to be trained there for whatever specific skills might be required. The English don't consider those who do that "dropouts." We do.

Germany has a continuous skimming process. So does Japan. But Japan also has a large suicide rate among kids who are cut from the educational mainstream. Others who continue moving up but don't get into, say, the University of Tokyo, the Harvard of Japan, are considered an embarrassment to their families.

So what about us? Should we continue to subsidize a relatively high rate of failure and the added burden of chronic misfits being disruptive, and even dangerous, classroom influences? Should we continue to pay so dearly for our scholastic duds? I think so, yes. I have some ambivalence on the subject, but I think there's a fundamental wrong — even an evil — in having kids identified early on as uneducable, effectively killing their chances for the American dream. Because you never can tell about potential.

See it from my experience: a high school dropout going nowhere, who nevertheless was picked up again and again by the system and finally allowed to make it through. Yes, I worked hard for it once I saw the light. But the system made it possible. I had the GI Bill. I had a National Defense Loan. Later, I was awarded a National Science Foundation Grant for postgraduate studies at Penn State University. I had an opportunity to salvage myself after messing up my first chance. The system allowed it.

I think free public education, and the push we make to educate *all* our children, at least through high school, is one of the underlying reasons for our greatness as a nation. That's not to say we always do a good job, but the mechanism is there. I think there's an inherent danger in allowing a segment of the population to opt out of the process, because that segment invariably will be minority, and the disparity between haves and have-nots will grow, presenting a real danger of creating that "permanent underclass" we talk about. All because of a dubious screening process.

At the same time, I think we have to be much more creative in putting the proper slant on vocational studies. Even at the elementary school level kids should be made aware of all the avenues of expression that make useful, fulfilling work. Let them know through career-awareness programs that not all the "good jobs" require a college education. In Dade County we used to send around portable career labs, set up in big semi-trailers. Inside, students could move from station to station to talk with representatives from various fields: a doctor at this station, a policeman at the next, a lawyer, a carpenter, and so on.

When kids advance into senior high, they need to have good information on the full range of opportunities. If they take the vocational route, it's up to us in education to make it a positive decision, one that they make by choice, not as a concession to expedience or a negative evaluation of their worth. I think that's a moral obligation on our part. Every kid isn't going to college, and one of the big mistakes we've made in this society has been to spread the notion that everybody who doesn't is somehow less valuable. In the process we have demeaned a lot of honorable callings: plumbers, carpenters, fishermen, mailmen, masons . . . even teachers.

We can change that by establishing early the values in all legitimate endeavors. In some cases, that means reactivating respect for the work itself. The analogy can be found, ironically, in what we're trying to do with the teaching profession: to reestablish its status *as* a profession. Because a lot of people see it as just another job and go into it (or treat it) accordingly. The redirection and refocusing are important.

How soon should we encourage kids to decide on a profession or vocation, so that they can point their studies in the appropriate direction? The best answer for that is to say there is no answer. For some, positively influenced by a dad or a mom or another role model, that step is taken almost from the time they first hear the ancient question "Whatta you wanna be when you grow up?" For the vast majority, no real channeling is likely before the ninth grade, but alternatives shouldn't be limited at any time, which is why schooling through the twelfth grade is important.

Interests turn. A kid might change his mind about a career ten or fifteen times from the ninth grade through the twelfth. He might develop new ambitions. Like me, he might suddenly see the light. The error would be in randomly deciding whose light burns brightest, the way some European models do, telling one group, "You're better students, so you're going to college and be professionals," and another, "You're behind academically, your best bet is blue-collar work." Chances are you'll then be dividing them exclusively by class or race, with those at the poverty level relegated forever to manual labor.

By the same token, I see every reason to provide helpful avenues of curricula to those who are comfortable with an early career decision. And we do. Because "choice" has become an educational byword, we're moving more and more toward an era of "theme schools," where the whole classroom emphasis is concentrated on one field. For example, we have high schools in New York City that are now devoted entirely to finance, to environmental studies, to music and art, to the performing arts, and to communications. We recently opened one that is geared exclusively to transportation and is tied to the transit system. Every kid who attends is considered a candidate for the NYC Transportation Department.

When kids finish at transportation school (grades nine through twelve), they can immediately move into jobs their diplomas qualify them for or go on to college for advanced study. Transportation is a profession that is now very heavily into computers, making more schooling necessary for some positions. So far, the idea is working. The school is very competitive, drawing about two hundred applicants for every one opening.

But we must be careful to keep the options open almost to the end. If a boy starts automotive courses in the ninth grade, say, and decides he doesn't like them, he should be allowed to switch. By the same token, he should not be *made* to change should a popular class close up and the adviser says, "Hey, we don't have anything left in automotive. How'd you like to be a welder?"

Theme schools in the vocational field would be a good idea if all they did was dispel the ridiculous idea that "working with your hands" implies an inferior mind. That has always been wrong because of the obvious: your hands don't work independently of your brain.

But sometimes we get more than we bargain for. We built the Queens School of Aviation especially to provide qualified people for the forty thousand aviation-related jobs that will have to be filled over the next five years at the three metropolitan airports: La Guardia, Kennedy, and Newark. We won't be able to fill the quota, however, because 98 percent of the graduates from Aviation High *go on to college* — to become engineers or some other kind of professional. The school lifted the kids' horizons right out of sight, to the detriment of its mission. I don't know whether to laugh or cry.

Meanwhile, one of the best dropout prevention programs we have going is the co-op arrangements with the business community that allow kids to work while continuing in school on a shortened schedule. When should youngsters be granted that right? When their need is established, to begin with, and at whatever stage they are deemed "old enough" to hold down the job.

In such an arrangement, several good things happen.

First, the youngsters are making money, maybe enough to ward off a family crisis.

Second, they are establishing themselves for later on, learning particular elements of the job, the degree of difficulty, what might be expected of them beyond their expertise, etc. Things you really can't teach them in school.

Third, on the job they are likely to be working with the most advanced equipment, too costly for schools to provide or keep up with. For the nation's school systems the rapid advances in technology create an ongoing fiscal problem. If I took you to most schools in New York or Miami, you'd find them still using old electric typewriters instead of word processors. We simply can't always afford to stay current, particularly with computer technology, which changes so rapidly it makes your head spin.

When we first started purchasing computers for schools in Miami, for example, we wouldn't buy them without the pad that screws into the table and locks them in place, as a measure against theft. Today, the pads are worth more than the computers. You can get PCs so cheaply it is no longer feasible to install the pads.

The key to all of this, of course, is to "educate" both sides on the importance of tying in to the process — and not giving up on it. Wherever I have authority you can be sure the business world is going to be told loud and clear how it helps itself when it helps with such things as career labs and co-op programs; how business's willingness to work with schools and school kids encourages the desire all around to be better qualified.

And what is that but a better way to resolve the failures of the American labor force and the indifference of those who will one day be in it? I know about indifference, and the casualties it can cause.

Which compels me to say that Joe Fernandez the father learned his lessons well from Joe Fernandez the son. Lily and I made it a point from the beginning to make sure that all our kids availed themselves of their opportunities. Realizing they might not get the second and third chances I did, we pushed them from the start — not to get a college degree so much as to be in a position to go for it if they wanted. We had mandatory study periods in the home. We made books available, encouraged trips to the library, and made priorities out of attendance and involvement.

And I have to say it paid off. All our kids grew up to make us proud, not only as good students but as responsible, loving human beings. Keith, now in his thirties, is a vice president with Dean Witter-Reynolds. Kevin was a construction official for Miami schools before deciding to go back to college for his business degree. He is now planning on law school. Kristin worked as a sales assistant at Dean Witter before she got married and had a baby.

Kami is in her last year of college and it is significant to note that she is the only one who plans to be a teacher. I shouldn't be surprised, considering the example I set. From the beginning I wasn't a teacher so much as I was a driver. I drove myself. I thought of ambition as having arrived in my life six years late — or, to put it another way, if I'd been on schedule, I would have been a superintendent six years sooner — so I did my damnedest to make up for lost time.

And I did, too, in some ways. One year into teaching, and still very green, I was made head of my department, albeit by a fluke. When I got to be a high school principal at thirty-five, I was the youngest to hold that position in Dade County.

But the higher up the ladder I went, the more I saw what needed to be done and the more I *wanted* to do. The harder I worked, the harder I drove myself. It became a way of life. I don't necessarily recommend it; you miss a lot of home-cooked meals that way. You also miss the rush-hour traffic, going and coming, but that's a small reward. When you sacrifice all that time you might have spent with your family, you can't get it back. I'm sorry for that. But I doubt I would have done it any other way, given the conditions. I'm not sure I'd know how.

My first teaching job in the Dade County public school system paid $4,500 a year. Now that I'm making almost fifty times that and have gained a measure of celebrity, it would sound ludicrous to say I was happier then. So I won't. But I will tell you that I was never happier as a teacher those first years at Coral Park High School. I knew almost immediately, however, that it was transitory. When I was a teacher, I knew I wanted to be a principal. When I became a principal, I knew I wanted to be superintendent. I had a passion for getting things done, and when my ways of doing them meant breaking new ground, I coveted the authority to do so.

But things happen to you as a teacher — sweet, significant things — that never happen to you in any other area of life, I'm convinced of it. You make a mark on young people, but they make a mark on you, too. It's wonderfully reciprocal, and indelible.

Steve Reinemund is the president of the Pizza Hut Corporation now. He was one of my students at Coral Park High when I joined the math department there in 1963, fresh out of the University of Miami. I was a brand-new teacher, and it was a brand-new school, state-of-the-art in every way and bristling with potential. The incoming class was made up entirely of ninth-graders, and Steve was one of them. If we suffered from some understandable stage fright, we suffered mutually.

I'd actually met Steve the year before when I was interning at Riviera Junior High. He came from a single-parent home, with a terrific mother, and from the beginning he was one of those kids you wanted to help because nothing came naturally for him, and nothing got him down. He had to work hard for every achievement. But oh, how he worked. And oh, how he achieved.

He wasn't a great student, certainly not in math. He was a plodder. But he got his B's and A's, I think, mainly out of sheer determination. He wasn't a natural athlete, either, but with the same drive he made the football team, first string. He made the basketball team. He was the best wrestler, the star baseball player, the homecoming "king." When I was asked to sponsor the Key Club, he joined and became its president. In his senior year, he was elected the president of the school's first graduating class.

Steve Reinemund did everything as if he had to prove himself. The best compliment I could have paid him was that I hoped my sons grew up to be like him, and I told him that when he graduated. He wound up getting a full ticket to the Naval Academy at Annapolis, and after his tour of duty he went to work for the Marriott hotels.

When he was gone, he sent me the page from the yearbook with his picture, on which he wrote: "I can't tell you how much you have meant to me for the last three years. Since I have not had a father, I have respected your opinion on matters as I would have respected my father's. Your understanding of my ability and your efforts to help me I will never forget. As far as I'm concerned, you are the teacher of the year because of your concern for our knowledge and your understanding of our problems."

Steve kept in touch as he made his mark with Marriott. When he took over as CEO of the Pizza Hut chain, he moved his home to Wichita, where he soon became president of the Wichita Chamber of Commerce. Every winter he invited me to his condo in Vail to ski, but I never had time to go. One year when I was superintendent he came to my office in Miami to talk about an agenda to help improve education in Wichita. He was still trying to do everything for everybody.

I ordered lunch to coincide with his arrival: Domino's pizza. I didn't say a word when the delivery boy came, just passed it around. "Try this, Steve," I said. "Best pizza you ever tasted."

He said he was glad to see I hadn't changed over the years.

We laugh now about the things that happened — that *could* happen — in a truly happy school. I knew I had the respect of my students from the start, so I could loosen up when I felt like it. Good teachers should be able to do that with their students — let 'em go, then reel 'em in, as the occasion demands. One afternoon a kid fell asleep in my class, with his head on the desk. When the lesson was underway, I motioned for everybody to bring their books and follow me. As we tiptoed out of the room, I switched off the lights and locked the door. We found an empty classroom and completed the period there, so I don't know how long the boy slept and can only imagine what he thought the world had come to when he woke up. (The fun of a good practical joke is mostly in the imagining.) But it was into the next period before he got out.

Coral Park was like the high school everybody would love to have attended. I remember when I was on the basketball team at Bishop DuBois High in New York, going to play a game at a Catholic school near Iona College, where everything seemed so perfect: beautiful campus, sparkling new gymnasium, flawless baseball diamond surrounded by trees. Coral Park was like that. A new jewel for the mostly middle-class Westchester area of southwest Miami.

Of course, for a starting teacher it wasn't the real world. The first assignment for most teachers in a metropolitan area is usually one of those blackboard jungles in the inner city that can smother enthusiasm and make you a cynic overnight if you're not prepared. Which is why I now insist on a thorough orientation and training program (and am in favor of "incentive pay") for new teachers assigned to such schools. But for me in 1963 Coral Park was another stroke of undeserved good luck: the right place at the right time.

Historically, it was the sputnik era, when the American space program was playing catch-up to the Russians and math and science were high priorities in the schools. With more openings than there were qualified instructors, a new math teacher could pick and choose. I didn't even have to go into the Dade County schools personnel office. I just filled out my application, sent it around, and kept saying no until I got the right offer.

Let me back up a half-step to make it clear how fortuitous this was. In my senior year at the University of Miami, I had decided to intern as a Spanish teacher. Despite my shortcomings in the language, Spanish was my minor and, well, Fernandez was still my name. Hope springs eternal. But when I got to my assigned school in Homestead and compared my labored Spang-lish with the flawless classical version taught by the department head, I ran screaming for a new assignment. Riviera Junior High's math department responded, and when I think of that good luck, I am reminded of the way other people's lives touched Jimmy Stewart's in *It's a Wonderful Life*.

The principal at Riviera was Jim Newmeyer, who went on to hire me when he was named principal at Coral Park. The math department was headed up by a retired Navy man from Tennessee named Fred Fuller. Fred was a methodical instructor; he taught algebra without really knowing why it worked the way it did. But he was a great guy and we became close friends (he pitched and I caught for the faculty softball team; we never lost), and when I became department head at Coral Park, one of the first persons I hired was Fred Fuller.

And it was at Riviera that I became friends with Joe Tekerman. Joe was teaching social studies at the time and serving as the school's representative to the Classroom Teachers Association prior to its melding into what is now a very strong and progressive Dade teachers union. He saw the need for it and worked hard on its behalf. I'll never forget him getting up at a meeting and calling the conservative faculty at Riviera "a bunch of hypocrites" for not joining the movement. He told them they could "stuff this job" and walked out.

Joe also came to Coral Park and, of course, wound up as my number one aide when I became superintendent. I still call him regularly because he is one of those "men of the people" who earned his ribbons on the front lines of just about every area of school management. When he was principal at Miami Jackson High, a tough inner-city school, Joe had a girl die in his arms after being stabbed in a fight over a 19-cent ballpoint pen. He said he used to wear blue jeans to Jackson to be "properly attired" for those times when he had to wrestle some of his more recalcitrant students into compliance.

But Coral Park was a joy. The Westchester area had a large Jewish contingent, which usually translates into strong parental involvement, and had taken in the first big wave of exiled Cuban professionals, who were also success-oriented. With those groups and a healthy mix of white-collar and blue-collar Anglos, we got outstanding support all around, and some outstanding students. Steve Reinemund was one of "mine." In my math class, I had two girls who were among the first female students to be admitted to MIT. A boy named Joe Harris became the statistician for the Washington, D.C., school system. Danny Perales, a poor Mexican kid who quarterbacked our football team, wound up a doctor on the West Coast.

The teaching staff was well-balanced, like a good football coaching staff. Newmeyer had people like me who rolled up their sleeves and went to work on anything that was needed, and he had elitists from Coral Gables High who knew their subjects backward and forward but *didn't* roll up their sleeves, just did what was required. That's all right, it takes all kinds. Young and old, hard-driving and soft-sell, queen bees and workers. One spinster teacher was a lieutenant commander in the naval reserve. Bob Wesley, who headed up the science and math departments, was a biologist who eventually quit teaching to take over his father's fertilizer business in Mississippi.

What kind of teacher was I? Involved, primarily. In the classroom I like to think I made mathematics come to life. I understood what I was teaching, I spoke the language (math has a vocabulary and syntax all its own, and you have to understand it to speak it), and I was a good communicator. There is a constant learning process in higher math; you seem to discover something every time you open a book. Sometimes, though, you can appear to be *too* smart about it.

At the University of Miami I had a professor named DelFranco who was a math genius. She knew it all — permutations, calculus, everything. I liked her, but I was in the minority. She was stiff and rigid, and forbidding. She'd begin a semester with thirty or thirty-five students in a class and end up with eight or ten. We had two math teachers like that at Coral Park: dry, on-course, undeviating. Kids who aren't scared off, who stick it out, often find they learn a lot from such teachers. So do other teachers. My feeling is that you need a DelFranco or two on every staff, for the expertise if nothing else.

Teaching at Coral Park removed any doubts I had about *being* a good teacher, and from the start I enjoyed the rapport and the give-and-take. I was the kind of teacher kids came to, for almost anything. If you passed by my room in the afternoon, there'd be a line waiting to see me after the bell. I was never an 8-to-3 teacher; I'd be there until the job was done and the last question asked, no matter how late.

I was also the kind of teacher principals love because if they needed somebody to sponsor a club or help out in athletics or at the stage plays, I'd do it. I helped organize the first chartered Mu Alpha Theta honorary math fraternity. I sponsored Key Club. I was piped into what was going on. Any time something went wrong, with the kids or with the staff, Jim Newmeyer called me. When he had problems with the coaches over gym time (they were all gung-ho guys trying to make their program the best), Jim would say, "Look, Red Berry's having trouble with Gene Stage over at the gym. See if you can talk to them." The football coach, Frank Downing, was terrific, but he thought anything that interfered with his team was the enemy. I had to chase him out of my office one day when he tried to get a better grade for one of his players.

Contentment at school didn't translate into the good life at home, however. A $4,500 salary didn't stretch very far even in the '60s. So I did a lot of outside tutoring, helping kids from other classes or from other schools for five bucks an hour. When the word got out that I could make a difference, I got so many calls I had to set up a schedule at the house. Parents from expensive private schools — Deerborn, Gulliver — brought their kids to me. My living room looked like the waiting room in a doctor's office. I was tutoring almost from the time school let out, seeing my own kids for nothing at school, then rushing home for the others. Popularity pays. I eventually got my fee up to $15 an hour.

I also taught military kids and servicemen at the Homestead Air Force Base at night, and adults in the adult ed program at Miami High School. My routine was a Chinese fire drill: regular hours (a full range of mathematics, from general math through calculus, including honors classes) at Coral Park; tutoring after school and on weekends; teaching two nights a week at the air base and two nights at Miami High (usually from 7 to 10). And just to make it totally crazy, I started work on my master's degree at Florida Atlantic University, commuting to Boca Raton to squeeze in one course at a time.

Six months into that first year at Coral Park, Jim Newmeyer made me a department head. The combined math-science grouping under Bob Wesley couldn't accommodate all the subject needs of so many bright kids. We needed more teachers, more classes. Wesley recommended me to head up the math division.

It was unheard of for a first-year teacher to be chairman of a department, and as far as I was concerned I really hadn't done anything to distinguish myself. But I'm a good organizer, and while a new school is exciting, it's problem-wracked, too, because it hasn't gone through an organizational shakedown.

My strength in such a situation is that I'm not a complainer. I go to work. That, probably more than anything else, won over the older teachers and in turn gave me a comfort level for doing what I had a mind to do. Over the next couple of years my management skills must have gotten some notice, too, because when the assistant principal for curriculum left to take a fellowship, Newmeyer asked me to fill in.

At that point I knew I'd probably never be a full-time teacher again, although I kept my hand in as long as I could, even after I became a principal. But what made those promotions so exciting were the opportunities they gave me to try things. Things I thought made good sense in the face of America's rapidly changing educational needs.

For example, I liked the idea (someone else's) that high school classes should be synchronized as much as possible along topical lines, tying subjects together so that students can make the connection between, say, math and science, or social studies and language arts. If they're studying Shakespeare in English class, it would be appropriate for their social studies courses to be covering the politics and events in Elizabethan England and the rest of Europe. If they're studying the Crusades, the geography department should be telling them about those parts of the world that were affected.

The trouble with high schools prior to this concept is *still* the trouble with high schools: at that level, teachers tend to think of themselves as "specialists." *We're not like elementary school teachers, dishing out little doses of varied information; we're better than that.* They're not, of course. Teaching is equally important at every level, if in different ways. My first year at Coral Park I tried to talk some of them into coordinating math and science with a computer education model, but nobody wanted to give up any territory.

As assistant principal, I had the clout I needed. I was able to push through a series of cluster programs, what I called "cooperative learning models." I got Bob Wesley in science and the new math chairman to form one cluster, and the language arts teacher to form another with social studies. And we started doing interdisciplinary teaching. We started *talking*, one department to another.

And it worked. The teachers got fired up about it almost as soon as it was suggested. Coral Park was an ideal place for such an experiment because it was loaded with enthusiasm. Once teachers were tuned to breaking new ground, to doing the unusual, they communicated. They made the connections. They rallied to team teaching like the good team they were.

We experimented with other ideas, some good and some not so good. One that clicked was a team concept for trigonometry, where we taught 125 kids at once in a college-type lecture-hall environment. I did the lecturing, and two other math teachers worked with individuals, answering specific needs. We were warned it would be chaos with such numbers, but it worked beautifully.

We also tried something I called "modular scheduling" (nomenclature does not always sing for new ideas) whereby we divided class time into 20-minute "mods," with teachers signing up each week for the number of mods they would need per lesson. If they had something that might run longer than the usual classroom period, say 80 minutes, they asked for four mods. The next day they might want only 20 minutes, or one mod.

I thought that would be especially good for science or shop teachers working on projects that needed a longer time continuum. With the mods we could also subdivide into smaller classes — fifteen to a group, say — for subjects within subjects. I never worked harder to make something work. The teachers seemed to go for it, too. But in the end, we were done in by all the movement. It was distracting. The school sounded like a department store in the throes of a year-end sale — you kept hearing those little bells, "ding, ding, ding," signaling the end of a mod, and kids tromping from class to class at odd intervals. Futuristic it was, practical it was not.

Probably the most meaningful thing we did during that period, in terms of shaping my thinking on major school problems, was to swap places for a semester with the math department of an all-black high school in a depressed area on the north side of town.

The idea wasn't mine to begin with, although some of my teachers were mad at me for agreeing to it. It was part of a "teacher exchange" program that was a precursor to the total faculty integration of Dade County schools by court order. This was 1967; in '69, the integration of faculties would become mandatory, with each high school faculty having to be 12 to 20 percent black, reflecting the number of black teachers in the system. The elementary school faculties had to be between 26 and 32 percent black. The Dade school board was trying to forestall a forced implementation of that order by showing its willingness to comply independent of pressure.

The first step toward compliance was to be a temporary exchange of teachers. The board worked out a formula and asked for volunteers. Coral Park was paired off with Northwestern High, one of the most trouble-marked schools in the system. As chairman of the math department, I suggested at one of our meetings that we do this thing together, as a team. None of us had taught any black kids; what I knew about mostly black high schools I learned at Commerce High in New York, hardly a reassuring memory. Most of my teachers had had no exposure at all. I said, "This can be a worthwhile experience. We can do it together, and have our jobs guaranteed for our return. It'll be fun."

Fun was not quite the word for it. But, yes, a necessary and worthwhile experience it surely was.

Northwestern was built in the early '50s, along a traditional model for South Florida: a series of one- and two-story wings off a central core, with louvered windows that mainly served to darken the rooms. It was really not a bad-looking facility, but it was dirty and run-down, with bleak, forbidding halls and an ominous and threatening air. It clearly showed a lack of pride.

It wasn't a matter of not caring, however. The school board knew how bad it was and kept trying to make it better. Years later, when I was superintendent, we spent more money trying to help Northwestern than we did on any other high school in the county and still had limited success.

My Coral Park math department — eleven men and women — was at Northwestern for a little less than three months. If it was an object lesson, it was a good one. The problems we know now to be universal in ghetto schools were there to see in abundance: absenteeism to the extreme, a 50 percent dropout rate, violence, drugs, low morale, low achievement, low respect, low everything. The sense you got was of a school under attack.

The orientation alone was enough to drive us away. A black assistant principal gave us marching orders: "Don't wear expensive jewelry. Don't drive expensive cars. Don't go to the bathroom by yourself. Don't be caught in hallways by yourself." I refuse to be intimidated by that kind of talk; it makes me want to push for ways to improve the situation, not run from it. Besides, I knew about ghettos. But she scared everybody else half to death.

We carpooled to Northwestern. One group of us drove in together in a Volkswagen. What we found from the first day was that the negatively charged atmosphere was pervasive. The white teachers were there primarily because they couldn't get hired, or had been dumped, by other schools. The bottom of the barrel. They made you think it was "Mission Impossible." The black teachers were obviously more able to cope and had more enthusiasm, but they were still part of the general malaise. They felt they got no support from the administration, so why fight it? Black and white, they were teachers who didn't want to be there, teaching kids who pretty much felt the same way.

It was obvious that the same standards used to maintain other schools weren't in force at Northwestern. Materials were sparse, equipment run-down. The school needed a good all-over scrubbing. Academically, in an environment like that, students who have any hope at all don't get a fair shake. The teachers' negative attitude, moreover, had to impact on the kids. When thrown into such a mess, they are likely to believe the evidence — that they're not worth salvaging — and perform accordingly.

Location alone wasn't the problem. Northwestern is on the far edge of Liberty City, a tinderbox for riots past, but it's still in a residential area with many single-family homes. Overtown, nearer the heart of Miami, is a lot worse. The desolation had more to do with the condition of the facility, the programs, the personnel — the messages they sent from the place. If I could have seized the moment when I had it as superintendent, I'd have torn down the school and built a state-of-the-art facility on the same site. Erase all memories.

My impression after a first-hand sampling was that it was criminal what was happening at Northwestern and that integration of *both* schools, Northwestern and Coral Park, was part of the solution. It was as wrong for the kids at Coral Park never to see a black teacher as it was for the kids at Northwestern to be deprived of the best teachers, black or white. When integrated faculties were finally implemented all over Dade in 1969, schools were generally better for it, if only as a signal of improvements to come.

As it turned out, we really didn't get any grief from the kids at Northwestern. I think they sensed we were there to help them, at least after they were exposed to us for a while. I know my students seemed surprised when I said, "If you have any problems, come see me after the last bell." They were probably even more surprised when I was there when they came.

The only trouble for me happened one day between classes. I was on a free period, heading for the faculty room, when a tall, stringy male student approached a teacher in front of me and said, "You already got yours" (meaning her diploma, the teacher told me later) "and you're not going to keep me from getting mine!"

The teacher had given the boy a failing grade, and he had decided to make her pay for it. When he grabbed her, I grabbed him, and it was sticky for a minute or two because he wasn't all that anxious to be taken to the office. We got him there anyway, with no real damage. I had a lot worse happen later when I was an assistant principal at a school where there was a "better" racial balance, Hialeah–Miami Lakes, and at Central, the inner-city high school where I eventually became principal.

In New York, such an episode today would be shrugged off as a trifle. Violence in our schools is epidemic, and extraordinary measures have had to be taken. Schools in Chicago, Los Angeles, Detroit — *all* the big metropolitan centers — now present the same image of an almost apocalyptic savagery.

The shame in this is stunningly obvious. Over the last two decades we have come to accept the unacceptable: American schools as war zones. Houses of fear and intimidation instead of havens of enlightenment. As if that's the price we have to pay for compulsory education. It's not. And the sooner we realize we do not have to pay that price, the sooner we will have better schools, meaningfully integrated.

The total picture should not be ignored, however. The vast majority of our schools are *not* in turmoil, at least to the degree that the daily headlines would make it seem. Moreover, if you knew the demographics of any big city, you could pinpoint with unfailing accuracy the likely trouble spots: those hives of despair in the teeming inner cities where the sins of the barbaric few (drugs, crime, etc.) and the dearth of opportunity for the many combine to perpetuate failure. In New York City, 14 percent of the schools account for well over half of the violence and thuggery that make the 6 o'clock news.

The long-term cure from *inside* those battlegrounds has always been believed to be integration, and I don't disagree with that as a major first step. But just moving bodies around to facilitate court orders isn't nearly

enough. And to do so late in a youngster's development, when perceptions and prejudices are hardened and his or her one prevailing form
of communication is hostility, only increases the odds that the "cure"
won't take.

In the metamorphosis of American school integration, one fact has
been made crystal clear: the earlier you start with kids, the sooner you
get them used to multi-ethnic and multicultural environments, the
better off they will be — and *you* will be as a community. If you let them
be isolated too long racially, there's a good chance of permanent damage, socially and psychologically. I don't mean to say there aren't one-
race schools that work; obviously some do. And I recognize the need
for people to have choices. That's what a free society is all about.

But if black kids go K through 12 and all they see are black faces
among the student body, and the authority figures — the teachers and
principals — are mostly white, it can't help but stunt their growth as
social beings. Neither will they be prepared for a positive interplay with
students of other backgrounds if their introduction to that noble goal is
to be yanked out of their ghetto environment in the ninth or tenth
grade, bused across town to an all-white school in an affluent suburb,
and told to "be a part" — until the bus takes them home again in the
afternoon.

If we're to teach kids truly to learn to live together, to resolve racial
tensions and bridge all the other differences, we must start the process
at the earliest possible level: in kindergarten. Every study shows that
school integration works best in promoting harmony and mutual respect (and, yes, even mutual achievement) where kids have been together for a long time. Literally grown up together. You'd like that to be
true of an entire community, but we've always demanded more of our
children in these areas than we were willing to do ourselves, so that's
still wishful thinking.

Busing was pretty much the invention of that dichotomy: putting
the burden on our kids to resolve the problems of school desegregation. Its successes now are openly disputed, even by those who benefited most. Generally and historically, busing's main flaw has been that
the lion's share was carried on the backs of blacks in America. For the
most part, it has *increased* tensions between races. Many blacks now
condemn the practice with as much ardor as whites, as well they should.
The consensus on busing was reached a long time ago: nobody is really
crazy about it or wants to give it much credit.

But I wonder if we are too quick to forget the awareness it created of the need for integrated schools. And the good it did in helping bring a new responsibility to the education of *all* our children in this country, especially in the South. I don't think it's any accident that when the National School Boards Association made a survey in 1991 it found that the South has a better-balanced integration of minorities in its public schools, a better integration record, than any other section of the country. But busing continues to get a bad rap, so we have had to become more creative with it.

Magnet schools, offering a curriculum of specialized courses to draw students from all over a district, were really invented to put a better spin on busing (and, ipso facto, integration itself). When whites get bused now, it's primarily to go into a black school where an attractive magnet program has been set up. What happens too often in such a case is not lost on black leaders — especially militant black leaders. The school had been a pariah, with hand-me-down books and hand-me-down teachers, unkempt, and lacking in materials. Then comes a fine-arts magnet to attract white kids, and all of a sudden money is being pumped in for new equipment, new books, the best teachers. Not all "equality of opportunity" is equal. Put yourself in a black parent's shoes. How would you feel?

But you must see it from the other side as well. Predominantly black schools, with all their problems and failures, are hardly reassuring to white parents. Their kids have only one life, too. You won't get white kids into these schools unless there's something special about them, and even then their parents will hesitate out of fear for their safety. It's a catch-22. So, to try for the kind of enrollment balance you want, you provide a tangible incentive. Until a better idea comes along, that makes enough sense to me for magnet schools to be continued.

The dilemma, however, is compounded by the wholesale shifting of the demographics in the big cities of America. In most urban school systems, children of color (African-American, Latino, Asian) *are* the majority of the student population. The "re-segregation" of schools in that light is a fact of life that you simply have to deal with at the site. You can't make people who have moved to Connecticut move back to Queens.

New York state is now second only to Illinois in the percentage of schools that are more than 50 percent black, and it leads all other states in schools that are more than 50 percent Hispanic. Almost 89 percent of the black kids of Illinois attend schools that have 50 to 100 percent minority populations. New York follows closely at 85.7, followed by Michigan at 84.6, New Jersey at 79.6, and California at 78.7. No southern state is in the top ten. New York has 86.1 percent of its Hispanic kids attending schools that are heavily on the minority side, followed by Illinois at 85.0. The gains of integrated schools have been allowed to dissipate in most parts of this country.

I'm for neighborhood schools. Certainly not for the purpose of fending off integration, but because I believe they can bring a neighborhood together to a mutual benefit, from the parents and kids and teachers to the shops and businesses and institutions that surround and support them. I think it's self-evident that kids appreciate a school a lot more when it ties into their whole life. I don't think you get that, or the pride that comes with it, when you're there on a pass and confined to a schedule that says you leave when the bus does. My preference is that kids be at their schools almost any hour of the day or night if there is something going on to interest them.

On the other hand, what keeps neighborhood schools from a natural well-balanced integration is the thing that has *always* been the sticking point: neighborhood housing. You don't change a ghetto by busing kids out of it. They come back every day to the dismal reality. Nor do you change it by lamenting its low economic state or its ethnic makeup. To tell you the truth, I don't know how you change it in a democratic society except perhaps through government-ordered restrictions on housing projects: by requiring a certain percentage to be set aside for minorities each time you plan one.

But let's not kid ourselves. There is no available magic to make neighborhoods ideally integrated overnight, no matter what percentages of race and ethnic mix the ideal is perceived to be. In the meantime, something needs to be done now to regain control of our schools in those hellholes where the uncontrolled 5 or 10 percent run roughshod over the rest.

I said earlier that the best answer to the failures of education in America is to improve *all* schools, to make them sensitive to every need and answerable to the highest standards. We're never going to get that if we don't free them from the tyranny of violence and turmoil that now menaces their existence. No matter how magnanimous the intentions of integration, or how much care is taken in carrying it out, kids aren't going to learn very well if their schools are boiling pots of hatred and intimidation. Teachers aren't going to teach very well if they are afraid.

I've known violence, I've *been* violent, and I've dealt with it in schools before. But I've never seen anything like the violence we now have in our big-city schools. Even with what I remember from my youth, and what I experienced in Miami, I could not imagine when I accepted the chancellorship in New York in 1990 that it would be so bad. It's not a phase, it's a malignancy. In the first six months of the 1991–92 school year, we had four students and a teacher killed in or near our New York schools. The teacher, Audrey Chasen, a beloved twenty-eight-year veteran of the city school system, was shot through her car window when she happened into the middle of a drug shootout.

In November 1991, at Thomas Jefferson High School on Pennsylvania Avenue in the East New York section, a fourteen-year-old boy, interceding for his brother in a fistfight, pulled a gun and shot wildly into a crowd of bystanders, killing a sixteen-year-old and critically wounding a teacher trying to break up the fight. At the same school three months later, in a second-floor hallway, a fifteen-year-old pulled a gun and shot seventeen-year-old Ian Moore in the chest and sixteen-year-old Tyrone Sinkler in the back of the head at point-blank range, killing both. Police blamed a long-festering feud and arrested Khalil Sumpter, who had run from the scene and was caught two blocks away.

Thomas Jefferson High is not your classic snake pit. It is, in fact, an attractive brick building with brightly painted halls and clean classrooms, and it's a school rich in tradition. But it now sits in an area that looks bombed out, with litter-strewn vacant lots and decaying tenements, and the families that exist there are hardened to the sounds of gunfire and the casual drug deals that go down on the street corners at all hours. In 1990 the area had the second-highest homicide rate in the city.

What happens on the grim peripheries of such schools as Thomas Jefferson can't be controlled by the schools themselves, of course. But the schools can't help but be affected.

In the four months between the killings, a fifteen-year-old girl was grabbed by two men as she waited at a city bus stop before school, driven to a remote area, and raped. An eleven-year-old boy was snatched as he walked to school on West 77th Street, raped, and sodomized by an HIV-positive parolee.

I could go on and on, reciting every imaginable form of depravity visited on the children of New York — too often perpetrated *by* the children of New York. A five-year-old kindergartner found packing a gun. A fifth-grader arrested with 411 vials of crack cocaine. A nine-year-old beaten and sodomized — by one of his schoolmates, age eight!

Thus the influence of the neighborhoods filters through. In the 1990–91 school year, there were forty-five incidents involving guns in or around the schools of New York. Eleven children were shot, one died. There were 2,170 incidents of weapons possession. In the first six months of the 1991–92 school year, we had fifty incidents involving guns, twenty-three inside the schools, two in school yards. Fifteen children were shot (including the four killed), and five teachers were shot. Immediately after the Thomas Jefferson killings, Mayor Dinkins put his signature on a $28 million appropriation to beef up security: to add metal detectors, X-ray devices, and whatever else it might take to keep weapons out of school buildings.

But don't be fooled. Such precautions are necessary, and I welcome any effort or safety device that technology can provide to reduce the arms race in our schools, but Thomas Jefferson High had thirteen security guards on the job when the first murder occurred in November. When the two boys were killed in February 1992, two armed New York City police officers were on duty *fifteen feet away*. Chicago has at least two police officers in every one of its seventy high schools and still staggers under the load of an expanding mayhem. Los Angeles has a security force of 300 in its schools, but still had 319 firearm-related incidents in 1991. High-tech surveillance and the deployment of more cops and more ordnance are *not* a sign that we're winning the war, but that we're losing it.

In our understandable eagerness to weed out the tools of the deadly acts, we miss another essential point: that kids now carry guns and knives as if they were pens and pencils not just to *do* harm, but to ward it off — to defend themselves.

School kids are getting mugged, getting robbed, getting bullied every day by their peers or by that vicious 5 or 10 percent that do most of the damage. In some neighborhoods, brazen "rat packs" (what one New York superintendent calls the roving bands of hoodlums in his district) routinely harass and threaten elementary and junior high kids. Newspapers tell of tougher, older kids beating up younger, weaker ones, taking their lunch money, stripping them of their jewelry and hats and shoes — and dignity. The fourteen-year-old who killed at Thomas Jefferson was small and baby-faced. He said he had been a victim long enough. He bought himself an equalizer.

No, not even an all-encompassing weapons shakedown will be enough. What it's going to take is a whole new way of dealing with the chaos in our inner-city schools. From the downtown bureaucracy to the blighted areas where the rubber hits the road, the malignancy has to be attacked by every concerned party, including those who stand to lose the most by its spread: the people in the troubled neighborhoods themselves. In effect, black leadership is on trial here. It has got to commit to working within the system on the proposition that *no* child, black or white, should have to fear for his or her safety in a classroom or a school yard; that *no* teacher, black or white, should ever be cowed or struck down by his or her students, under *any* circumstance; that it's an insult to the black community that the worst schools are always perceived to be in their midst.

Those gallant soldiers of such honored organizations as the NAACP need to quit fighting wars they've already won and concentrate on the one that now threatens the deliverance of their children. Schools are where you go to get the credentials to improve your lot in life. If children are to learn, schools *must* be safe places to learn in, not trauma centers. They must be able to employ (and keep) the best-qualified teachers, and not lose them to battle fatigue, or worse. Inner-city schools need every resource we can muster, and not be held hostage to fear and intimidation. When they are deflected from their purpose, the damage is long-term. It doesn't take much digging to find the consequences. At the end of 1991, only 10.6 percent of New York City's black teenagers, aged sixteen to nineteen, had jobs.

I meet with black advocacy groups all the time, and I listen with a sympathetic ear because I want what they want: a better chance for their children. I tell them to put my feet to the fire — if I don't demonstrate the proper sensitivity to their schools and children, call me out on it. If I am ever shown to be acting in the best interests of one group at the expense of another, I'll resign in a minute.

But all too often I find that when some groups talk up their agendas, they are more concerned that police acted "hastily" in reacting to a violent act than the fact that the violence had profoundly disturbed the learning process at the school. They are more concerned with the "intimidation of students through the use of police" than the daily specter of children intimidating other children and beating up on teachers, to the detriment of learning. They're more concerned that the principal I fired for drug use or the superintendent I replaced for incompetence was black than with the harm their actions were doing to their communities.

You can trot out all the excuses you want for the aberrational behavior in inner-city schools, and chances are I'll agree with every one. You can blame the poverty, the drugs, the unemployment. You can blame absentee fathers and illiterate mothers. And you'll be right. They are terrible handicaps. But that still doesn't make sociopathic behavior right, and to excuse it gets us nowhere.

Review the dispassionate accounts of "incidents" that cross my desk any week of the school year and judge for yourself. Taken at random, a summary from a week in January 1991: fifty-four cases of assault, forty-eight incidents of harassment, thirty-seven charges of larceny, thirty-one cases of disorderly conduct, five robberies, one sex offense, eleven cases of "criminal mischief," nine charges of "menacing" behavior, sixteen cases of "reckless endangerment" . . . and sixty-four cases of weapons possession.

A full rundown of the box score for an entire week would require too much space here, but even *one day's* report is a fairly suffocating thing. On one day that January, we had twenty reported acts of violence, beginning at 8:30 in the morning at a junior high school in Brooklyn where a fourteen-year-old was asked to remove his hat by a security officer, refused, and, according to the report, "repeatedly struck the officer." The student was suspended.

At 9:05, in the staircase at a high school in Brooklyn, a sixteen-year-old male student was robbed of four gold rings and an earring by an unknown male who threatened his victim with a knife. At 9:30, in a high school in Queens, a female student was slashed in the face with a belt buckle in a fight with another girl and rushed to the hospital. Her antagonist was arrested.

At 10:25, in a high school hallway in Brooklyn, one male student hit another "repeatedly on the head with a book bag," causing contusions that were treated on the scene. The attacker was suspended. At 10:40, at a high school in the Bronx, a sixteen-year-old male student was caught brandishing a knife. The weapon was confiscated, the student suspended. At 11:30, in the bathroom of a Brooklyn elementary school, a ten-year-old female slapped and punched a nine-year-old, who suffered a swollen cheek and bruised stomach.

And so it went, all day long: a female student arrested after slashing the heads of two males with a box cutter in a Queens junior high school; another female cut in the face by a male in a junior high classroom fight in Brooklyn; three female high schoolers in the Bronx caught carrying knives; a volunteer assistant punched by a female teacher in a Brooklyn elementary school; a Manhattan middle school teacher hit by a chair thrown by a teenager when the teacher asked for identification. According to that report, the teacher chased the student, who then turned and "struck the teacher repeatedly with a broom stick." The teacher required stitches. The student was transferred.

It must be emphasized that these were only some of the incidents *reported* on that day. How many actually happened — twice as many, five times as many? — we have no way of knowing, but you can be sure that the unreported cases far outnumbered the reported ones.

There's a tragic mistake we make — meaning all of us: school administrators, community leaders, parents, the school board, everybody — in not ganging up on this contamination. Not just because too many bad guys win, at the expense of too many good guys, but because right now in this country blacks have more opportunity than ever to make it in life.

I would be the last to say that the least qualified among them have an "equal" opportunity; there's still plenty of prejudice and bigotry out there for the more persistent racists to feed on. But proof can be found everywhere that those who are qualified — meaning those who are educated in one field of endeavor or another — do not just get hired, but get to the top of the highest-paying and most-prestigious jobs in government, in business, in the professions, in the military — in just about every walk of life. You don't have to be a running back or a blues singer to be black and be a star in this society anymore. You can be governor of your state, or a U.S. congressman, or a justice on the Supreme Court. You can be president of the National Baseball League or chairman of the Joint Chiefs of Staff, or own the Oakland *Tribune*. Blacks now hold all those positions.

Many big-business leaders will tell you forthrightly that given a choice in hiring they pick the qualified black almost every time, for whatever good reason, even if it's just out of conscience for past neglect. Newspapers and television stations, and the media in general, bend over backward to hire blacks. Not just to fill a hole, but to be a station's anchorperson or a newspaper's lead columnist. I am not so naive as to believe that all employers are acting along those lines, but enough are to make a difference.

Meanwhile, we in education see it in the numbers of qualified black teachers we *don't* get. Across the country school districts are crying for good black teachers and administrators, but we all have a pipeline problem now because even the black colleges that traditionally turned out prospects are producing graduates who opt for other (and more lucrative) careers. It's a mixed blessing, and ironic. The shortage is alarming, but the reason for it is encouraging.

In any case, to miss this window of opportunity, to fail to stress that education can get black kids into the mainstream, and to fail to make them more agreeable to the process, is an unforgivable mistake on all our parts. And when the very places that can make the difference are turned into asylums of violence and fear, we have allowed our black children, in effect, to cheat themselves. If I were a black leader, I'd be screaming. Screaming in demand that my schools be models of decorum instead of armed camps. Some black leaders are, and their voices are welcomed.

Why is this so urgent right now? Because there is an element in the mix that at this moment in time is at once the most alarming and the most depressing of the inner-city problems and it is as tied to the chaos in our inner-city schools as a man's hand is to his wrist.

The single most tragic figure in American education is the dysfunctional black male, and if we don't do something to turn him around, the dire statistics he creates will get much worse. Already they are frightening. The leading cause of death for black males aged fifteen to twenty-four is homicide. Unemployment among black male teenagers is two out of three in those blighted core areas where life is so cheap. Their high school dropout rate is about the same. More young black men go to jail than go to college.

I am among those educators who believe that one emergency measure worth exploring further (if we can find a way to satisfy civil rights laws) is all-male academies for inner-city blacks. Schools that would offer a specialized multicultural curriculum, aimed at raising self-esteem, while providing a more disciplined environment geared specifically to boys and free of the sexual distractions that contribute so greatly to the turbulence in these urban hives. In short, schools that could attack the needs of this troubled legion through a streamlined and more focused learning process.

Why would I be for such a measure if I'm against school segregation of any kind and have just told you how important it is that racial de-isolation, for the benefit of *all* kids, should begin in the earliest grades possible? Because we're not talking now about five-year-olds. We're talking about thousands and thousands of hostile, tuned-out young adults, men-children who have been locked into a social and scholastic time warp and been made prey to every evil influence poverty and its wicked antecedents (broken families, broken dreams) can inflict. They *require* our special attention and special schooling, if we can provide it.

The problem is that you can't make such a school mandatory, for all the hard-won civil rights mandates that have been correctly applied to prevent discrimination in the schoolhouse. But clearly something must be done, and if an all-boys school is worth trying, as many experts agree, a summit meeting of educators and civil rights leaders needs to be called to explore the possibilities.

Feminist leaders who object to excluding girls from such schools might be persuaded to consider all-girls schools as well, on a trial-option basis, for pretty much the same reasons. Almost three thousand black teenage girls become pregnant every day in America, and fifteen hundred drop out of school. Those who know the psychology (*and* the physiology) of the situation argue that some separation of the sexes during school hours for those traumatic first years of puberty and adolescence surely can't make matters worse, and may make them better.

Single-sex public schools are not new, of course. Almost every big city has had them in the past. Boys & Girls High in New York was a Boys High *and* a Girls High before "separation" of any kind became a lightning rod for civil rights activists. Many parochial schools are still single-sex, a Catholic tradition. Research shows they do better with classroom deportment. One would have to think, too, that the explicit sex education courses we now must teach could be more openly and specifically dealt with in a single-sex environment.

Knowing all this, the city of Detroit put together a plan for an all-boys inner-city model in 1991. Ninety percent of Detroit's public school students are black. Fifty-four percent of the black males who enter the system do not graduate, lagging behind in every area of study and causing an overwhelming majority of the discipline problems. Detroit planned to open three all-black male academies, starting with elementary-age kids. Proponents called it a "last desperate measure" to rescue the city's male population — and thereby the city itself.

But from the reaction they got, you'd have thought they had declared war on the Bill of Rights.

The American Civil Liberties Union and the National Organization for Women charged "discrimination" against female students and sued the school board. A U.S. district court judge ruled that all-male elementary schools were "unnecessary and unconstitutional." And Education Secretary Alexander, delivering the coup de grace, said Detroit would have to find other ways to help black males without "segregating them in violation of federal law."

Beaten down by the odds, Detroit's Board of Education backed off from an appeal of the judge's order and finally dropped the idea altogether. Although twelve hundred parents signed their kids up for the 536 available slots at the three schools, the board decided it could not justify a costly court battle over an issue it had "little chance of winning."

Advocates of an all-black, all-male academy in New York City almost got past the talking stage with an alternative high school its founders called the Ujaama Institute (after the Swahili word meaning "familyhood"). The plan was initiated when I got there and was modified a number of times under pressure before settling on a collaborative effort with Medgar Evers College. Opponents argued that it was separatist and racist. After it went through the wringer a few more times, Ujaama was reduced to a multicultural school with no sexual barriers, and as of this writing it is still "in development."

I wasn't crazy about the original Ujaama game plan (it had a number of flaws), but I remain sympathetic to the strategy even as it languishes. Baltimore and Milwaukee have launched similar efforts, with similar rebuffs. When Spencer H. Holland of the Center for Educating African-American Males first presented the idea in a 1987 article in *Education Week*, one of my elementary school principals in Dade County set up two all-male, all-black classes, but the feds found them in violation of sex discrimination laws and we had to abort the effort. So it goes.

Meanwhile, the search for a more stabilizing environment for inner-city schools goes on. I have completed a student-conduct code for the school board to approve for the public schools of New York City. I want to have it spelled out, the way we did in Miami, exactly what is expected of our kids and what action will surely be taken if the expectations are not lived up to.

I intend, too, that all the teachers we place in those most troubled schools go in prepared and be appropriately compensated for their efforts. But most important will be the help we get from all those who have a vested interest in making schools better, because they won't get better without their help. If it's a cooperative effort, we *can* have safe schools in unsafe neighborhoods. We must. Because the alternative is unthinkable.

There was a banner on display over the second-floor balcony at Thomas Jefferson High School when the two boys were killed there in early 1992. With an almost uncanny appositeness, it read: "The choice today is not between violence and nonviolence. It is either nonviolence or nonexistence."

With all the running around I did to make a buck those first years in Miami, and with Lily working full-time in the comptroller's office at Burger King (while at the same time handling the chores of child-rearing), we gradually moved up economically. Lily was the family's backbone, much as my mother was. She had been the one who saw the dead end I was heading for as a stubborn teenager, and had it not been for her willingness to work I'd never have been able to go back to school. She always saw the need for those things clearer than I did.

Kevin was born in 1962 and Kristin in '65, and we knew then that we would be Miamians for good. Keith's health was much improved. We had no intention of moving back to New York. So we splurged and bought a larger home on a corner lot (that matters in Miami) at Point Royale, paralleling Old Cutler Road, not far from Biscayne Bay: four bedrooms, two baths, and a family room. We kept the little house as an investment and rented it out.

My third year at Coral Park, I was offered a National Science Foundation Fellowship to take advanced studies in mathematics, a benefit promoted by the government in those days as part of the catch-the-Russians effort in the schools. The deal included a $4,800 stipend — more than I was making as a teacher — and granted a leave of absence with credited time, so I went for it, applying to Penn State and LSU. I got accepted by both, and chose Penn State. Lily's boss was from the State College area and offered to let us use a house he had there that he said was "close to the school, right by a river."

The fellowship was for a full school year, so we sold the house in Point Royale, moved all the furniture into my mother's house, loaded up all we thought we'd need, and went on our way. As it turned out, the house we were graciously given to use was more like a big, one-room hunting lodge, so far out in the woods that I faced almost an hour's drive going in to Penn State every day — when the roads were passable. The neighbors said that for me to make classes in the morning during the winter, I'd have to leave at 3 A.M.

We tried to find an alternative, but everything was taken in and around State College. We found a temporary apartment, then moved again when we were able to rent the second floor of a two-story house in Pleasant Gap, right off a main highway but still forty minutes from the

Penn State campus. It wasn't a good choice. Pleasant Gap is Amish country and did not live up to its name. The Amish almost by definition are clannish people. They didn't speak to our kids and barely nodded at Lily. We pretty much stayed to ourselves.

I studied in a program for teachers, all advanced math skills, in a class of about thirty-five from all over the country. We stuck it out only until the winter of 1966, a bitter cold one up East. By then we were all anxious to get back to Miami. We packed the car and a big U-haul trailer (in our eagerness to save a nickel, we'd even taken a washer and dryer to Pennsylvania), and like the fools that you are when you're young and scratching for every nickel, we decided to drive straight through. Lily stocked one cooler with fried chicken, sandwich meats, and bread and another with milk and soft drinks, and we took off.

We were in the mountains of Virginia, well past sundown, when the storm hit. It was Korea all over again. The snow came right at us, obscuring my vision and slowing us down as it began to stick. The road shrank in front of us. I finally had to pull off. I inched onto a side road, and when I couldn't see enough of a track (I couldn't see pavement at all), I stopped. We were near a place called Natural Bridge, but we didn't know it at the time. We just pulled off the side and stopped, taking our chances.

And we stayed right there. The road was impassable, no traffic coming from either direction. We slept in the car. We were probably lucky we didn't freeze to death, but when I got up and stumbled outside the next morning, I realized how lucky we really were. Snow was piled high all around, but we were right on the verge of a steep cliff — and one of the back wheels of the trailer had slid off the edge. If we'd continued the way we were going, we'd have surely gone over or been pulled over by the trailer.

I hustled everybody out, and we plodded up the road through the snow in search of help. About a mile away we came on an old motel that had closed because of the storm. I pounded on the door, and the proprietor came out, blinking at us like we were specters. When he understood the fix we were in, he invited us to stay, at no charge. We stayed two days, eating out of our coolers. When the roads were cleared on the third day, we got AAA to pull the car out and get us going. Looking back on that episode and the one in Korea, I know now that God makes provisions for drivers like me. They are called "chauffeurs."

My job at Coral Park was filled when I got back, so I spent the rest of that term and summer of 1967 at Palmetto High School in the affluent

Kendall area of Miami, with the OK to return to Coral Park in September. Which I did, as a math teacher and head of the department, but not as assistant principal. The A-P whom I had replaced had returned. I wasn't unhappy about it because it still allowed me three more years at a school I truly loved.

Before the 1972 term, however, I was advised by the superintendent of schools, Ed Whigham, that he would prefer I move back up to assistant principal, which was my sentiment exactly, and when the principal at Hialeah–Miami Lakes High School told me he would be needing an A-P for curriculum, I applied. At the interview, I was responding to questions by a group of people in his office and barely noticed a handsome black man sitting in a dimly lit corner. He just sat there, blending in. The interview was almost over before he spoke.

He said, "How would you plan for a school to switch to a quinmester schedule?"

Taken by surprise, I said the first thing that came to mind: "I'm not sure, but before anything else, I'd involve the students. They're the ones who'd be most affected." My answer, simple as it was, seemed to perk him up.

The man in the shadows was Johnny Jones, then the district superintendent (Hialeah–Miami Lakes was in his jurisdiction) and a rising star in the school system. Jones later was to succeed Whigham as superintendent of schools — and to become the most tragic figure in all my experience as an educator. With his talent, Johnny Jones could have wound up Secretary of Education. I came to know him as a charismatic leader and a brilliant communicator, but at a critical time in his administration, a part of him emerged that I didn't know at all — the part that put him out of a job, in disgrace. He was to play a key role in my life over the next several years.

The following Monday I was accepted for the job at Hialeah–Miami Lakes, a school about the same age as Coral Park, but light-years behind in operations. The principal, Marvin Griep, was a first-timer, and was ill, and he had a weak administrative staff. The school was overcrowded and on double sessions, going from 7 in the morning to 5:30 at night. It had a strong academic program, and its student body was divided almost perfectly along ethnic lines: well-off white kids from Miami Lakes, blue-collar Latinos from Hialeah, and a large group of blacks bused in from a rough area in Opa-locka. But instead of being a model of racial harmony, it was torn by racial strife.

The school building itself was actually on the Hialeah side of 138th

Street, the main drag that divided the two communities. The kids called it the "38th parallel," after the demarcation line dividing North and South Korea. The image was appropriate. Even before the school was built, there had been friction between the whites and the Cuban-American kids, and some pitched battles. Add the Opa-locka black kids, who didn't want to be there, who had, in fact, spent all their school lives being shuttled around to desegregate other schools they couldn't call their own, and it was like busing in nitroglycerine.

Moreover, it was the age of "black militancy" and the "black power" movement in America, when schools going through desegregation were especially ripe targets for making havoc. The black kids came in spoiling for a fight. The Cuban kids obliged. They weren't as quick to turn the other cheek as the white kids. And not only would they fight back, but they'd bring their relatives and friends into it, too. There'd be a spat, and then later four or five guys from the neighborhood of each combatant would show up for round two.

Interracial dating was a hot issue then, and we had fights over that and over drugs. But they really didn't need much encouragement: a harsh word in the locker room, an accidental bump in the cafeteria, and the next thing you knew somebody was in the hospital. We had little gangs of kids lashing out, going through the halls whacking people. We even had a gang of black girls running around with razors, trying to cut white girls.

Sometimes the conflict would simmer two or three days before we got to the bottom of it and collared whoever was responsible. Then we'd have to call in the parents, which could be just as dicey. On one occasion we rounded up a group that had been pounding on kids, and when we brought in the parents, the parents wanted to fight *us*. We had to call the police.

Stiffer punishments would have helped at Hialeah–Miami Lakes, but Johnny Jones was trying to discourage suspensions, so our hands were tied. I was getting to know and like him then because he at least had the guts to visit the schools that were in turmoil. A lot of administrators talk a good game until the fur begins to fly, then make themselves scarce. Of course, given the national mood, that year was a mess everywhere. Other Miami schools, like Central High, were having wholesale riots.

As often as not authorities would find adult activists right in the middle, egging kids on. At Hialeah–Miami Lakes we had a huge common area that was easily accessed from the outside, so you couldn't always tell who belonged and who didn't. The spark could come from anywhere, at any time. A group of older Cubans waylaid some of our kids in the parking lot one night and opened up the skull of one boy, a pretty scary sight.

Actually, it was all scary. But sometimes it was scary *and* funny.

We had a fight break out in the commons area one afternoon, and the public address system announced a "code blue" emergency, which meant a certain number of us were to drop everything and rush to the designated area. The catch was that the school was laid out poorly; it had a fourth-story planetarium in the middle, and you couldn't always get from one side of the building to the other without going back down and around. That made it especially tough for security, even when we brought in walkie-talkies. Today when we lay out new schools in New York we get security people to advise us on access and routing so that kind of thing won't happen.

Anyway, we got this code blue, and I stopped whatever I was doing and ran to the commons area. Vinny Hines, the assistant principal in charge of discipline and an ex-football player, was the only other staffer who got there in time to face the problem: three Latin males waving machetes at some of our kids. When they saw us coming, they ran for the parking lot, and by the time we made it there, they were in a car moving out. So we hopped into Vinny's car, gave chase, and were soon right behind them, just like in the movies.

Then they came to a red light. And suddenly it all got very civilized. They stopped, just like you're supposed to. And we stopped right behind them. And Vinny and I looked at each other as if to say, "What now?" I mean those were *machetes* they had been waving.

But the adrenaline must have still been pumping, because we got out simultaneously and approached the other car from either side. And just as we reached for the door handles, the light changed. They took off, leaving us standing there, empty-handed and staring at each other. We had to laugh. There wasn't anything else we could do.

I was still pretty hotheaded in those days, so tackling a problem physically wouldn't have been out of character. But I realized I was getting older one afternoon when a buddy of mine in the math department, Joe Novas, came into my office, plopped down in a chair, and said, "So-and-so says you're overdoing it," naming the chairman of our special ed department, a lazy sucker whom I was always scolding for something. "So-and-so says, 'Who the hell does this spic Fernandez think he is, coming here upsetting the applecart.' "

I didn't wait for another syllable. I ran out the door and down the hall, across the commons to another wing, then up three flights of stairs. Boy, I wasn't going to let this guy call *me* a spic. I was raging. But when I got up to his classroom and confronted him, I was also out of breath. I waved my finger in his face and tried to tell him what I was going to do, but the words wouldn't come.

"You . . ." Nothing. I took a breath and started again. "You . . ." I gasped for air. He must have thought I was having a seizure. Finally Novas, the instigator, burst into the room and grabbed me. My target still didn't know what was going on, he was just standing there, bewildered. And Novas said, "Hey, take it easy, Joe. I was just kidding. He didn't call you a spic." Well, if I was going to get anybody at that point, it should have been Novas, but the only thing that made sense for me to do was leave, which I did.

With Griep ill so much, I pretty much ran Hialeah–Miami Lakes High. Vinny Hines was a good administrator, but he'd take forever counseling some kid while a line of people waited for him outside. We'd have been fine if Griep had had a couple more Vinny Hineses and Joe Fernandezes around to pick up the slack, but the other two assistant principals weren't coordinated into the effort, so we were a lopsided operation. I suggested to Griep we divide our responsibilities by grade: I'd take the twelfth, and each of the others would take a grade, and that way, if something went wrong, we'd know whom to go to instead of having to stop and figure out who was doing what.

But Griep was on the way out, and by the time I had him convinced, he was being replaced by a new principal, Russ Wheatley. For me it was a fortuitous change. Russ and I were on the same page from the start. We're still close friends after all these years. He made me his senior A-P and put me in charge of the master schedule, which meant I had more control over the budget, together with the departments I oversaw: math, science, the language arts, as well as the school newspaper and the adult programs. It was all good training.

And despite that year of turmoil, Hialeah–Miami Lakes became a first-rate school. The violence was more a fashion than a fixture, and it slowly diminished. Thank God, we had a good academic program going, because Russ Wheatley was able to build on it, improving the staff and providing excellent extracurricular activities for the kids. Like me, he was a sports buff and recognized the positive attention and unifying spirit a good athletic program can bring to a school. Athletics helped us get over the rough spots. Everything began to jell.

But what I learned then about successfully integrating schools only marginally pertains to what I believe today. I think first and foremost you have to involve yourself with the community as a whole and seek to convince every kid and every parent and every faction in it that even if they can't tame the streets and the neighborhoods, they can — and *must* — tame the schools. That education is the one best hope for all disadvantaged kids who want to make it in life, but they won't get it if their schools are in chaos. That the ideal is not to have the neighborhood influence the school, but vice versa. Schools should make neighborhoods better, not be beaten down by them.

The first ingredient for making it work is an active community relations board, representing every group and open to every faction. A cadre from the school should work through the board to reach out into the neighborhood, knocking on doors, talking to people. Letting them know what the goals are and calling on *their* leadership to help find solutions to problems. Encouraging participation. Tying common bonds.

If the only time you involve yourself with the community is when you have a problem, it's not going to work. If you don't do anything to prepare for crises, if you don't foster outreach and a reciprocal concern, you won't change anything.

Of course, there isn't much sense in reaching out to the neighborhood if the kids come from somewhere else, way across town. Then you have to rely more heavily on leadership groups and work for boundary changes that can be made to effect a more compatible pairing of neighborhoods for meaningful integration.

But the real key is what I said before: starting early. Bringing kids together in kindergarten if possible. The volatile atmosphere at Hialeah–Miami Lakes was not helped by the fact that the kids were strangers one to another, with the blacks especially suspicious and hostile, having been routed from their neighborhood and bused into four different high schools, with no hope of finishing with the kids they had started with. Given the sensitivity of the times, conflict was probably inevitable.

And yet, again, the trouble we experienced then was a Sunday picnic compared to what we now face in our big-city schools every day. All things are relative. The solution nevertheless remains the same. It's all in our willingness to make the application.

When I was just starting out as a teacher, I heard a speech that changed my life — or at least my thoughts on what I should do with it.

Four or five hundred new teachers were gathered for orientation at the Dade County Auditorium and to be greeted by Joe Hall, then the superintendent of schools. We were appropriately awed because Hall was a Miami legend. At another time and place, he might have been the subject of a song by Woody Guthrie or a book by Damon Runyon. He was a big, slow-talking, slow-moving southern gentleman who carried a glass of iced tea around with him on the job and ran the Dade schools like an absolute monarch.

Joe Hall had been Miami's school superintendent for what seemed like forever. He had started out as an elected official, a one-man operation in a one-room office, when the Dade system was thought of as a backward, good-old-boy network where relatives of people on the inside got the jobs on the outside and what mattered was who you knew, not how much. When the county made the superintendency an appointed position, Hall rolled on with the tide, helping the school board grow into a force that eventually required a cast of hundreds and a whole building to run its business.

Hall was a gutsy, hardheaded, hardworking administrator, with a sixth sense about school needs, and in his thrall the Dade school board gradually became more progressive and representative. It added a black member, Bill Turner, and a Jewish woman, Phyllis Miller. Ed Whigham was brought in to be groomed for Hall's job, and Leonard Britton as a second assistant. But on that day in the auditorium, Hall was still very much in charge.

It wasn't so much what he said, but the way that he said it. He talked about the mystique of the educator and the importance of the classroom teacher — how they should "never be sold short." He talked about initiatives he was taking to make schools better, and how *we* should get inspired to do the same. And I *was* inspired, on the spot. I was invigorated.

In those days, whenever I wanted to try something new, I'd run into the old intransigence. A principal or a vice principal would say, "You can't do that. It's never been done." But hearing Joe Hall, and sensing the clout he had, I remember thinking, *That's* the kind of authority you need to get things done in the schools.

From that point on, whenever I had an opportunity to involve myself in the system's workings, I took it. At Coral Park, I was active in politics and was voted union steward. In 1969, Florida had the first statewide teachers strike in American history, and I took my whole math department out with me. The issues weren't all that sophisticated. A salary increase was the main thrust, not working conditions, or bargaining powers, or grievance procedures, or anything complicated.

I don't recall what we were making, but my annual salary after six years in Miami wasn't much more than $6,000, so I suppose any strike was justified. My empathy now for teachers in New York surely had its roots in those leanest of times, when we had to battle for every penny. We stayed out three weeks and won a small increase. But more important, the Classroom Teachers Association emerged as a stronger organization. There were some hard feelings against the teachers who didn't strike, but we had sailed successfully through our first big storm.

In my second year (1973–74) at Hialeah–Miami Lakes, I was elected secretary-treasurer of the Dade County School Administrators Association. About that time, the Florida legislature passed a collective bargaining law that allowed public employees to negotiate terms and conditions of employment. As one of the officers in the association, I was involved in reviewing the bill, to see what it meant to our organization and the school system as a whole. As a result, I was somebody to turn to for expertise in labor relations. It eventually became expected of me.

At that point I wasn't thinking about a downtown job at all, but events kept moving me in that direction. Dr. Whigham had finally succeeded Joe Hall, and one of his first moves was to bring in a labor attorney, Gavin O'Brien, to head up a new division he called the Office of Legislative and Labor Relations. Gavin, as an assistant superintendent, would serve as chief negotiator and lobbyist to the legislature in Tallahassee and the federal government, something Dade had never had, and he would have another lawyer as his assistant and an executive staff of six directors for each of the county's school administrative areas.

I was asked to apply for one of those six spots. I did, but with some trepidation. Johnny Jones had blocked me the year before when I had been recommended for the principalship of an adult education program at another high school. I had made something of a splash by inaugurating a class for school secretaries while moonlighting in the adult ed program at Miami High. I contended that as the first point of contact, the secretaries could make a real difference in promoting school harmony by the way they treated visiting parents. The class's success gave me some status with the adult ed people, and when the principal's job became available, I applied. It wasn't exactly mainstream, but it meant a principal's salary. As an assistant principal I was still making only $11,000 a year.

A few days later, Marvin Griep came to my office, very nervous. I loved Marvin, but he was like Don Knotts when he got nervous. "J-J-Joe, I gotta talk to you about this job."

"What about it, Marvin."

"Dr. Jones told me to t-t-talk you out of it."

"Why? I'm a finalist. It's going to the board."

He said, "Jones won't let you go. He says you've been an A-P only a year and a half, and he needs you here." I was ticked, and for a long time I resented Jones for it, even though I knew it was because he wanted to keep me on his team. But it turned out to be a blessing in disguise.

Because when the job with O'Brien came open, Jones couldn't block it. He tried, but Whigham overruled him. Whigham said, "You can't keep Fernandez forever. Let him go."

Ironically, there was another budget crunch on at the time, and it worked to my advantage. O'Brien was allowed to hire only two district assistants: an elementary school principal named Lillian Peterson and me. Lillian wasn't a self-starter, and she didn't like working overtime, so she was content to follow my lead. And with so much to do, and all of it new, and with people clamoring for explanations, I did what for me comes naturally: I dove in. That summer, O'Brien was away lobbying in Tallahassee, and I spent every spare minute studying school law. I became an expert on certifying unions.

I was downtown for two years, operating out of the School Board building on the same floor as the superintendent. I answered to Gavin O'Brien, but he was hardly ever there, so when anything came up I dealt directly with Whigham. As it developed, that little office of four people — the two lawyers, who weren't school people, and Lillian and I — wielded tremendous clout. We negotiated Dade's first union contract. Dade schools had never known such things as "grievance procedures." We went a step further by advocating councils in the contract to encourage interplay between teachers and the administration at the earliest stages, the idea being to foster future harmony.

We certified all the unions, beginning with the United Teachers of Dade County. We certified the food service and bus drivers unions and a consortium of the trades unions. It was two years of nonstop activity. I had responsibility for the teachers, the largest union, which in turn put me in regular contact with principals, with whom I had equal rank. But the principals came to *me* for counsel, and as we were also involved in training senior staff members, the whole thing put me in the unusual position of directing people of much higher rank and seniority. It was pretty heady stuff.

But even as I gathered the experience, and accumulated the knowledge, I knew it wasn't a job to last. A phase-out period was built in. Once we got to a certain point, that would be it. I told Whigham that when it was time for me to move on I wanted to return to the schools as a principal. He said he'd remember it when the time came.

When it did, however, it was not only unexpected, it was a shock, with several aftershocks. Like an earthquake.

It came in September 1975. I had used up the whole summer negotiating the teachers contract, so I had taken a late vacation with my family on Sanibel Island on Florida's west coast. Gavin O'Brien tracked me down with a phone call.

"The superintendent wants to see you."

"What for?"

"I don't know. But he wants to see you now."

We drove back to Miami that afternoon, and as soon as we hit town and picked up a newspaper I learned the reason. Jim Newmeyer, my principal and patron at Coral Park and a dear, dear friend, had suffered a fatal heart attack. I would never have wanted it to happen that way, but I couldn't help but think that Whigham was calling me back to take over my "old school." Even if realized under painfully sad circumstances, it was a wish come true.

I had, in fact, once confided to Whigham that very thought. He had asked me what my ambition was in life, and I said, "To be principal of Coral Park High School." What I didn't tell him was that I wanted to be a principal only until I could become a superintendent.

When I got to his office the next morning, Whigham ushered me in, closed the door, and got right to it.

"I know how close you were to Jim Newmeyer, and how much Coral Park means to you, all the ties you have there and all."

I was right. The job was mine.

Then he said, "But what I really need is somebody very strong to go take over at Central High. All that school has known in the last few years is dissension, and riots, and confusion. I think you're the guy to straighten it out. I'm moving Dan Wagner out of there, to take over at Coral Park. I want you to save Central for me."

I was stunned. In my mind I framed the answer: No, sir. Not me. I wanted to be where the chances for success were a little better, not at a school under siege.

Then Whigham started detailing all the problems Central had. An inner-city school, with racial conflict. A split faculty that didn't communicate. Almost no community relations. Overcrowded classrooms. A high dropout rate. He kept loading me down with horror stories. Then he said, "However, you'll have carte blanche. You can try your own methods and bring in your own people wherever and whenever there's an opening."

That cheered me a little bit. I said, "How long do I have to be there?" I was thinking of it as a sentence.

Whigham smiled. "You haven't even taken the job and you're already talking about leaving?"

"Well . . ." And we laughed.

"You stay as long as it takes to clean it up, Joe. It won't be a two- or three-year job, though. It'll probably take five years at least."

I thought, Well, nuts. That's all I need to hear.

But I took it. Actually, Whigham asked me to apply for it, so it would appear to be my idea, and I did. And the next week I was on the job.

Classes had already been going for two weeks. Central was ridiculously overcrowded, with an enrollment of forty-six hundred, so it was in double session, meaning the first period started at 7 A.M. In the fall, that means dark as hell.

And when I walked into the main building that first morning, all I could see was the lit tips of cigarettes lining the hallways. And all I could hear was loud music booming out of those big-box radios.

To say the least, it wasn't Coral Park.

Geographically, Central wasn't really central, either, and it was anything but your typical, cramped inner-city campus. It had been founded fifty-odd years before as a downtown vocational school called Tech High, but in its reincarnation it had been converted to a comprehensive curriculum and moved to an eighty-acre track stretching from the far side of Liberty City, from 95th Street north to 103rd Street, and from Northwest 17th to Northwest 19th avenues, making it one of the largest facilities in the system. Mirroring the ethnic makeup of the area, the student body was about 85 percent black, with the rest white and Hispanic, and all at the lower end of the economic scale.

Spread out like it was, with courtyards between the wings and wide expanses of lawn that even included a lake, Central had the potential for great beauty — and for major control problems. Unfortunately, it wasn't taking advantage of the former and was regularly victimized by the latter. It was a mess physically and totally lacking any sense of order or discipline. Somewhat symbolic of the conditions, the lake eventually had to be filled in after a car was found at the bottom. With a body in it.

I stood there that morning and watched as the first-period bell rang, and all those kids in the halls barely moved. It was as if the bell was a suggestion instead of a command. They stood around smoking and listening to their radios, and straggled into their classrooms only as the mood struck. It was that way pretty much throughout the day, and every day. And it wasn't just the indifferent attitude of the students. It was also the attitude of most of the teachers.

They came to school with no sign of caring, no real respect for their jobs. Especially the white teachers. One former priest used to teach in tennis shorts until I cracked down. I had one young social studies teacher who thought it was "liberal" to be sloppy and two hippie types from the Woodstock days who were suspected of using drugs with the kids. On the other extreme, I had a vocational teacher who told the black kids they couldn't cut it as electricians because they had an "extra bone" in their hands, and a carpentry teacher, a big, tough white guy, who called them "jungle bunnies" to their face. "All you jungle bunnies get in here!"

I mean, racism without pretense. I had a science teacher who openly referred to his black students as "niggers" when he wanted to put them down. He was another big guy, too, with a chip on his shoulder, and actually got in fistfights with the kids, usually one-on-one where there weren't any witnesses. I was convinced he picked most of them. I must have had ten instances where parents threatened to come in and kill him. He had tenure, so I couldn't fire him right away, but I kept bringing him up on charges. One day he went out to the parking lot where he kept his little blue Volkswagen all spit-shined, and it was covered in white paint. Ruined. It was poetic justice.

What it boiled down to was no more than teachers proving to be what they seemed: the bottom of the barrel. It's not so unusual. Inner-city schools get what other schools don't hire or newcomers fresh out of college who'll take anything. Teacher assignments and transfers are based on seniority, so a good teacher who happens into a school like Central will usually transfer out at the first opportunity. It becomes a self-fulfilling prophecy of inexperience, mediocrity, and incompetence.

You could make a chicken-or-the-egg argument out of it, of course. With inner-city schools there's a tremendous burnout factor as even

those teachers who *do* care get worn down by the discipline problems
and the lack of motivation and achievement. Sometimes they quit out of
fear. All of which contributes to the reason why I say teachers unions in
America should be pressured into salary differentials in their contracts
that would allow for giving good teachers more incentive to stick it out
in those schools.

So, how bad was Central High on my arrival there? This bad: most
principals start their Monday mornings going over curriculum with
their staff. My Monday mornings began with an inventory of what had
been stolen or damaged over the weekend. There was always some kind
of loss, some kind of vandalism to inspect, sometimes even a dead body
from a neighborhood fight. With two teeming housing projects near
the school, no doubt drugs were a factor in the violence and theft.
There was a steady stream of break-ins.

But the campus was so big, with so many points of access and egress,
that it was almost impossible to seal off. For an "inner-city" school, it
was actually a crazy layout. The parking lot was on the far edge of the
property, out of view of the main traffic, which meant kids could come
and go and do their dope at will. One side butted up to an agricultural
school. We were always having to chase cows off our football field. On
another side was an alternative school, MacArthur North High, where
the incorrigibles went when they were kicked out of other schools. A lot
of our more violent problems came from there. A fence the students
called the Berlin Wall divided the campuses, but it didn't keep the
MacArthur kids from infiltrating. Among other routes, they could
come right into one of our main buildings, Carter Hall, through the
exit doors on that side.

But the main problem with Central you could fathom in a heartbeat.
It was a school drowning in its own poor leadership. It hadn't been
there long, but already it had had four principals (I was the fourth).
One had been relieved after only six months. Worse, there was no
rapport between the administration and the teachers.

Teachers who wanted order, who wanted their classes started on
time and no fooling around, wouldn't take their problem kids to the
principal or the assistant principals because they knew they wouldn't
get support. The assistant principals were literally afraid of the kids.
They'd turn the other way if they saw a fight start, and when you
wanted them they were not to be found. I eventually issued walkie-
talkies and made them keep them open at all times, just so I'd know
where they were. The teachers, left to their own devices, survived as

best they could. Some took to locking their doors to keep kids in and renegades out. Definitely a siege mentality.

Well, why not? The school had been ripped by riots, one after another. One of its previous principals, Cleophus Allgood, was assigned there specifically for that reason — to stop the rioting. He couldn't do it. It was a self-perpetuating thing. After one outbreak, the president of the black student union at the University of Miami was identified as a riot leader; he'd been a Central graduate. But nothing was done. He was practically a hero. The violence had become routine. It was "expected" at Central.

I remember one incident early on, after a white Jewish girl at a Miami Beach high school had been badly mauled by a black student, her necklace ripped off and her face pummeled. The Jewish community clamored for action. The politicians followed suit. A grand jury issued a report, and a commission was chosen to study the violence in Dade schools. The newspapers were full of it.

Right at that time we were hosting a big workshop at Central, for about six thousand teachers and administrators. Our kids weren't even in school. A television crew came to interview me on the Beach situation and the grand jury report, which was virtually an indictment of school safety. We were talking in the courtyard right outside my office, with the camera rolling, when a workshop session broke for lunch. And as the teachers spilled into the courtyard, one of them fainted.

The TV cameraman immediately refocused on the lady on the ground. People were flocking around, trying to revive her. And when the interview ran that night on the 11 o'clock news, the channel juxtaposed my remarks with footage of the woman on the ground, as if she'd been assaulted. They didn't say she had, but the implication was clear.

So that's what I faced. I don't say my way of turning things around in such a school would work for everyone; each school has its own character, and there are thousands of troubled schools in America. But there are some common grounds to work from, and even if you sometimes have to wing it (there being no manuals to cover most of what happens), you can be sure you're on the right track if you remember what you're there for: that your priorities are the kids and their parents. *Those* are the people you have to get to. Everything spins off their understanding of what a good school is all about, beginning with the fact that it belongs to them, not to the principals or the teachers or the school board.

And to get that understanding, you have to reach into the community, not wait for it to come to you.

One of my first moves at Central was to find out who the area's strongest leader was: a black priest at one of the Episcopal churches named Father Majors. (With a name like that, he had to be a leader.) I made an appointment to chat. I told him I wanted to go into the community, to preach *my* gospel. He said, "How about if you and I take a walk in there together? Knock on some doors. I'll say, 'Here's the new principal. He has a plan.' "

I said, "Lead the way."

For four days we canvassed the area, from one boundary line to another, talking to parents and neighbors, giving them the full picture, inviting them to the school. If they weren't home, we left notes. The response was immediate. We were able to create the school's first parent advisory board and brought the board in once a week to talk.

I called a special assembly of the kids in the school auditorium. There were too many for one session, so I met with them by class, beginning with the seniors.

When they were seated, I asked all the teachers to leave.

I said, "All right, I've been here long enough to know what's wrong with this school. Here's my conclusion." I gave them both barrels, telling them that this was *their* school they were screwing up, not mine, and outlining what they'd have to do to change it. The rules they'd have to abide by. The good that would come from it if they did.

I said, "As I see it, you have two choices. You can go on the way you are and when you graduate, *if* you graduate, you'll do so from a school you'll always be ashamed of, the laughingstock of the community. Or you can go out with a future, from a school with a good reputation that makes you proud."

Having made the point that a true sense of order was a must for education to work, I put in a whole new agenda of conduct requirements, after first making sure the teachers and staff understood that they were responsible for enforcing them, too, and if they didn't, they'd have to answer to me. No more loitering. No more straggling into class late. No more hats. No more boom-boxes. If a kid was caught with a radio, it was taken and he'd have to come to me to get it back. If he was caught twice, he'd have to bring in his parents. In no time, kids stopped wearing hats to class. The radios disappeared.

Administratively, the first thing I did was get Central off double session. I told Superintendent Whigham, "The only way we're going to get this school functioning as a unit is to have one faculty, one student body." We had two — one group checking in at 7 A.M. and finishing at 12:30, the other starting at noon and finishing at 5. There was no connection. Ships passing in the halls. To change to one session, however, we had to reduce the classroom load, so all the ninth-graders were relocated at the junior high schools in the area's feeder pattern.

I bootlegged like mad to get things done to improve security. I didn't want to wait for requisitions to creep through channels, so I got my shop to make grates for all the windows. Without the fire department's approval, I had the doors on the far side of Carter Hall chained shut.

With money I could squeeze from other departments, I was able to hire a local contractor to fence in the parking lot, but we ran out before he could enclose the whole area. We were left with an odd-looking, L-shaped divider that was open to the campus at either end. Funny thing, it worked — somewhat. It discouraged anybody who wanted to get in but didn't want to walk all the way around. The flow of infiltrators waned. But I never really shut it off completely until years later when as superintendent I moved MacArthur to a new facility on 130th Street.

The worst riot we had while I was there started when a MacArthur boy came into our cafeteria and grabbed a cigarette off the ear of one of ours. Two or three Central boys jumped him, and he ran back to MacArthur, only to return in less than an hour with a posse of his own. A free-for-all spilled out onto the campus. One of our teachers called the police, and before I could stop it there were motorcycle cops on the scene, roaring their engines and using their cycles like sheep herders. It was a mess — kids screaming and falling down, fights breaking out.

There was a lot of blood, but only one kid was seriously hurt, cut by a razor. When we were able to sort it all out and haul in the instigators, the consensus was that the greater damage was done in not containing the original fight and by panicking into calling the cops too soon. I reached an understanding with the precinct commander that from then on they wouldn't come on campus unless someone in my office called.

Meanwhile, I made student monitors out of the Central football team, the toughest guys I could find, with the sure knowledge that the best way to police a school is by taking a proprietary interest and policing it yourself.

Some things I did with reluctance. I had to declare a moratorium on the regular weekend dances when I discovered they weren't all they were supposed to be. The dances were a popular means to raise money for extracurricular activities, but you could get high on the marijuana smoke, and if you went into the boys bathrooms, you could break your neck tripping over the card games and the dice.

I called a meeting of the student government we had formed and said, "No more dances until you prove to me you can have them without gambling and smoking and using drugs." I got my "monitors" to back me on it.

To better control access and identify traffic, I closed the campus, making it mandatory that the kids stay in for lunch. It was unpopular at first, but the parents supported me. When you take something away, however, it's smart to give something back. We softened the rule with a lot of little niceties for the kids. We put kiosks around the courtyards and tables with umbrellas for them to eat under. We brought in a lunch wagon that sold hot dogs and all the wrong stuff kids love to eat.

To inspire some pride in the place, I set about improving the looks of it. I bore down on the custodians to clean up and spruce up. When I got the books straightened out (the finances were a mess) and could free up some funds, I started wheeling and dealing for landscaping. We put trees and shrubs around the main entrance, items I got mostly for nothing, some from a prison farm. I got the Air Force to donate the shell of a space rocket and we set it up out front with a bed of multicolored flowers spelling out the school name: Miami Central Rockets. We beautified the dusty, barren courtyards with trees and shrubs, and fertilized like mad. A few of my staffers came in on Saturdays to help me. We planted more than two hundred trees, anywhere and everywhere.

As quickly as I could, I reconstituted the teaching and administrative staffs, but it wasn't easy. I'd been promised a free hand in filling some of our key openings — an assistant principalship, a student activities director, a couple of department heads. But they were filled for me. I was furious. I immediately began moving to reverse some assignments I thought were mistakes, knowing I'd make some enemies in the process.

One opening, in student activities, had been filled by a black man named Matt Lawrence. I didn't know him, and his résumé didn't tell me much. He was a big-chested ex-football player who just naturally seemed slovenly: tie off to one side, shirttail blousing out. He *looked* lazy. I called him into my office.

I said, "Look, Matt. With all due respect, I don't know you. Who's your rabbi? How'd you get this job?" I said, "I gotta tell you, I'm fighting to get you out of here, and a bunch of others as well. I want to open these jobs up." Matt said he understood, but he'd do his best to change my mind.

Well, as it turned out, after about a month of having Matt Lawrence on the job, I got permission to move him — and I didn't want to. He was terrific. Good with the kids, a strong disciplinarian, a loving guy. I made him an assistant principal. He was the best one I had, and the next year when I went downtown, I backed him for the job and he succeeded me as principal at Central.

I wasn't so lucky with the rest of the staff. I wound up having to "surplus" twenty-seven teachers, including the science teacher with the Volkswagen. I remember that number, twenty-seven, because I had to go down to the business office one day, and Steve Moore, an assistant superintendent, said, "What's wrong with you, Fernandez? You can't move that many teachers." So I went to Whigham and explained my reasons, and instead of getting on me, he jumped all over Moore. And the next time Moore saw me, he got on me again — for the ragging he got from Whigham.

Wherever I could, I brought in or promoted qualified blacks. The school hadn't had a single black department head, and all the administrative staffers were white. That was unacceptable.

I promoted blacks to head up the language arts and math departments. I made Rudy Barber the school's first black football coach, and Gene (Choo-Choo) Clapp my athletic director. The kids loved Choo-Choo. He could spot something going on at the far end of the eighty acres, blow a whistle, and it would stop. Like the others, he cared, and in caring understood the need for tightening up the rules. For Gene, the tougher the discipline the better. He didn't hesitate to swat kids who got out of line. But as far as the kids were concerned, they were love taps.

That was one thing I had to get used to: the black disciplinarian's appreciation for corporal punishment. I'm not in favor of it, but black teachers generally are. They may have a point. I know Gene Clapp didn't hesitate to lower the boom, and the other good disciplinarians on the staff would often do the same, regulations notwithstanding. My most graphic experience with the practice came one afternoon when I caught a persistent truant the staff called the "Silver Fox," in honor of a line of stark white hair down one side of his head. His real name was

Hendrix, and on this one day I checked his schedule and was right there to grab him the moment he tried to skip out. I took him to my office and called his parents.

Within five minutes, they were there. The father loomed over me, boiling mad. I thought, Uh-oh. He said, "What's the problem here, Mr. Fernandez?" I told him his son had a long history of cutting classes, and we'd finally caught him.

Without a word the father turned and smacked the kid on the side of the head, sending him sprawling across a coffee table and onto the floor. When peace was restored, the father said, "My son's been coming to this school for four years, Mr. Fernandez. He's a senior. You're the first person in all that time to tell us about this. The next class he cuts, you call me, and I guarantee you he won't bother you again." The Silver Fox never cut another class.

My base support, as it turned out, came from the black teachers, who genuinely wanted something better for their kids. Given Whigham's permission to make changes without worrying too much about the rules (seniority guidelines, for example), I didn't hesitate to move when I saw an opening. With better teachers, we were able to tighten up the curriculum and even inaugurated some honors classes. I started what we called an "in-depth curriculum cluster" in which we combined with three other northside high schools for a kind of mini-magnet program of advanced placement courses. Each school provided a specific area of expertise, in Central's case math and science. Except for the downtime traveling, the idea worked out pretty well.

When the reality of revival set in, and teachers and students saw what was happening and knew I was seriously committed to making things better, they began to turn around. I wasn't a white guy *trying* to change things, I was a white guy, supported by just about everybody from the community leaders down, *changing* things. School pride becomes a tangible force when that happens. It acts as a catalyst for getting *more* done: good things mushrooming into other good things. There was so much evidence of improved attitudes that I reinstated the dances.

When I think of it now, I have to say I'm probably more proud of the job we did at Central than anything I could have imagined doing at Coral Park. My staff, in a breathtakingly short time, proved that you could forge meaningful change even within a context where the student body was mostly poor, mostly minority, and largely underachieving. The dropout rate went down significantly, and although academic scores didn't shoot up, there were enough signs of improvement to augur well for the future.

We started a school newspaper, and our yearbook won a blue ribbon. We got the school represented at the Science Fair for the first time. We started the first swim team. I appointed the district's first female athletic business manager, whom the kids adored. Our basketball team won the state championship that first year, and the gym was packed for every game. Like I said, sports can play a major role in bringing a school together, and that team galvanized school spirit like I've never seen. We also had a fantastic band, led by a three-hundred-pound taskmaster named Ken Tolbert, who wouldn't settle for anything but the best and the classiest, and we put the wheels in motion to add a chorus.

Some of the things that were improving at the time didn't bear fruit until later. The band, deserving for so long, got invited to a music festival in Germany when I was superintendent. I got the school board to advance $25,000 for expenses, and the band went and won top honors. The letters of praise from the Germans could have filled a scrapbook. The year after I left, Central was a winner in a school beautification contest. I was there when Matt Lawrence got up to accept the award. He said, "One of the problems we had to overcome was having too many trees and shrubs. Some idiot planted 'em too close together, and they were killing each other off."

When he sat down, I leaned over and said, "Matt, I was that idiot."

I enjoyed my two years at Central more than I would have ever believed possible. I would certainly have stayed longer if events hadn't once more moved me along, but I doubt I'd have wanted to stay forever, as I might have at Coral Park. The frustrating part, the thing that kills you in inner-city schools, is the amount of time you have to spend doing things that aren't directly related to school. The theft, the violence, the vandalism. You just get something fixed, or you get new equipment, and you take another hit, reel from another setback. You have to keep going back to the kids and teachers and community leaders, telling them why it's wrong to let these things happen, how it hurts everybody. You take three steps forward, then two back.

As a child of the ghetto myself, I could empathize with the Central kids, although the experience helped me gain fresh insight into all those poverty-related problems that make life in the slowest lane so frightening today. Funny, though, I have to say I was never afraid for myself at Central, not even on that first ominous day. To the end, security remained a problem, but I was one with the school, and I felt we were family. Somebody threw a brick at me outside Carter Hall before a function one night, but it missed badly and I didn't give it a second thought.

The only time I was in real danger I didn't even know it. Matt Lawrence had to tell me later.

We were into a code-blue emergency, with those of us who were alerted to it converging on the parking lot where an outsider had been found breaking into cars, stealing radios. When we tried to get the thief to come to the office, he balked.

I stepped in because I wanted to get it over with before we drew a crowd. Sometimes a crowd can do dumb things when it misinterprets what it sees. Matt and I grabbed the guy and started walking him to my office when we were approached by a group of kids just getting out of a shop class. One of them wanted to know what was happening. I said, "No big deal, fellows. Just go on about your business. Everything's under control."

But with my attention diverted, the guy somehow pulled a gun, and though my head was turned and I didn't see it, Matt and the others said he pointed it at me and pulled the trigger. You could hear the click as the cylinder advanced. There was no bullet in the chamber. Matt quickly grabbed the guy's hand, twisted it, and the gun fell to the pavement. When he checked it out, the gun was a couple bullets short of being fully loaded. My time hadn't come.

I know now, of course, that the Central High experience was anything but the dead end I feared it would be when Ed Whigham tapped me for the job. If I'd gone back to Coral Park, chances are I would be there still. At Coral Park, I wouldn't have had to make waves. I wouldn't have had to call attention to myself. I could have gone merrily about my business, unchallenged, uninterrupted, and unnoticed.

But that's not the way it worked out. The Master Plan kicked in, and at Central, I *did* make waves. Big ones. And the attention I got put me in position for the next major turn in my life, the one that led into the fateful administration of Johnny Jones and then to the superintendency of the sprawling, never-say-dull Dade County school system.

Life for the Fernandez family, meanwhile, was definitely looking up. For one thing, I didn't have to work three and four jobs anymore to make ends meet. As a first-time principal I was up to the $27,000 range in salary, which meant Lily and I could splurge. We sold the little house we'd bought for $11,000 for almost three times that, and using the proceeds we had put aside from the sale of our second home in Point Royale, bought a four-bedroom, two-bath ranch-style house in an area of Miami called Pine Acres — paying, as I recall, just under $40,000.

Then we sold that and bought a larger four-and-two on an acre in the Suniland area for $90,000, and as far as I was concerned we'd made our last move. The Suniland house today, after extensive improvements, would probably bring $250,000 on the Miami market. I am reminded of that now when we're taking flak for the "million-dollar mansion" we occupy in Brooklyn Heights, which some of the New York media delight in depicting as a sign of executive extravagance in the face of all those budget cuts, and I think, Fellas, if you only knew.

The Suniland house that we loved had a two-car garage and a swimming pool, and backed up to a neighbor's tennis court. The ancient brownstone in Brooklyn — which serves as the official residence for school board functions, and we don't own and will have no stake in when it's sold — is three stories high and creaks in the night, has a backyard big enough for a barbecue pit but not much else (certainly not a pool), and we park on the street, when we can win the daily battle for available space, or in a garage a quarter mile away.

It is our required residence and was chosen because it is big enough for my whole family and is within walking distance of my office. The city had to spend about what our Miami house was worth to make the brownstone comfortable. But every hammered nail or swish of plaster brought cries of outrage from the media — none of whom ever saw the inside of the place. Too bad. It would have been a revelation. Ed Koch or David Dinkins would never have mistaken it for Gracie Mansion.

Please know I'm not knocking the house or the generosity of my New York contract. It was more than any public school administrator would ever dare hope for. But a condition I made in moving from Miami was that my family wouldn't have to take a hit in living standards. No CEO would settle for less. The irony is that the Brooklyn Heights residence provided for New York City's chancellor of schools wouldn't hold a candle to what we lived in on a principal's salary in Miami.

It gives me something to think about when it's 20 degrees in New York and snow has covered the barbecue pit.

PART IV

THE DADE COUNTY SCHOOL SYSTEM is unlike any other in that it is a little bit like so many others — here a dash of Atlantic City, New Jersey, there a touch of Corpus Christi, Texas, over yonder a pinch of Greenwich, Connecticut.

Florida is the only state in the union that delegates school control on a countywide basis — by comparison, it has sixty-seven school districts to California's seventeen hundred — and though this makes for a more consistent handling of such testy issues as desegregation by all but eliminating "district hopping," it also makes Dade County a monolith of a school area: two thousand square miles of problems as widely disparate as its demographics.

In the rural southwest, migrant workers and their children bend in the sandy fields to pick tomatoes while their distant neighbors in Coral Gables and Kendall play tennis on backyard courts. From neon-lit Miami Beach on the east, across Biscayne Bay to spicy Little Havana and the mean inner-city streets of Overtown and Brownsville, and on to the edge of the Everglades on the far west, Dade is a swelling, turbulent polyglot that hasn't known a moment's peace and understanding in decades.

The ongoing invasion of poor immigrants from all over Central America and the Caribbean, walking in out of the ocean from leaking boats, speaking no English and barely literate in their own tongue, is a factor that will keep Dade's scholastic achievement scores down into the next century no matter who the schools superintendent is. In some parts of Miami, teachers are actually helping write a heretofore unwritten language: Haitian creole.

Dade's schools since the '60s have been rocked by every kind of unnatural disaster: rampant drug problems ... race riots ... deadly violence ... a crippling teachers strike ... the Cuban refugee influx, compounded by the Mariel boatlift in 1980 ... and in that same year, a major scandal involving the county's first black superintendent, Johnny Jones.

You'd have to say I first came to real prominence in this cauldron as a troubleshooter for Johnny Jones. Later, I would become the deputy of Jones's successor, Leonard Britton, who was a single shade of gray as an administrator and went on to become the superintendent of the Los Angeles schools system, only to lose that job about the time I wound up in New York. In the Machiavellian world of school management politics, there really is a logical line of ascent in all this, but it takes some explaining.

The trigger was the sudden decision by Ed Whigham to quit the Dade superintendency and return to academic life at the University of Alabama at Birmingham, for reasons unclear to me then and now.

It was all quite out of the blue. One day Whigham was my boss, with my full appreciation for his abilities. The next day he was gone. Leonard Britton became acting superintendent, with the understanding that he could not be a candidate for the job. When it was crunch time, however, Britton applied anyway. But neither he nor the other two candidates, Gavin O'Brien and the superintendent of the Dallas schools, Linus Wright, had reckoned with the pulling power of Johnny Jones.

Neither had I. I backed Gavin O'Brien.

Gavin was convinced he'd be the new Dade superintendent. He thought he had the votes of five of the school board's seven members, and all he needed was a simple majority, so he went ahead and put together his reorganization plan. He was a wonderful organizer, O'Brien, always projecting ahead to cover the contingencies. He'd go nuts today with all our big educational organizations because they *don't* plan ahead. It's one of their biggest failings — actually, one of the biggest failings of *all* of education.

I learned how to "work out of books" from Gavin O'Brien. He'd sit down at a meeting, and if somebody said, "What are we gonna do about the trades unions?" he'd pull out a plan and plunk it down — all worked out in advance, scenario by scenario, neatly typed and in a folder. I do that now. If, say, I'm dealing with plans for new alternative high schools for our discipline problems, I'll have a three-ring note-book right there, filled with the answers I need. Preparation can be crucial. With so much at stake in education today, you can't afford to be caught wielding a garden hoe when the job calls for an earthmover.

Gavin's shortcoming was that he was trained as an attorney, not an educator. But he had had me for that. I'd been his alter ego on education issues when I worked with him before. Whenever he didn't have a sense of how an issue might be viewed in the field, or how it would impact on the schools, I provided it for him. So when he said, "If I get this job, I want you to be one of my assistant superintendents," I said, "Love to."

But he *didn't* have five votes. He had only three. Jones won the super-intendency on the third ballot. I know it caught Johnny by surprise, too, because when they exchanged congratulations and condolences after-ward, Johnny admitted that he didn't even have an organization plan. Typically, because he was a team player, Gavin said, "No problem. You can have mine." And he turned over his plan to Jones — the one that included bringing me in as an assistant superintendent.

The election of Jones was on a Wednesday in May 1977. I had two days to think about all the reasons Johnny would leave me hanging at Central High. I was O'Brien's man. I'd politicked for him, to the point of lobbying a couple of the board members on his behalf. With the credibility I'd built up in the black community as Central's principal, I'd even gotten the teachers in that area to support him, which *had* to get back to Johnny, who was as plugged in to the black community as anyone could be. He'd come up through the system, from teacher to principal and on.

But true to the size of the man, Jones didn't let any of that bother him. On Friday, he called. He said he wanted me to serve as an assistant superintendent, heading up a new Department of Community Affairs. The thrust of the job would be to set up a whole network of parental involvement and at the same time bring in the business community for help and cooperation. Exactly the kind of thing I had come to believe in — and believe in now more than ever — as critical for the future of America's schools. Naturally, I said yes.

Johnny Jones was almost everything you'd want in a leader. Smart. Creative. Charismatic. One of the most talented administrators I've ever been around. But probably the thing that made the greatest impression on the way I do things now was that he never let up. He believed you'd get root-bound if you didn't keep moving, keep agitating, keep pushing. For him it came naturally because he was so hyper. He fairly quivered with exposed nerve endings.

Jones's management style was probing to the point of being confrontational. I liked that, too. He called it "conflict management," pitting one bureau against another, one division head against another, so that sparks would fly. The sparks he wanted were ideas and answers. The thing he *didn't* want was lethargy. His cabinet knew it had to stay on its toes because he'd go after you if you didn't. If you were smart, you'd get embarrassed only once.

Johnny had a phenomenal memory. He could remember something you told him a year ago, and if you were imprecise the next time you brought it up, he'd say, "That's not what you said last winter!" A good memory can be a major asset when there's conflict. One time we were in a senior staff meeting, which I always found fascinating just for the sake of watching him work on people's minds, and one of the directors of the Chapter I program was into a report when Johnny said, "How many Chapter One kids do we have now, Ed?"

Ed said, "Forty-one thousand two hundred and eighteen," some exact number like that. I knew right away he was faking it. So when we were further along in the meeting, I said, "Excuse me, Ed, but how many Chapter One kids did you say we have? I didn't catch the number."

Ed said, "Forty-three thousand six hundred and twelve."

Johnny sat straight up in his chair. "What's going on here! A little while ago you said forty-one thousand two hundred and eighteen! What is this?"

I meant it to be a joke, but the one thing Johnny Jones *didn't* have was a sense of humor. Life was an ongoing battle with Johnny, and he wasn't about to make light of it.

For example. Before every school board meeting he would invite five principals and five assistant principals to witness the proceedings. He believed you had to develop leadership abilities early, at the school level, and he was right. It's not enough that principals know about their schools, they should know about the school *system*, the whole operation. It was my job then to brief them, explain the agenda, identify the hot political issues, etc.

Then after the meeting, Johnny would bring us together for a debriefing. For the visitors, all of it was new and exciting, but for the rest of us it was a drill. The board meetings alone could go well into the night, and usually came on the heels of a whole series of long days (nobody in Jones's cabinet worked 9 to 5), so we'd go into the debriefings dragging our tails. Not Johnny. He'd be up, spoiling for a fight, still high from having just dealt with the board. His favorite opener then was, "What did you see at the meeting, Mr. Fernandez?" Heaven help you if you hadn't seen anything.

Anyway, this one afternoon during a board meeting a case came up involving a black undertaker who'd been burying his bodies on a piece of school property. Little grave markers began to appear in a vacant lot on 27th Street where we had a maintenance terminal. The lot was sometimes used to store surplus buses.

At the debriefing, Jones said, "We gotta stop this guy from using school property as a cemetery."

We were all tired, and nobody really wanted to get into that one so late.

So I said, "I have an idea."

Johnny said, "What's that?"

I said, "Why don't we just put up a fence and a big sign: 'No Body Allowed.'"

The room broke up. Everyone except Johnny. He said, "This is serious business, Fernandez!"

Well, it was also midnight. You can get pretty giddy at midnight if you've been going since 7 A.M.

I'd do that, try to loosen things up with a laugh, whenever I thought it necessary, or even if it wasn't necessary. Johnny put up with it because he liked me and because he needed that kind of thing. I was always needling him, reminding him that he was black, telling him, "You can't do that, you're black. How's that going to look on your record?" Sometimes he'd get mad, but he'd never stay mad.

And the truth was, Johnny operated adroitly within the power structure. He knew he had to work with *all* the factions to get things done, and he moved in the inner circles like a favored son: quick, charming, politically astute. He could lunch with the CEOs downtown, then spend the afternoon rapping with the brothers in Liberty City. He was tied into the black network of educators nationally, including a group of superintendents who had come out of the Rockefeller internship program. There was no end to his connections.

One of the men he hired as a speechwriter was Ernesto Ramos, the nephew of the Philippines' celebrated General Ramos. Ernesto was a brilliant writer, and Johnny loved intrigue, so it was a perfect fit when the cabinet was going through the initial reorganization and there were guys Johnny wanted to ease out. He had to do it one careful step at a time, and not always up front.

That was the part about him that made you wonder — that love of deception. You practice deceiving people long enough and it becomes a way of life. Johnny was good at it. But from my perspective, knowing what I know about the job and the man, it wasn't necessary. My belief is that the better way is *always* to be up front, if for no other reason than it makes it easier to keep your stories straight. For running schools it should be a cardinal rule. Johnny Jones was strong enough and smart enough not to need to play games with the truth. But his whole era was shrouded in secrecy, and play he did.

We were having our first strategic planning session at a Holiday Inn in West Broward County, but the group included those Johnny wanted to ax as well as those he wanted to keep. So he'd hold regular meetings during the day, then at night meet with the *real* cabinet on the q.t. The problem was we each had a roommate, and not every roommate was part of the inner circle. So after dinner we'd slip into the parking lot to be picked up by designated drivers to go to a nearby home of one of the group.

I'll never forget the scene as long as I live. We're all sneaking around, trying not to be conspicuous. I'm waiting near a streetlight on the far side for my ride when I see another car driving slowly around the periphery of the parking lot. Each time it comes to the entrance of the motel, the lights go out and the car passes — and there's nobody driving! Or so it seems. The guy behind the wheel is ducking down each time he passes so he won't be seen.

He does it two or three more times, then finally stops down the way, and Gavin O'Brien emerges from the shadows and gets in. Meanwhile, I'm still waiting with another guy for our ride. But no car comes. Then suddenly the bushes behind us rustle and I hear this thick Filippino accent: "Psst! Psst! Hey, Fernandez, over here!" We turn and the bushes spread, like Arte Johnson used to do wearing that German helmet on "Laugh-In." And there's Ernesto. "Psst! Over here!"

It was so ridiculous it was funny. We doubled over laughing.

Ernesto lasted through the reorganization, then went back to the Philippines to run for the senate. He needed to be where the skulduggery was better orchestrated.

Johnny Jones got off to a fast start as superintendent, deftly moving out the "good old boys" on the staff. He didn't trust Leonard Britton and would have liked to have dismissed him, too, but it wasn't politically sound, so he did to Britton what Britton later tried to do to me: he separated him from the pack. He made him permanent legislative liaison to Washington. A deputy in exile.

But Johnny's executive style was neither vindictive nor small-minded. A whole new sense of excitement percolated through the system. Johnny welcomed new ideas, and he had sound priorities of his own. His genuine concern for the education of poor kids led to a pilot program that extended the school day from 3 to 5 for Chapter I kids, the most at-risk of all, and provided them an afternoon snack out of the food subsidy budget. He set it up for the central staff to interview and handpick the teachers for those after-hours classes, so we would be sure to get the best available, and then paid the teachers handsomely: the equivalent of fifteen hours a day for the ten they worked.

He gave me almost complete freedom to try things in my areas of jurisdiction. The Dade Partners program we initiated, pairing local businesses with the needs of neighboring schools (the needier the better), grew from nine participants at start-up to more than nine hundred companies and institutions over the next several years. For me it was not just a revelation (I already knew there was plenty of help out there waiting to be asked), it was a portent of what could happen in any school system if the right buttons were pushed.

I believed it then and am convinced of it now: American businesses will respond to almost any legitimate appeal to help America's schools, especially at the grass-roots level. I had it verified those first years of Johnny Jones's administration. The Dade Partners became a force growing almost on their own. They sponsored scholastic contests and donated equipment (copying machines, telephone systems, etc.). They taught special classes, served breakfasts at meetings, recognized honor roll students with gifts, provided jobs and services to individual schools.

We could pick up the phone and get a bank to fund publication of a study. Or a mom-and-pop store to mentor a kid, or provide a part-time job, or come in on career day and talk about small businesses. It all counts. Dade's partners contributed everything from free tickets to cultural events (opera, ballet) to free hamburgers for good attendance records. Later, when I was superintendent, American Express donated $485,000 to *its* partner, Miami Springs High, for an academy of tourism to train students to be hotel operators and cruise directors. The implications of such a specific involvement are vast — made to order for cooperative networking with businesses. What could be the downside?

I enjoyed working for Johnny Jones. I was uncomfortable with all the intrigue, and I couldn't fathom the need for all the deception, but I have to say I liked the fact that accomplishments were made. We worked hard, and things were popping so fast you could barely keep up. We didn't know what regular hours were. At one point when we were moving a lot of principals around, Johnny had us calling in candidates at 11 and 12 o'clock at night for interviews. In that kind of environment I thrive because I don't mind going beyond my responsibilities. When you're moving that fast, vacuums get created that most people are afraid to fill. Even if it's part of their turf, they'd rather let someone else do it, because it's safer. I don't believe you accomplish as much playing it safe.

So it happened that I wound up coauthoring Dade County's first strategic plan for schools: a five-year outline for attacking the problems and achieving the goals in those areas of education deemed most important — from test scores to achievement tracking, from levels of literacy to the dropout rate. Nothing is more valuable to the running of a school system than a good strategic plan.

I have to admit, though, that I'd be embarrassed to match it against what we do today when there are so many resources at our disposal and reams of computerized data to tap into. Ours was a cave drawing by comparison, but it was vital because it was first.

Angie Welty and I put it together. Brought into the cabinet in that first reorganization, Angie was an English teacher from West Virginia who had also come up through the ranks. She had headed up an English television teaching lab, then became a district administrator, and was finally tapped by Johnny for downtown. Angie and I and our families became close friends, and I don't think any two people ever worked better together. Or longer. Or harder. We were fortunate to have understanding spouses.

Today it takes a whole battery of experts to put together a strategic plan. Then it was just Angie and me, doing it on top of all our other duties. Every day after hours we'd meet in her office or mine to gather and sort the information from the field, shaping it into plans, then writing it out. The material we got from the various offices and departments was often spotty and usually sparse, but it was the only game in town. We'd sift through and bounce things off one another, then run to our separate typewriters and write whole sections of the plan simultaneously.

We'd work that way until we were exhausted, which usually meant when everything we did sounded funny or crazy. By that time it was 11 or 12 o'clock. For safety's sake, we carpooled so Angie wouldn't have to drive home alone. One night I dropped her off at her house and was almost home when I realized I was driving her car. Then, halfway through the whole ordeal, Angie had to be hospitalized for a gall bladder operation. I called her up the night before and reminded her of my deep admiration for the beautiful grandfather's clock she had in her office. I said, "Angie, I wish you well, but if you don't make it, can I have your clock?"

She said, "You bastard, Fernandez!"

When I became superintendent, Angie gave me the clock as a token of her esteem. When I left for New York, I gave it back as a token of mine.

It took us six months, but when we finished, the school board loved it: Dade's first long-range plan to deal with the growing demands on education. But Johnny Jones deserves as much credit for it as anybody. It was his idea. I wish I could say it saved him when his star began to fall, but it didn't. For all his charisma and style, when Johnny went down, there was no saving him.

When the scandal first began to unfold, I was up to my neck in another hot item Johnny had laid on me. If I always got the toughest jobs under Jones (and later under Leonard Britton), as long-time board members like Holmes Braddock and Janet McAliley used to say, it was because I wanted them, and Johnny didn't hesitate to oblige. The toughest at the time was redefining school boundaries as a means of implementing desegregation orders.

Johnny had started the implementation himself with his own plan, but it blew up in his face. His called for a tremendous amount of cross-busing, putting the burden (rightfully) on whites as well as blacks but affecting so great a percentage of Dade schools that the whole county was up in arms. It was much too ambitious, and it came to an ugly head when white parents on Miami Beach rose up in protest over the pairing of their schools with those in Overtown, the roughest area of inner-city Miami. Black kids for some time had been bused to Miami Beach, and their parents weren't all that crazy about it, either.

It had been so one-sided, in fact, that the shrinking population of some of the Overtown schools made it likely that we'd have to close them down. And *that* didn't sit well in the black community, either, because Overtown is where the hoi polloi used to congregate for a brush with the stars of black culture in Miami. Famous athletes and black entertainers who couldn't stay in the Beach hotels where they performed frequented the old Sir John Hotel in Overtown. It wouldn't have been unusual to see Ella Fitzgerald or Sugar Ray Robinson or Louie Armstrong walking out of the Sir John. And the area's high school, Booker T. Washington, was its pride and joy.

Blacks would come from as far away as West Palm Beach to go to Booker T. Prof Williams, Booker T.'s last high school principal, had practically achieved sainthood. To shut down that school would have been a disaster. In the end, however, the problem of desegregating it wasn't solved until I was superintendent and was able to close down nearby Robert E. Lee Junior High, rebuild Booker T. as a state-of-the-art middle school, and move in Spanish kids from neighboring areas to achieve the appropriate balance. Hispanics are classified as "white" in Miami for desegregation purposes.

Anyway, when the Jones plan (actually written by a cabinet member named Sonny Gross) sank in, the community as good as shouted it down. The reality of the changes had a domino effect on people's confidence in the plan, especially as it related to the high schools, which had always been untouchable. Both sides came to the board meetings by the busload to protest and demonstrate. The politicians jumped in. The activists jumped on the politicians.

This was Jones's first negative encounter with the community, and the board collapsed on him. Bowing to the pressure, the board ordered a year's moratorium on boundary changes "so that a process can be worked out." Jones turned it over to me, and I immediately went about trying to regain community support. Gerald Schwartz, an attorney, and Mattie Bower, one of the leaders of the Miami Beach protests, had a big hand in helping me turn it around. Mattie once threw a pie in the face of a city official so I especially wanted her on my side. I sure didn't want to be on her hit list.

Jones left it for me to come up with a new game plan. I didn't have to. I already had one, virtually in writing. When I was going for my doctorate, I had three working theses that had to do with school reform. One was a plan to head off any tax referendum that would cap funding of education, something that came in handy when we blew the roof off with that record $980 million bond for building new schools. The second was a plan to reverse the flight of talented students from an inner-city middle school by better utilizing magnet programs.

And the third was what I called Attendance Boundary Committees, what came to be known simply as ABC. The plan was unusual in that it called for groups of citizens (parents, primarily) around the county to help implement school assignment changes in their area by actually participating in the process. Why not? They had a stake in it. My feeling was that you gain more by bringing people in than by trying to keep them out. You really *can't* keep them out, not in a free society. You shouldn't even try.

Nothing that I know of in school governance is more incendiary than boundary changes or busing mandates. They tend to inspire the worst in people. When the board first made proposals to pair Coral Reef Elementary School, in the silk-stocking district of Perrine in southwest Dade, with F. C. Martin, in a black enclave called Richmond Heights, the meetings held at Coral Reef were notoriously ugly. People yelled and screamed; white parents and agitators called each other "nigger lovers" and came close to blows. Joe Tekerman's wife, Barbara, was president of the Coral Reef PTA at the time and after she spoke in favor of the plan she and Joe had crosses burned on their front lawn.

You could have characterized the whole negotiation in a single word: disgraceful.

But look at the unfairness the board was dealing with. The schools in the area were F. C. Martin, all-black, and Coral Reef, Howard Drive, Palmetto, Leewood, and Vineland, all-white. The plan called for black kids to come to the white schools from 1 through 5, meaning for five years. In return, the whites would bus to Martin for grade 6, or one year — if their parents let them. Many white parents chose to move their kids into private schools for grade 6. The burden was obviously on the blacks.

But even in that scenario, considered the best of a bad lot, nobody seemed willing to agree. Our temporary solution was to allow F. C. Martin to keep its segregated kindergarten for one year, then start advanced academic programs at the school to make it more attractive to whites. It still involved busing, of course, which never satisfies everybody. It just ofttimes happens to be the only answer.

Anyway, my hope for Attendance Boundary Committees was that if we got parents to see for themselves the need to make changes — the racial imbalances, the overcrowding, the unfairness in the busing, etc. — they would accept the solutions without having to be dictated to by a central office. At the very least it would make the process more palatable. Boundary changes in some cases satisfied desegregation demands *without* busing. But more important, ABC allowed for bottom-up decision making instead of top-down, much the same as what would one day be the heart of School-Based Management.

What I didn't want was to shove a process down the parents' throats. Administrators have to remember that these aren't sacks of potatoes they're moving around, they're the flesh and blood of concerned moms and dads. And when you have to tell them that their children may be ordered to a school they don't want them to go to, in a place they don't think is safe, the burden is yours to show how it could work out to everybody's satisfaction.

Conversely, it's also up to you to prove to parents that under existing conditions their kids may not be getting the best shot at an education. If there are three hundred too many kids in a school, the school can't function properly. It means you'll be serving lunch at 10 in the morning and keeping the kids out at phys ed longer because of the demands on classroom space. It means holding classes on the stage of an auditorium or in a supply closet. It means everybody suffers.

When you can prove that in the long haul — four or five years down the road — their kids' chances will be improved, parents will come to the conclusion that boundaries have to be changed. Then you can present the alternatives, which don't always mean busing. Often it's just a matter of swapping classes with contiguous schools. A grade configuration change, say, where you move the sixth grade from the elementary school to a nearby middle school, and the ninth grade of the middle school to a nearby senior high. Boundary changes don't have to impact the kids that are already there, either, only the incoming class. It would vary by the case.

In order to make it clear what we were up to, I created guidelines for a "school profile," whereby every school in question could determine what capacity it was at in utilizing its facility. I gave them a formula. If the formula indicated a school was at 115 percent, it meant it was 15 percent over capacity. They'd work from there.

I had an oversight committee made up of citizens instead of educators. I commissioned a task force of parents, administrators, and various staffers in the system to establish a road map that showed how to go about gathering the data base, how we'd meet, how we'd pinpoint the problems and resolve them. We laid out a series of steps to be taken, leading up from the ABC at the school level, then to the district, then to us at central headquarters for hearings. We were thus able to take the school board out of the process entirely until the final sign-off, which was good because boards tend to worry too much about the political ramifications. Politicians can screw up a plan quicker than anything.

With the parents made to see the problem, and the ABC hammering out the boundary change, we would then take it to the board to sign. At that point all the heat was off, all the emotion banked. The decisions had been made on data, not prejudicial rhetoric.

Sometimes, of course, the parents *wouldn't* see, and when I sailed out into the storms, it was left for me to open their eyes. I got used to hostile crowds. Usually it was a matter of facing down people who just wanted to be heard, who weren't interested in solutions. At one meeting at Edison High, a black activist named Taylor started scolding me and I said, "Wait a minute, Taylor. Number one, you're not my mother. Only my mother can scold me. Number two, if you don't want to listen, I'm out of here. We'll send you the directive."

Most of the time they listened, and when we had the ABCs in place, we succeeded much more often than we failed. I couldn't always be Mr. Nice Guy, however. Sometimes I had to get pretty testy. Holmes Braddock, the senior member of the school board and a native Miamian (the one who had the high school named after him for a lifetime of serving education in Dade), was there one night when it *really* got hot. As he tells it, the New York street tough reemerged. I held up my hands and said, "All right, that's it. This is *my* meeting, and we're going to run it *my* way. You can talk all you want, but if you disrupt us one more time, it's over." I really don't remember what I said, only that I was teed off, but when they calmed down, we went back to the schedule and before long the boundaries were in place.

In time we learned to be very creative encouraging parents to volunteer for changes. At Pine Villa Elementary, an all-black school, we put in a Montessori kindergarten, with the idea that the incoming first-graders would be there on a six-year plan. Since the requirement with any of those special programs is that they be racially balanced, it meant that the white percentage would increase progressively throughout the school as the kids moved up in grade. We got their number up to 20 percent, then 25, then 40, and so forth.

Most schools, however, were apt to go the other way, and that meant a different approach. Miami Shores, an upscale white enclave along the bay in northeast Dade, had a terrific elementary school that was so popular it was bulging at the seams. It was racially mixed, but the blacks were pushing up to the 50 percent mark, which usually leads to whites pulling out, and they were. Traditionally when that happens, the school winds up with parents who don't have the time to be as supportive, and who then become indifferent or suspicious and hostile, and before long it is wracked by all the problems typical of schools in turmoil.

So we did this:

West of Miami Shores was a middle school, Horace Mann Junior High, where most of the Shores Elementary kids would go if they continued in public schools. Horace Mann was a beautiful old facility, but with a mostly black enrollment. There was tremendous resistance from white families to sending their kids there. Some had rented apartments elsewhere to use as subterfuges to get their kids into different schools; others had given up entirely and put them in a nearby private school.

After a review, I realized that even if I had 100 percent success convincing white parents through ABC that sending their kids to Horace Mann would mean three years of not having to pay private school tuitions, and even if I promised to throw in some advanced academic programs, we still wouldn't create the balance we needed. It would still be only 20 percent white.

So instead we worked out a plan where we would move the entire sixth grade from Miami Shores to Horace Mann and make the latter a magnet school in computer technology. Moving the Shores sixth grade and concurrently shifting the Horace Mann ninth grade to Edison High automatically brought the balance to almost fifty-fifty. It also meant that with the ninth-graders gone the younger kids wouldn't feel quite as threatened. We figured the rest would take care of itself. We got the local ABC to buy it, and the school board did, too. The only catch was they wanted *me* to announce our intentions to the suspicious parents of Miami Shores.

There must have been two thousand people jammed into the three-hundred-seat Shores Elementary auditorium the night I presented the plan. They were standing shoulder-to-shoulder all around. I had a number of my staff people there, scattered through the auditorium, but it was not a friendly crowd, and when I started to walk them through the plan, every time I'd open my mouth they'd interrupt me. When I said something they didn't like, they booed and yelled, and my people booed and yelled right along with them. (Later they explained that they didn't want to "blow our cover.")

But I stuck it out. I said the process was meant to find solutions we could all live with. That if they listened they might realize that it could be a good thing. And when I had laid out the full scenario, and they saw the possibilities, they came over to my side. At the end of the evening, we might not have been one big happy family, but we were agreed that the plan was worth trying.

Afterward, we made a lot of physical improvements at Horace Mann. We put in a computer technology program and got it linked with nearby Barry College as a partner. Eventually, we built a new building next to the existing facility and created an academy for computer science that was state-of-the-art. I also put together an advisory committee for the magnet school to make sure it worked out. It did, and it's still working.

Pivotal to ABC's success was the sensitivity it demonstrated, the spirit of compromise it brought to the boundaries problem. I like to think ABC helped create a much better feeling about schools in Miami and the ongoing need for change. The thing you can't get away from, however, is that in such matters somebody is always viewed as the winner (from the parents' standpoint, the kid who doesn't have to move) and somebody the loser (the kid who does).

But we worked hard to keep harmony, and every plan was tailored to the circumstances. If, in fact, we wanted to change a boundary for a high school, we often said, "This will only take effect with the incoming ninth-graders, kids who aren't part of the school yet." In other words, we grandfathered in the students who were already there, letting them have the option to stay.

We didn't solve all the problems that way, of course. But there are just so many solutions available to deal with overcrowding and desegregation: grade configuration changes, portable classrooms, program enhancements, boundary changes, busing. Long-range and short-range solutions, but all with an eye on the longer view. Basically, I think, the key to success was in taking the politics out, removing the shadow of the board from the process. We diffused the potential for major objections at the final point of decision. Our line in the sand had been drawn, and compromises reached, before the board even got into the act.

Yes, we had intentions aforethought. We felt we were the experts, and we were, because we did our homework and came armed with maps and surveys and studies. We could tell you by the block how many black and white kids would be impacted if we moved a boundary just so much. From our data base, we could tell you everything you needed to know about a school without ever having been in it. We were sophisticated with our information, and we were consistently able to say: "This is the best way to resolve the problem."

Admittedly, we orchestrated a lot of things, and ofttimes the community didn't know it was being orchestrated. But we were planting the right seeds, and we made our position stronger by always giving them honest information. We didn't throw any curves or doctor up anything. We thus established a high level of trust and a broad range of contacts in the field to get our ideas to surface. We were willing to accept some modification, but by coming in armed with facts and being careful to show tact and communal concern, we were able to get the plans through that were needed.

I don't know if Johnny Jones had expected that kind of result, but it really didn't matter, because he was long gone by the time we really got rolling. Leonard Britton, who succeeded Jones as superintendent and kept me in charge of the ABC program (I think anticipating that it would fall on its face, and me with it), wanted no part of it then. Certainly at the beginning it looked like a quagmire only a fool would put his foot into. I was to learn soon enough, however, that what Leonard really didn't want was me, I suppose for obvious reasons. I was considered a Jones man.

Even when ABC turned out to be a success (my first as an assistant superintendent) and school boards from all around the country were sending representatives to Miami to see how it worked, Britton ignored it. That intransigence alone helped save my future when push came to shove in the aftermath of the Jones scandal. Britton couldn't fire me then even if he wanted to.

A skeptical clerk at a plumbing supply house called down the avalanche that got Johnny Jones. The principal at MacArthur South High, Solomon Barnes, had used school funds to purchase some gold plumbing fixtures, ostensibly for vocational classes. The clerk gave the order a second look. These weren't gold-*plated* fixtures the buyer wanted, they were *gold* fixtures. She called Barnes and asked a leading question: why would a school need such expensive equipment?

The clerk said Barnes told her it was to be used in a "demonstration bathroom" MacArthur was putting together for a public showing.

The clerk didn't buy it. She leaked the particulars of the order to the press.

The Miami *Herald* investigated and found that not only the gold plumbing but also various materials previously purchased by Barnes were nowhere to be found in the schools. Missing items included some expensive photographic equipment.

In the face of a suddenly intrigued media, the lie began to unravel. An aggressive investigative reporter for Channel 7, a young man named Ralph Page, came to me first.

"Solomon Barnes ordered gold fixtures for a plumbing class, all right, but they weren't for the class and they weren't for him. They were for Johnny Jones."

"That doesn't make any sense," I said. "But I'll check it out."

Sure enough, Johnny said there was nothing to the story. I believed him. Moreover, it didn't seem like all that big a deal. More like a clerical misunderstanding.

A day or so later, Page was back in my office. He said he had learned that Johnny Jones was building "an expensive vacation home on the Florida Keys," and did I know where he got the money for it. I said no, but I didn't think it was something he'd keep from me — or *could* keep from me.

I went back to Johnny. He said no, he certainly wasn't building a vacation home on the Keys. Which was technically correct, but as good as a lie, because what he *didn't* say was that he was building a home in Naples, on Florida's west coast. I hadn't asked the right question.

It didn't take long for the Naples home to be discovered, which immediately put me in a bad light with the press for having given out "deceiving information." One of my jobs at the time was to brief the media on issues — not to keep a lid on, but to be sure correct information got out. In this case, I became the "official spokesman" because as soon as the seriousness of the situation was realized, Johnny's attorneys wouldn't let him talk to the media.

Johnny hadn't been implicated, but Barnes was a longtime friend of his and the lawyers thought it best that he hold his tongue. I was left somewhere in the middle, not really sure what was happening.

Each day brought a new revelation. The builder in Naples conceded the whereabouts of the gold plumbing fixtures: he had installed them in Johnny's vacation home, along with a lot of other expensive items he'd gotten through Barnes. It was reported that Jones and Barnes may have been getting kickback money from a friend through the school board's purchase of Chapter I materials. The friend was the wholesaler in the deal.

Even as the noose tightened, Johnny continued to deny everything.

Each time I had to run down an allegation, the people who might have been involved or had some knowledge of it also issued denials. Considering the implications of the crime, and what a conviction could do to him, I suppose I can't really blame Johnny for stonewalling me, but I kept getting put into the position of backing up lies without knowing they were lies. When I relayed Johnny's explanations to the press, or went on television or radio, I was the fool in the middle.

"You said Jones wasn't building a vacation home."

"No, I said he wasn't building one on the Keys. But he *is* building one in Naples."

"Oh, come on, Fernandez, you're giving us the runaround."

"I'm telling you what I know."

When it got worse, and inferences started to fly, members of Johnny's cabinet began to wonder if we shouldn't start worrying about our own reputations, not to mention our jobs. But even then I thought it was going to prove to be a big misunderstanding. I couldn't bring myself to take it seriously.

At a staff meeting one morning, Red McAllister, our head of security, brought in a brown envelope stuffed with all the bills and catalogues for the plumbing fixtures. When I reached for the "evidence," as a joke I spread my handkerchief over the envelope before I grabbed it, as if I was concerned about leaving fingerprints. Something you'd see watching *Perry Mason*.

It was supposed to be funny, but everybody was so dead serious, maybe thinking we really *shouldn't* be touching this stuff, that when they took it and passed it along they also grappled with the handkerchief. Only Angie Welty laughed.

Jones wasn't at the staff meeting. As it turned out, he was at that moment in conference with Bill Frates, a prominent Miami lawyer who at one time handled libel cases for Time Inc., and numbered John Ehrlichman among his clients. I should have known then that Johnny was in trouble, but I kept thinking that a man so smart couldn't have done such a stupid thing and that the investigators would finally take a turn that led nowhere and the case would die.

But it didn't die. I kept getting calls, and Johnny kept issuing denials until the whole sad mess was laid out. The gold plumbing was just the tip of the iceberg. Investigators found thousands of dollars in cash hidden behind the chimney of Johnny's house in Naples. They uncovered a skimming operation with Chapter I moneys where a local publisher was paid for books and materials and then kicked back large amounts to his "partners." In several instances the same man bought property under assumed names for some of those involved. Investigators also found a minister who had purchased land in the Bahamas for the accused. It went on and on.

The open arms that the world of education had been extending for Johnny Jones as he headed to the top closed on him fast. The day the story broke, Shirley Hufstedler of the U.S. Department of Education was in the school board building, having breakfast on the top floor with the board and the senior staff, including me. The scuttlebutt was that she was there to feel out Johnny on the possibility of his becoming undersecretary of education. Jimmy Carter was in office, and Johnny was clearly a man any liberal President could draw on: a brilliant administrator and the only black with such high visibility in American education. But Hufstedler left town the next day without a word.

Shortly afterward, Jones was indicted. Trial was certain. With Jones on the ropes, it didn't take the board long to make a move. Johnny was suspended, and Leonard Britton, back from exile, was made acting superintendent.

I don't think anybody who liked him ever completely got over Johnny Jones's disgrace. He had been such a talent. He was the son of a Baptist preacher and spoke with that kind of fire, except with considerably more polish than you might expect. He had been a language arts teacher and used impeccable English. If you turned in a sloppy report, he'd edit hell out of it in bold strokes. If you had an idea for some project, chances were he'd have a better one. But he was also good at giving credit where it was due.

His charisma was undeniable. Johnny could play a crowd like a Philadelphia politician. We'd come into a room, Johnny in the lead, and he'd just light it up, slapping backs, moving from table to table, making conversation. People would pop up in front of him and he'd be happy to see them, and then as we walked away he'd say, "Who was that?" Somehow with Johnny that didn't seem phony. He could do it. I wouldn't even try.

Bill Frates, the lawyer, who is dead now, once said that one of Johnny's problems was that he was trying too hard to *appear* successful, in keeping with the crowd he aspired to run with. Frates thought part of that might have been to impress his beautiful wife, Mattie, but I don't agree. Mattie is a handsome lady, no doubt. But Johnny was in control.

No, I think what turned Johnny's head was nothing more complicated than the oldest con in the business: power. You get to a certain point with success when it makes you think you're infallible and entitled to things whether you've earned them or not. Johnny got caught up with the power. He had people around him who made it too easy for him to cut corners. I say that, yet I think, But he was still too smart to do the dumb things he did. So the bottom line is I really don't know.

Johnny left quietly. He never apologized to me for the lying, but I didn't expect it. That wasn't his style. He was convicted of unlawful use of funds and a number of other things, including soliciting perjury and witness tampering, and sentenced to from three to five years in jail. I don't know how much time he actually served, hardly any at all, according to the stories. He did work some of it out with community service, and then the unlawful funds conviction was overturned on appeal when it was found that the prosecution deliberately kept blacks off the jury. Solomon Barnes was convicted and went to prison.

I didn't see Jones for a long time after that. He got back into circulation in Miami by selling meats to the school system. Johnny loved to cook, loved to eat, so he was a natural for the food business. When he was superintendent, he'd call you into his office around noon and sit there eating a big bowl of rice and beans, and you'd be salivating like mad, but he'd keep eating while you talked as if it were a perfectly natural way to conduct business. The only way he kept his weight down was by being constantly on the go.

To this day, Johnny Jones is the greatest tragedy in education that I've known. The schools of this country need great black leaders more than ever, especially on behalf of those dire core areas where the failure to communicate with the establishment is chronic and the tendency toward nihilism among the young grows more frightening all the time.

I read the other day where the rap singer M. C. Hammer, one of the few positive role models modern music has produced for black kids (or for any kids for that matter), said that "the biggest threat to the black man today is not the white man, but the black man." *Time* magazine did a story about urban schools where black kids now have such little respect for scholarship that they actually harass — threaten, intimidate, beat up — other black kids for trying to do well in school. Those areas are desperate for role models to tell them they deserve better than that, and for qualified black leaders like Johnny Jones to stand up to the underminers and troublemakers and be appreciated when they say, "How dare you ruin our kids' chances!"

So it wasn't just all that talent that was lost. The Jones debacle was a spiritual loss, too, and I think that was the most hurtful. When it comes to education, I'd argue that we *all* have a stake in turning these things around, but it's also true that we need the Johnny Joneses to speak for us in the process. To speak from the highest levels of authority and tell how education can make the difference.

Even with his conviction overturned, Johnny kept having problems. He accidentally killed a child in an auto mishap going home from a restaurant he ran in Little Haiti, and that got him back in the news for a while, negatively. I hadn't heard from him for at least five years when, in 1991, I got a letter. He told how he was back in business with the schools, selling meat through his processing plant — "Johnny Jones' Smoked Something-or-other" — and said he was doing fine. But that he was undercapitalized. He wanted to borrow $2,000.

Undoubtedly realizing that Jones would never be back, Leonard Britton started reorganizing immediately after the indictment. And when he was officially named superintendent, he moved with a vengeance.

Those who had been brushed by the scandal — that is, who were considered close to Johnny — were the first to feel the lash. Joe DeChurch, Johnny's deputy in charge of operations, was demoted to assistant superintendent, then later moved out of operations entirely to "staff development," a dead-end street. Angie Welty was dropped from assistant superintendent to executive director. Leonard gave me a tiny little office out of the way and tried to bury me with things nobody else wanted, but I wouldn't let him demote me. He tried, but with a little help from a friend I made it too difficult.

As a new boss is wont to do, Britton first asked for everybody's resignation. Angie and I thought it over and decided not to give it to him. My feeling was that a resignation in the wake of Jones's dismissal was tantamount to an admission of guilt, if only by association. Besides, I said, "If he doesn't want me as an assistant superintendent, fine. But I'm not going to make the decision for him. He'll have to do it."

The Saturday after he took over, Britton called. He said that in his reorganization plan he "needed help" in the vocational department. I said, "Tell me about it."

He said that it was an "executive director's job," which automatically meant a demotion.

I told him I wasn't certified in vocational studies and would rather not take it.

He said, "OK, but at least think about it over the weekend."

I said I would.

He called back that afternoon. "Joe, you're right. You don't need to be in vocational education. I've got a better spot for you, in labor relations."

Labor relations was something I liked, an area where I had some expertise. But again, it meant I'd be under another assistant superintendent, as an executive director. I didn't tell Leonard, but I was beginning to think I'd just as soon go back to being a principal, because there I'd have more control of my destiny. If you're good enough, sharp enough as a principal, you can get things done in spite of the constraints.

Finally, he offered me a job I *did* accept, at first. He said he'd put me under Joe DeChurch in operations (this was before he demoted De-Church a second time), working in tandem with Earl Wells, a black administrator who'd been a valued assistant superintendent under Jones. Again, it meant being an executive director. But I agreed.

An hour later I got a call from Wells. He said, "I'll be damned if Britton's going to demote me. Just because I'm black, and Johnny did all that stuff, doesn't mean he can kick me around." Earl was a bright guy with a spotless record and wealthy in his own right. He and his wife, who was a longtime principal in the system, and a good one, owned property in various places, and with their kids grown they had a comfortable life. He didn't need the hassle.

He said, "Joe, if we accept these jobs, it's going to look like we did something wrong and this is our punishment."

I said, "OK, then what do we do?"

"*We* don't do anything. Let me check around."

Well, I know exactly what Earl did then. He "checked around" by going to Athalie Range, a respected black county commissioner, and some of the other high-profile people in the black community he knew had downtown clout. He also knew what we all knew about Britton, that he'd back down from the first rebel voice with any authority to challenge him.

When Earl Wells called back, he had the word. "The powers that be are moving. They're not going to let this happen to me, and they won't let it happen to you, either."

Sure enough, on Monday Britton called. "You know, Joe, I've been thinking about it. You really haven't done anything that would make me take this out on you. I'm not going to make you an executive director, I'm going to keep you as an assistant superintendent. You and

Earl will have the same jobs, reporting to DeChurch, but with no demotion."

I thought to myself, Sure, out of the goodness of your heart, and nothing to do with the pressure Earl Wells's buddies put on you. Who do you think you're kidding? But all I said was, "Fine."

It was the beginning of seven years of working directly under Britton. Seven years, as Holmes Braddock used to say, "of getting all the dirty jobs," beginning with the boundary changes. But I never really saw it that way. I saw it as an opportunity to take the lead in finding ways to get things done — to make schools better. If Leonard threw me to the wolves, I learned to dance with them. If being where the action was while he stayed safely in the office meant being where I could do the most good, then that was where I wanted to be.

In the end, it was the tack that would make me Britton's deputy in spite of everything, and then his successor.

I recount all this intrigue to remind myself as much as the reader that too often in education leadership gets so wrapped up in its own selfish interests that it forgets what it's there for — if it ever knew. Johnny Jones, taken in by his own deviousness, was a chance-taker who in a last confusion of twisted priorities took one chance too many. Leonard Britton was a gatekeeper who played it so close to the vest that you had to think survival was his only real interest. Whether he had ideas to offer we never found out, because he never offered any. One thing you have to say about Leonard in that context, however: he didn't steal from the children. Johnny did.

They were opposite poles, Jones and Britton, but in the final analysis each in his own way had less of the schools' interest at heart than he should have. It's a problem throughout education, this inability to keep in focus the basic idealism that should separate the leadership of schools from that of just about every other institution. But I have to say that nothing I experienced in Miami could compare with the cynical manipulation of power, the outright corruption of the process, that I have had to deal with in New York City. How some of the people there ever got into education in the first place is beyond me.

By the time Britton demoted DeChurch and put me in charge of operations, I was already handling most of the "dirtier" assignments. Besides boundaries, I was required to do the disciplining of principals and administrators (something that prepared me well for New York). When there was no other recourse, I had to call them in and tell them they had to retire or we'd have to fire them. A very hard thing to do when it's somebody who has been in the system twenty years. Britton didn't want any part of that.

Whenever there was a dispute, I tried to keep the damage under control by summoning all interested parties to get them to see the reason behind my actions. When you make a habit of openly dealing with these things, you head off a lot of trouble later on. On one occasion we got an audit from the feds on our food service program that showed some major accounting breakdowns in districts where we had black principals. I didn't want it to become a racial thing, which it really wasn't, even with tensions being what they were after Jones's departure, so I took two or three of the worst audits, brought in the principals, and convinced them to retire. That gave the others enough of a scare to volunteer their help straightening out procedures generally. The feds were satisfied, and the damage was minimal.

As day-to-day head of operations, I involved myself with everything from the budget to labor negotiations, from networking with the PTA to finding linkages to improve our relationships with the business community. I didn't hesitate to bring in anybody I thought could help, at any time. I had gotten high grades for the ABC results, and the Dade Partners program I'd started under Jones was booming, but in both cases my success was really in enlisting the help of others. You're a fool in this business if you think you can do it alone.

Despite everything, Britton knew he could count on me. I worked harder and was there later than anybody. I had good relations with the unions, the teachers, the principals, the administrators, the press. The people in curriculum liked me. I had gained the confidence of parents groups by being out there for ABC. Britton and the others knew that I was honest. If I was tough, I didn't always speak from a set position — I was willing to listen. Most important, I believed in making decisions based on the common good. That's key.

Part of Britton's problem was that so much of his first few years in office was marked by a general paranoia over finances. In the post-Jones period, every procedure was in question. The focus was more on how we did business than on needed reforms. It really wasn't until we had a banker on the board, Paul Cejas, who as chairman put in some excellent checks and balances to avoid future fiascos, that everybody began to breathe easier. In the meantime, though, Britton drew more and more inward, and I got more and more involved in the problems and initiatives that were actually the superintendent's responsibility.

As for being in the middle, I was caught right there — on the roof of a surrounded school in Overtown — during the Miami riots of 1980. *Not* a place I wanted to be.

A number of things had happened to put the black community on edge. You couldn't blame the Jones case, but it was probably part of the resentment that had been festering, together with other political issues. What triggered the riots, however, was what appeared to be the senseless beating of a black insurance man named McDuffie by Miami police after a high-speed, late-night chase. Those kinds of things always get maximum media attention, as Los Angeles (and the whole country) found in 1992 with the Rodney King beating in a similar circumstance, and are thus inherently volatile.

The riots began on a Friday with school in session. One of my tasks was to oversee emergency procedures for getting the children and the staff in and out of the worst areas: Liberty City, Overtown, and some parts of Coconut Grove. By the following Monday, it was a national story as the rioting got worse, so we closed the schools in those sections.

Closing schools is usually a last resort in such a crisis, not only because you have to make up the days, which is costly, but because you don't want the kids out in the streets with the rioters. On the other hand, nobody wants to risk bringing them and their teachers *into* a dangerous situation, either, so it's a catch-22. Several white motorists who happened into the most dangerous areas during the worst of the rioting were waylaid and beaten — two of them fatally. Los Angeles knows how that can happen.

A state of emergency was declared and lasted for several days, but part of the city's strategy was to try to make everything appear "back to normal" as quickly as possible. It wanted the schools reopened and kept open. I coordinated the effort through our closed-circuit TV station, acting as the on-air "anchor" and bringing in Britton and a couple of black administrators to encourage our teachers to stay at their posts wherever there was adequate police protection. Actually, we did a good job of it. The schools were reopened in two days and kept open. Nobody was hurt, and no real damage was done, although some teachers' cars were hit on the way in and out.

But at one point early on I was in Overtown trying to decide whether to close an elementary school. You could tell by the noise and the sirens that the rioting had gotten worse. We had already sent the kids home. I went up on the roof of the school to see how bad it was and was greeted by a nightmare scene: rioters clogging the streets in all directions, running in packs, wielding bats and sticks and throwing bricks through store windows, looting and fighting and setting fires. Anarchy.

What made it doubly scary was that I could see the police, too — *backing away* from the area, giving up territory in order to establish a line of defense. And there we were, inside the territory they'd given up!

I immediately called our security people to tell them our predicament. We had walkie-talkies to use during the emergency, so I was able to communicate from the roof, where I could also help coordinate the rescue, if one was ordered. Many of the teachers and administrators were still in the building. I had no way of knowing what the rioters would do if they broke in, but I really didn't think they would. Mobs like that are usually more interested in finding something to steal than someone to hurt. But who could be sure?

Security told us to stay put until it could get the police to work out an evacuation. We stayed put, and waited. A very long two hours later, the police brought in two school buses under the escort of six patrol cars and took us out. They made teachers who had cars there leave them behind, and when they put us on the buses, they made us hunker down away from the windows. Some rocks were thrown, but nobody was hit.

I would like to think that there was a deference shown the schools during those riots that kept us safe and that maybe the confidence we had tried to build in the black community was a factor, but I doubt it. Mob violence is a mindless thing, driven only by passion for whatever it is the mob wants. The schools just didn't happen to be something that qualified.

Whatever their justification, if there was one, the riots that year and the lesser ones Miami had several years later could not possibly have had any salutary effect on education, unless you count making the places under fire more forbidding than ever. Such images hurt the schools, and therefore the children who attend them, more than people realize because of the damage they do to the perceptions of life in those bombed-out areas. I shudder to think what they do to the trust and hopes of young people. (School? Look around, man. What's the sense?) Certainly they don't make teachers any more comfortable.

But when it was over, it was over. There was no time to dwell on it one way or the other, so much was going on. I'm not talking about just in Miami, where every day brought a plumber's list of new leaks to plug in the system. Nationally, education was on the hot seat. If you could stand the heat, it was an exciting time. *A Nation at Risk* had come out, indicting the whole of American education but really saying the things we already knew.

Wherever you went, change was being discussed. Educators are boring that way. It doesn't matter if we're meeting at a big curriculum conference in the Chicago Hilton or by chance on a street corner in downtown Newark, the only thing we want to talk about is education and its needs. From what I had seen in my travels, Dade County was in many ways a replication of what was going on, and what was going on generally was that public education was taking a bashing. The air was charged with all kinds of brilliant reasons to be depressed.

And a lot of the carping was out of ignorance of what was *really* happening.

I didn't hear anybody say, for example, that the dramatic shifts in demographics were a huge factor. That the incursion on the curriculum of all the social-awareness and problem-resolution courses, rushed into existence to deal with all the new threats to our children's well-being, was a huge factor. That the growing alienation of the black underclass, sinking farther out of the mainstream, was a huge factor, together in some areas with the assimilation of large numbers of poor immigrants and political refugees, themselves destitute and barely able to communicate even in their own language.

No one really appreciated all we were being asked to do — and with the same old tools that we'd always used.

The stage was being set to make education the fall guy in our national dilemma, and the blame would be without regard for all the factors. A bum rap.

But, ah, not entirely a bum rap, either, because education *needed* a new direction, and unless you were blind to its problems, you could see even then that to make it viable in a radically changing society new resources had to be uncovered and a new awareness created.

You could see that we'd have to pursue a political agenda, with as much clout as we could muster, and do more to involve government (and government spending) if we were going to keep pace with the schools of our international competition.

That we'd have to bring in the business community for support to an even greater extent than we were doing in Miami.

That we'd have to get more involvement out of parents and coordinate our efforts with higher education so that goals and resources could be synthesized to produce better results on graduation day.

And perhaps most of all, that at the point of attack, at the schools themselves, we'd have to make changes in the decision-making process in order to answer with dispatch the shifting, elusive needs of the classroom.

It was about this time that I began to sow the seeds of School-Based Management in Miami. What I knew about its first forms was just enough to make me want to go further. Hammond, Indiana, and Rochester, New York, had made stabs at it, but without really relaxing the reins and letting the horses run. Giving a school or group of schools only 10 percent control of the budget is not really a "school-based" operation.

I started a committee to look at school-based budgeting, with a former junior high principal, Dr. Gerald Dreyfuss, who was then executive director of the budget, as chairman. Gerry was a keeper. I later made him my assistant for SBM when I was superintendent.

Britton pretty much left me to my own devices, to try the waters, to throw out suggestions. I published a manual on the "beginnings of School-Based Management" with his knowledge, but without his endorsement. I created a professional library in every cluster of schools that made up a feeder pattern, and for a year inundated them with literature on school reform, the idea being to get material in the hands and heads of teachers and parents and administrators so that they would be ready for anything. Then I prepared an extensive memo, inviting schools to consider participating as "SBM schools" and telling them how to proceed if they were interested.

Leonard wouldn't sign the memo. He thought it was "too controversial."

But he didn't want to squelch the idea, either. It might turn out OK. So he said, "You sign it."

Much later, when he was on the way out as superintendent, he told me, "I made a mistake. I should have signed that memo. Now you're associated with School-Based Management, but I'm not."

I tried something else at the time that would have gotten Britton some accolades, too, but he backed away again. Believing as I do that the time-honored (and failure-dominated) confrontational approach to contract negotiations between unions and management was outdated, Pat Tornillo and I put together a "unions" conference and invited the school principals and the union stewards — lions and lambs, who almost never meet agreeably on anything.

I rented hotel space and a conference room at the Miami Springs

Villas, and Pat got Albert Shanker, president of the American Federation of Teachers and a guru of school reform, to come join the fun. Shanker and I were the speakers. Britton should have been, but he begged off.

At the meeting, the principals sat on one side of the room and the stewards sat on the other, but they listened to suggestions of collaborative action they'd undoubtedly never heard before from a union leader, things about finding a common ground to work from, and why that was more important than ever. I laid out the basics of School-Based Management. I explained some of the ways it could promote trust and cooperation and result in any number of mutual benefits.

Tornillo was there, providing support, and afterward he and I produced a dog-and-pony television show that mainly focused on answering questions about SBM. Gerry Dreyfuss moderated, and Pat and I acted as his "guests," with principals and teachers as audience and inquisitors. The idea was to allay initial fears about SBM and try to explain the basics. To talk through the changes it would mean.

The "show" went over well. Pat and I were up front about how limited our knowledge was as to what might happen. "Look," I said to a question that we couldn't readily answer, "we're going to be writing the book on this stuff. It's all brand-new. We're the Mayflower Company, touching shore on a new land. We don't have all the answers yet. And some of the answers we're giving you now might be different later on."

Primarily, we said, the message was this: "Dream! Be risk-takers! And we'll support you doing it."

That's the way we sold SBM.

Why did I think it would work? How had I come to believe that giving more say to teachers and administrators and parents would prove a better way to get things done? I think it went back to my days as a department head at Coral Park High School. My math department functioned well because I got teachers involved, got them talking, got them making suggestions. It's common sense to me that ownership in an idea gives it a better chance of succeeding. That when people are attached to something, they work harder to make it fly.

Second, when I was an assistant principal and wanted to do something that was a departure from tradition, I knew a lot would depend on what kind of risk-taker my principal was. I was frustrated more than once by principals who refused to venture into the passing lane. When I was a principal, I found the same thing applied to my district superintendent. You have to take risks if you're trying something different, and you have to have support from the top. Much too often *I* was willing to take the risk, but my superiors weren't.

But even with those promising early responses, and the excitement I could see being generated on the subject of School-Based Management, I felt I was usually either preaching to the choir or to deaf ears. It was ironic. I had come up with the idea of satellite schools — schools at the workplace — when we were in a cabinet meeting and Britton was discussing the tremendous overcrowding problems we had, including the lack of funds to build new schools.

I said, "Why don't we look at getting the business communities to provide school space for us, right where the parents of these kids work, or close to it. Maybe even under the same roof." I'd never heard it done before, but I thought, what the hell, it makes sense.

Granted, the concept got expanded considerably later on, but I was looking at it as a means of finding relief for the numbers. But no one, not a single cabinet member, responded. Not even a "Hey, Joe, nice idea." It didn't discourage me. It just made me wonder.

Meanwhile, Joe Tekerman had come on board downtown, having finally called it a day as a principal, and I had him on my staff — a valued friend with ideas of his own that I could play off. I had him start a file on the things I'd do if *I* were superintendent — SBM, satellite schools, and so forth. I don't remember which suggestion I'd just seen die in the thin air around the superintendent's office, but I remember telling Tekerman, "Joe, I've got so many things we ought to be doing, but I'll be damned if I'm going to waste any more of them on Britton."

Actually, at that point I was just getting over being mad at Leonard for something else he'd done — not to me, but to Tekerman. When I think about it now, however, I realize I should have thanked him for it because it wound up putting Tek on my team.

Ryder, the trucking company, had done a one-year pro bono study of Dade's school transportation department and found some alarming abuses. The maintenance shop was stealing tires, people were ripping off equipment and skimming from the service bills. The buses weren't being inspected according to regulations, the Florida Highway Patrol failed a bunch of them on inspection, and when the records were examined, it was learned that entries had been falsified.

Ryder made recommendations that led to our restructuring the entire maintenance operation. As I would today with any large school operation, I recommended that private vendors do some of the work and that the auditing be done by qualified outside firms rather than in-house. But Britton wasn't satisfied. He wanted to pass it off as poor management, and since transportation was partly in the realm of Tekerman's responsibility, he tried to make Joe and a man named Alan Olkes the scapegoats.

He demoted Olkes. But when he tried to do the same to Tekerman, Joe got his back up. An honorable career — decades of service as a teacher, principal, and administrator — wasn't going to be trashed if he could help it. He told Britton, "I'm suing you."

That changed everything. Britton came to me. He knew Tek and I were friends and he didn't want to get sued.

I said, "Don't demote him, then. Just let him come work for me."

I talked to Tek, and he agreed to the compromise, reluctantly at first, but then enthusiastically when he realized the possibilities in our teaming up again.

And I believe at that moment I began thinking about being superintendent of the Dade County school system. I began to think my time had come.

It was obvious from a whole series of events that Leonard was rapidly losing ground. He had gone through some personal crises of his own, including a divorce, and in his hands the system had gone stale. There was no doubt he was looking elsewhere. Articles in the Miami papers began insinuating that his days were numbered. The board's attitude was visibly changing, and much of it, according to the innuendos, had to do with Leonard's fainthearted ways.

Board members had been after him from the start to name a deputy, but Britton kept putting them off. I think he felt that appointing a deputy was tantamount to naming an heir-apparent, and he was too insecure for that. But the board had taken a reformist bent with the addition of Paul Cejas, Dr. Mickey Krop, and Janet McAliley, and kept pushing him.

When he finally named me deputy in 1986, I think he thought of it as the easy way out. I had delivered on things that made him look good, and in his way he appreciated that, but I think he also felt that I still bore the stain of Johnny Jones and would never be considered for the superintendency — even though I was the only assistant who had been a principal, the only one who had worked in labor relations. I had been a department head. I had been in charge of operations and dealt with personnel. I knew the budget inside out.

As Britton's "surprise" deputy, I had come prepared whether he thought so or not. I told him up front I wouldn't be a deputy in name only. I said I would be "everything the job calls for, and be ready to take over if the situation arises." I told him that without realizing how close we were — less than two years away — to that happening. He said he wanted it that way, too, because he needed "to mend fences" with the community and the board.

But for Britton, the situation only got worse. The last year or so saw a generally demoralized staff, with Leonard trying to accommodate the often opposing positions of single-minded members of the board. Things we thought were nailed down would change from meeting to meeting. Whoever was the last to get his ear got their way. At one point, he publicly announced the promotion to the personnel office of a man everybody knew was a white racist. A black board member challenged him on it, and not only did Britton back down, but he agreed to give the job to the board member's nominee — a *black* racist. He had to back down again when the flap made the papers.

As Leonard faltered, my time was mainly spent putting out fires. Word got around that he was feeling out other cities for a move. Tallahassee was rumored as a possibility. Without fanfare, he entered into negotiations with Los Angeles. I got an inkling that the board itself was preparing for a change, when out of the blue Paul Cejas, then board chairman, invited me to lunch in Little Havana and said, "I think Leonard's on the way out, and I want you to know you're my choice for superintendent."

Not long before then I had been interviewed for the superintendency of schools in Long Beach, California. Holmes Braddock told me about the opening, and I put my name in, not really thinking it would lead to anything. But Long Beach sent representatives to Miami to talk, then had me come out there as one of the "two finalists" for the job. They put me up on the *Queen Mary* and showed me all the courtesies, but I knew when I got the full picture that I didn't want the job. I wanted to stay in Miami. The other guy who was interviewing was a local and turned out to be the only one they offered it to.

But the experience had gone well, and I came back thinking if something else came up, I might still consider moving on. I had gotten some national celebrity with the ABC program and Dade Partners. School-Based Management was showing signs of coming to life, and when the movers and shakers of Dade wanted someone from the school system to take to New York to speak to groups about bringing business to Miami, they usually chose me.

So when Cejas indicated that I was his preference, I had to think that the planets were in line. Within days, Britton announced he had been offered, and would take, the superintendency of the Los Angeles school system. He had six months lead time and remained on the payroll in Miami, technically still in charge, but he deferred to me on the budget we had been working on for the next fiscal year, and all but turned the entire operation over to me as he flew back and forth to L.A. In effect, then, I had six months to prepare for the job, even though I had been given no official word.

On July 1, 1987, having overridden a tentative move for a national search, the Dade school board opened the floor for nominations for a new superintendent. Mine was the only name offered. I had a good idea it might go that way because every one of the board members had wanted to meet with me one-on-one beforehand. Each let me know what he or she expected, and I told them what *I'd* expect, including full responsibility for selecting my staff.

Florida has a sunshine law, and when my nomination was put up for vote at the meeting, a large crowd was on hand, including the press. Each board member was obliged to comment, and other comments came from the floor. I had to sit through it all. Fortunately, none of the feedback was negative. Pat Tornillo, God bless him, said I was "the right man, in the right place, at the right time." The Miami *Herald* used his remark in an editorial supporting me.

The vote was 7–0, first time around. I look back now and realize how lucky I was to have that kind of support, and how much easier it was on my nerves than if I'd had to wait out a split vote. Three years later, when I left for New York, it took seventeen ballots for the board to name Paul Bell as my successor.

I said nothing profound in my acceptance, just thanked everybody and went back to work. But at the very next board meeting two weeks later, I put them on notice. I said I wanted to be held accountable, but I didn't want to have them publicly criticizing me or my staff the way they'd done with Britton. I said if they had a problem with anybody on the staff, come to me. I said I didn't want any surprises.

I laid out the areas we intended to concentrate on: my plans for "professionalization" of teachers and principals, to make their jobs more respectable and better compensated. I talked about moving the agenda ahead, improving the workplace, recruiting and training better teachers, more parental involvement, what we had to do curriculum-wise, and what we *would* do about overcrowding, including some of my ideas on building plans that would later take shape as the controversial $980 million bond issue for new schools.

Some people told me afterward that I'd been a little too strong. I didn't think so.

I did have one major regret. My dad wasn't there to see any of it. I'll never forget getting the B'nai B'rith Award for outstanding community relations that year. Actually, Paul Cejas and I got it jointly, but I was supposed to make an acceptance speech, and when I looked out at the audience, I saw my mom there crying, and I thought of my dad. He'd died just before I was named deputy.

It was such an untimely thing, Dad's passing, even though he was seventy-five. He'd been diagnosed as having an aneurysm, but he had kept it from us. The doctor had advised against surgery because of his age, but I learned later that they *should* have operated on him when the clot was discovered. He was still a strong, wiry guy, and very active, and would have had a good chance of surviving it.

Mom called at 2 in the morning when the aneurysm burst. I called 911, got dressed, and was at his side when the rescue squad came. I went with him to the hospital and lived there for the next seven days. I slept in the waiting room, going home only to shower and change clothes.

They operated right away, and Dad came through it OK, in a way proving the point. But the damage had already been done. He wasn't conversant until the fifth day, and we talked. He was very calm, but he had a funny look in his eye, something I'd never seen. That night I went to sleep on the waiting room couch, and about 3 in the morning the nurse woke me. "Come quick." When I got to his bed, he was already gone.

I hadn't been all that close to my dad growing up. He worked so much he was rarely available for the traditional stuff that I eventually did with my kids — playing ball, going fishing, taking little trips. But we grew a lot closer when he retired and moved to Miami. We were together a lot then, mainly a matter of our involving him and Mom in almost everything we did as a family. He loved puttering around our yard, doing things for Lily and the kids. He was a terrific grandfather.

And I thought of him as I got up to give that speech to the B'nai B'rith. I thought how fitting it was that I would be honored by this liberal group, because Dad was a sucker for liberal causes. I said, "I only regret my father isn't here to see this . . ." and I choked up. For the first time in my life I was speechless. Angie Welty came to my rescue. She stood up and applauded, and then everybody stood and applauded. And I sat down without saying anything.

I still get choked up thinking about it.

I took over the Miami school system with none of the fanfare, and virtually none of the attention, I got in New York. Comparing the two, I prefer the quieter approach. But I made a mistake in Miami that I didn't make in New York. I didn't clean house. I made some structural changes, but I left in the loop a number of people I knew would just as soon have seen me disappear, but I thought they were talented enough to deserve my support. I just didn't have the presence of mind to consider the consequences. I doubt many people would agree, but I was too nice.

I named as my deputies Paul Bell and Tee Greer, and then Angie Welty, all of whom had been assistant superintendents under Britton. But Angie was the only one I really wanted. I didn't think I'd get the kind of enthusiasm or creativity I needed out of the other two, but I figured a little laissez-faire wouldn't hurt for a while and in the years to come I'd get my people in through job attrition.

I know it was a mistake, because we would have been able to move a lot faster getting our programs in gear, and Miami wouldn't be experiencing the backsliding it is now when so much of the work we did is withering on the vine — even School-Based Management, although it's probably too firmly in place to succumb to neglect. But the truth was I didn't think of any of them as important enough to be considered obstacles. Besides, there was just so much going on, and I was so full of energy for the job, that I couldn't take the time to worry about it.

And it was fun, because we were a tonic to the system, infusing it with ideas at every level. It was like a three-ring circus, with perpetual-motion acts in all three rings. I was primed to make decisions; right or wrong, I made them, moving the agenda along at top speed. In the field, Tekerman and I brought new meaning to the term "hands-on management."

At first I had put Joe under Tee Greer to give Greer some help, but I decided I needed him more and made him my executive assistant. I basically ran everything out of my office, but from the beginning I'd made up my mind that I wasn't going to be desk-bound. I saw that failing in others. If anything, I was probably too willing to deal directly with problems. If there was an attendance snafu, I didn't go to Bell, who was in charge of that area, I went directly to the person responsible.

If that's a sign of not being altogether trusting in the ability of others, I plead guilty with an explanation: chains of command are in place for a reason, and usually they are good reasons. I don't recommend breaking chains of command. But when a system (a bureaucracy) is clogged by inertia, or people in it need to wake up or stand aside, you will always find that the job is getting done — *if* it's getting done — by those who have found ways to avoid "channels."

My style, undoubtedly spawned by the urgencies I have felt in headlong efforts to break out, is *not* to pay much attention to chains of command. It drives some people crazy, because I do it in New York now as much as I did it in Miami, but I have a thing about time (I'm always running out of it), so I pick up the phone, or I get in my car and go right to the source. In Miami I didn't have the faith in some of those I'd left in place below me to follow through, so if I had a principal I wanted to get in line, I'd do it myself or send Tekerman. "Get this guy straightened out, Joe." And Tek would bypass three or four bureau chiefs to do it. But no, I don't recommend it, except under extraordinary conditions.

One of the things I knew I'd be is a visible superintendent, not at press conferences or banquet halls, but in the schools — those being the places where we were supposed to make a difference. That first year, usually with Tekerman at the wheel, I visited sixty schools. More often than not we popped in without warning. When classes opened in September, we started at the southern extreme of the county, in Homestead, and worked our way north, and were into our sixteenth and last school of the day at 7 P.M. We finished at a school so far north that the principal said no superintendent had ever been there.

Just after lunch, we drove into the parking lot at Citrus Grove Junior High, and I threw a fit. There were graffiti everywhere. I am very sensitive about graffiti. Tekerman says it's the Puerto Rican in me. Actually, I hate them for what they represent: careless, mindless, stupid vandalism. I said, "Look at those graffiti," except in words much less delicate, and stormed into the school.

When I got to the principal's office, I walked right in unannounced, and there he was with his feet up on the desk. I said, "Do you realize you have graffiti all over hell out there?"

"Yeah, I wanted to tell you about that."

"*I'll* tell you about it. It's now two-thirty. I'll be back by five o'clock. If that stuff is still here by then, you won't be."

We got back at 6 o'clock, and there was paint slopped all over the place. Actually, the graffiti looked better than the paint job, but I couldn't complain. The principal had done what he was told.

At one elementary school in Coconut Grove, I walked into a class where the kids were huddled around a fishbowl, crying. Their goldfish had died over the weekend. Tekerman was waiting for me at the car when I got back outside, and he must have thought I'd finally cracked. I said, "We need to get the kids in room so-and-so some goldfish." Joe gave me a look, and then did what any good soldier would do with an order like that: he called his wife. "Barbara, go get some goldfish and take 'em to room so-and-so at Coconut Grove Elementary right away." And *Barbara* did the flipping: "*What?*"

But the highlight of the day, in both our estimates, came when we dropped into a class of second-graders at a northside elementary. The teacher's glowing introduction of the visiting dignitaries from downtown was greeted by polite applause — and a piercing raspberry from an unidentified male scholar in the back row.

I pretended not to notice, but when Joe and I got back to the car we laughed so hard the tears rolled down our cheeks. I said, "Tek, let's go back and give that kid a diploma! He might be the smartest kid in Dade County."

Actually, the word had gotten out even before then that I was not going to put up with grubby-looking schools. Three days before classes started, I walked into Shadowlawn Elementary and found the grass knee high, unopened boxes of supplies and books piled in the hallways, a stench in the building that would knock you down, and a baby grand piano teetering dangerously on three bad legs. When I went into the office, the principal was sitting there eating lunch and watching a soap opera on television. I fired him on the spot.

Unfortunately, he was a black man, in a mostly Haitian school, so to avoid problems, I made him come downtown with us. Then I called in his community leaders, took them to the school, and showed them the reason for my action. I said, "School starts Monday. Here it is Friday afternoon. Books are still packed in boxes. The place is filthy. Is this what you want for your kids?" They shook their heads.

I told them we were going to do something about it, and we did. That very weekend. We brought in a custodial SWAT team to spruce up the place. We did an industrial-strength cleanup job. We planted some shrubs. And I replaced the principal with a sharp black woman out of our executive training academy.

Word on those kinds of measures gets around fast. I wanted the grapevine to twang with the news that we would be visiting schools without warning, so watch out. The principal at one school had her husband mow the entire playground over a weekend for fear that I'd show up on Monday morning. I used to accuse Tekerman of tipping schools off, especially if the principal was somebody he liked, so on the days we'd venture out I wouldn't give him our destination until I got in the car. Then I'd hand him a sealed envelope.

That was in fun, of course. And the idea of our visits wasn't to cause fear and trembling; it was to show concern, and be receptive to problems, and get people thinking about how proud they should be of their schools. Most of the time the action taken was nothing more than pointing out a need for some attention. Even if we only passed without going in, I'd make a call to the school or send a memo: "Your walkways need sprucing up. . . . You could use a paint job out front."

I do that now in New York City, even though I can't be on the scene nearly as much because of a far greater office commitment, at least for the time being. But in New York I'm facing only 322 square miles to cover instead of the 2,100 in sprawling Miami, so when I'm out I carry a laminated list of our 1,100 school buildings, and when I pass schools — sometimes three within a few blocks — and I see something wrong, I call the custodial manager on the car phone: "What the hell's going on at PS so-and-so?" And I lie to them a little: "That's the third time I've been here this month and the graffiti're still there!"

My feeling from the beginning in Miami was that if I was willing to take the time to do it, and to tell them what was right with their schools, the principals and the custodians on the scene should be willing to hear what was wrong. And I told them that. I wasn't just interested in the program, I wanted to know that the environment was right for kids, too, and that the place looked like people cared about it.

They knew up front I was going to be frank with them. After a while it got to be funny, because I'd come in and the first thing they'd point out was how clean the place was, so I'd call in the custodian and the maid and tell them what a great job they were doing, and I'd go around to the classes and thank the kids. I'd stick my head into classrooms to talk to teachers, and sometimes parents would be in there, too, and I'd thank them. And even if it was only a whirlwind visit, they got the sense that this guy from the superintendent's office really did give a damn.

Soon enough, there was a kind of spirit out there that you could feel. Things were happening. If you were a principal in the schools, it could affect you either way: you were either afraid of me coming, knowing you might be criticized, or you liked the idea that things were going to get better because of this kind of involvement. Generally, the feedback was positive. I got a little flak from board members when somebody complained to them, but it wasn't hard to get them to see the logic in my efforts.

And if I left a principal gasping, I tried to temper it with a follow-up letter, suggesting in gentler words what plants he could add to make his school at least *look* better ("dracaenas would be nice, something with a shallow root structure") and making arrangements to provide the plants and trees. But under the circumstances, whatever I did was not likely to be mistaken for appeasement. I was determined to have Miami's schools better perceived, and properly and smartly run. I replaced or transferred twenty-nine principals that first year.

Which wasn't as easy as it sounds. A couple of hot topics when I took over were the new contract we were hammering out with teachers and the reclassification of principals. The teachers were upgraded to true "professional" status, with a three-year contract that sent salaries soaring by 28 percent, to an average of $39,600 by 1991 (figures so much better than the New York contracts I first dealt with that it was embarrassing, especially when you consider the cost-of-living differential). Again, where once we were lucky to get two applicants for every opening in the ranks of the fifteen thousand Dade County teachers, we were getting eleven or twelve by the time I left.

But I'd always thought that a problem Dade had with control was in its inability to move principals around without their district's approval — and, conversely, the inability to move out weak district directors. So as a first move I reclassified *all* the principals in *all* the schools to director's level. Which meant that senior high principals went up one grade, junior high principals two, elementary principals three. Until then — as did most school systems in the country — Dade operated under the dated and farcical belief that a senior high principal is somehow more important to the educational process than a junior high or elementary school principal. Nothing could be further from the truth.

Salaries were not equalized immediately but were worked out over a period of years. The idea was so well received that the state of Florida followed suit. Any principal would henceforth have the same status as any other principal, at any grade level, and be equal in rank to the district directors.

Which gave me the hammer I wanted.

With the principals now operating at their level, not only couldn't the directors block a move, but I could move the *directors* out and make them principals if I wanted. This gave me openings to move in some of my more talented reform-minded people, as both directors and principals. People who had an understanding and an appreciation for School-Based Management. The best result of all.

PART V

SCHOOL-BASED MANAGEMENT was like a battle plan for the ages for me.

I didn't have to be in a prominent school area to wage it, because it would be just as applicable in Miami, Oklahoma, as it was in Miami, Florida, and just as timely in Manhattan, Kansas, as in Manhattan, New York. But certainly Dade County and New York City presented riper, broader fields for its testing and follow-through.

Would I have been as good a superintendent in Miami without SBM? Or would I have been as attractive to New York without it? (Or attracted *to* New York without it?) I think so. I'm confident enough in the quality of whatever methods that develop out of what has been called my "find-a-way" approach to education that we — meaning the supporting casts I've had around me in all my efforts at reform; I've been lucky to have them — would always get the job done somehow.

But out of SBM there congealed in my mind's eye a vision for *all* the schools of America. Not because my hand was on the switch, but because in its mature form SBM was so obviously an answer for the masses. Other things we introduced wouldn't work everywhere. Satellite schools — schools at the workplace — would not be viable in most rural areas or in some smaller metropolitan cities. Bilingual education programs aren't needed in many cities. And all the other things we did pale in significance, because the tide of change with SBM could affect reform for a lifetime through any school area, under any set of circumstances.

But before I go any further, let me clear up a misconception. I didn't "invent" School-Based Management. Not the components of it, anyway. I didn't wake up one day and say, "Eureka! SBM!" SBM is a process, evolving over time and through a variety of influences, and any number of people have contributed to it — even unwittingly. Anybody who ever bought into the idea probably added something to it, because the nature of SBM is to act on your best instincts.

I certainly wasn't the first to discover that a school system, like everything else, works better if people talk to one another, if people plan together, if people apply what they know at the source of a problem *to* the problem. I didn't "discover" that people work harder making something happen if they have a proprietary interest, a "sense of ownership." All those simple truths are vital to the success of SBM.

But you can't separate the theory and its application from the experiences of the man. As a maverick classroom teacher and a department head, I wanted to do things that continually ran contrary to the "traditional" way. Often my principals would let me try, but *more* often I'd either get shot down at that level of authority or at the levels above it — up where the names have no faces and you never get your day in court.

As a principal, I did a lot better job pushing ideas, but even then my best tool was the school system phone book because I often bypassed district superiors and went right to the top with my problems. If I needed a budget decision, I called the budget director. If I wanted an OK on a transfer, I went directly to the associate superintendent for personnel. I got to be on a first-name basis with those people. I was convinced that if I had to go through the technocrats in the middle, it would take months for anything to happen. Seeing this, a CEO would be smart to say: "Uh-oh, my people are having to work *around* the system instead of through it; the system needs changing." But at the time I wasn't worried about the system, I was worried about getting projects moving.

Thus I became hardened to the belief that the fewer controls a dedicated educator has to deal with, the better job he or she can do. But with my own growing sophistication, I also realized it wasn't enough just to say, "Let me try, I'll take the risk." Because sooner or later you have to answer to somebody. You can't arbitrarily and indiscriminately bend the rules again and again because that can create even *more* problems when people find you out or the wheels fly off.

So in time, I came to appreciate two things about running a school: local control is the best control, but you better be accountable. School-Based Management embraced both principles.

As for the name, we could have called it anything. On-Site Management. Shared Decision Making. Or, like Ted Sizer, Essential Schools. Sizer, the guru of education rethinking at Brown University, has a whole network of schools following his lead, and much of what he does with Essential Schools is similar to what we do with SBM. I'm not even sure School-Based Management is original with us. Hammond, Indiana, though a relatively small school district, had been doing a lot of innovative things in the decision-making process for years and the name could have come out of there.

But the name's not important. The importance of what you might call the "generic prescription" for SBM is that it came from a distillation of the processes many of us learned as classroom teachers and school administrators, picking out the things we knew (or had an inkling) would work to make schools better if we'd only had the authority to put them in play.

In that sense, nobody has approached SBM exactly the way we have, or taken it to the extent we have. That's as it should be, because the genius of SBM is that it is adjustable to the conditions, not only from town to town or district to district, but from school to school. When it's humming, SBM can take any number of forms. Thus, what we fashioned in Miami is different from what we have now in New York . . . which is different from what they're trying in Rochester, or Hammond, Indiana, or any other place that has seen the light. There are some commonalities, to be sure, but for SBM to function it has to fit the ethos of the community and the problems peculiar to the school. In short, it needs to answer to its own.

So, what do we have to have at a school to make a solid launching pad to get SBM off the ground? First, some obvious things that boil down to teamwork:

We have to have a good principal who is secure in his or her job and not afraid to share the budget and the decision-making with the SBM "cadre."

We need a faculty that will appreciate the sense of ownership of new methods and will have the ability to coalesce with the staff in forging a strategic plan for the school.

We need parents who are willing to be active partners in the venture.

And most pivotal, we need a central office that not only will create the organizational model to make the SBM operational (and accountable), but also will be willing to stand back and let the baby bump and stumble through its formative first steps.

Which brings us to the qualifiers we will have to deal with:

1. Inevitably, we *will* make mistakes.

2. So to ensure that we won't keep making them, we will evaluate everything we do.

3. But as our administration will always be open to question, because we are doing those evaluations ourselves, we will have an external evaluator validate *our* evaluation.

4. And although we will be expected to show results immediately in academic achievement — the whole point of reform of any kind — it won't always happen. We can expect encouraging signs and some early triumphs, but chances are we won't see startling results overnight. In most cases, it will take several years to make a difference.

And there is one advisory that should be etched in stone for all SBM models: because the effort will usually require people (teachers, principals, administrators) to go well beyond what they are normally expected to do, we will take pains to recognize them for that effort and, whenever possible, reward them for it. Commendation and compensation. The American way.

Our final game plan came about this way:

While a deputy superintendent under Britton, I had made Dr. Gerry Dreyfuss the chairman of that first committee for exploring the possibilities of School-Based Management, expanding on Gerry's own ideas for "school-based budgeting" at the junior high school where he was principal. Gerry had worked under Whigham in the budget sector and as a veteran of the system had a reputation for being a great conceptualizer. I made him my assistant in charge of exploring SBM.

From Gerry's original ideas at Nautilus Junior High School had come what was called the Computer Assistance School Allocation System (CASAS), a mouthful to describe computer monitoring of the budgets. Whigham, as superintendent, had worked from the earliest days of computer technology toward a wide-ranging data collection and utilization program for Dade. As a result of CASAS, I could sit in my office downtown and call up in a flash the budget of every one of Dade's 260 schools, and on a visit to the site I'd be armed with a printout that told me where the money was being spent or transferred, where the personnel vacancies were, etc. (New York, amazingly, didn't have computerized school-based budgets at all when I came. We will.)

The school-based budget plan was mainly intended to give a school principal the discretion to change line item expenses. In other words, if the budget allocated for 100 teachers, and he only wanted 95, he could trade in those five teacher units for something else of equal value, provided he got approval. That approach was a natural fit for SBM as a whole. Gerry's committee started there.

To get good information, the committee had to have broad representation from the four Dade districts, including principals, superintendents, their directors, etc. — a task force, actually. But it was soon slowed by internal disagreements. Gerry isn't a driver, he's an idea man, and his committee factionalized on him. The area superintendents and directors saw SBM as undermining their authority as middle managers. They were right. If we gave their essential budgeting power to the schools, the directors would wake up one day and say, "They don't need us anymore." Which was what I had in mind — to redefine the job of area director completely. (As it turned out, I ran out of time on that one.)

I kept getting bad vibrations, so at one point, when Gerry called and put me on his conference phone to hear the committee's "ideas," I blew up. He had the whole group in his office, and as I listened I realized they were undermining the direction I wanted to go. I chewed the tail off the director I knew was the ringleader. This was a long-range plan, I said, not meant to hurt anybody unnecessarily, but what we were going to do meant a wholesale revision of the decision-making process and he damn well better work with that in mind. Everybody heard me. From then on, the area people stopped giving us problems.

Gerry and I still had to modify substantially the final report. Just giving principals some control of school spending wasn't nearly enough. Our SBM plan meant bringing the teachers (and, therefore, their union) and the staff into the loop and making a tie-in with parents, and this would change the whole modus operandi to reflect an unprecedented cooperation. Some committee members never really embraced the premise (bedding down with the union was especially odious for administrators), but from that report grew the predicate for SBM.

And from there came the agenda to get the show on the road: joint meetings with the union stewards and school principals (we broke every taboo in the book with that kind of synergism) and a series of dog-and-pony shows around the county with Pat Tornillo, the two of us tap-dancing to "this thing called 'Professionalization,' " SBM being the central jewel of the piece. The union was easily won over because Pat, who had himself emerged from the ranks to become one of the great innovative union leaders of our time, saw what it would mean for the stature and working conditions (and wages) of teachers.

Everything was in line now for what I wanted to do. All principals from elementary to high school were equals. District directors were neutralized. Teachers and their union stewards were informed and poised to be involved. And I had allies in court to share the driving: Gerry Dreyfuss and Pat Tornillo, Tom Cerra and Alex Bromir, the south area superintendent, and Joe Tekerman, who had run what was virtually an SBM shop when he was principal at Miami Jackson High years before. Later I brought in Frank Petruziello out of labor relations to be my associate superintendent for SBM.

We got a grant from the state to help fund implementation and met with the principals and union stewards to lay out initial SBM requirements. We weren't deliberately vague, but it helped in the beginning to make it understood that the game plan was not a dry document, that we were still open to changes. But basically we said that the operation within a school should be run by a cadre, a management team of about fifteen to twenty-five people, including the principal and representatives from the teachers, the administrative staff, the clerical, custodial, and cafeteria staffs, and the parents.

The cadre would have a say in all matters from budget control to curriculum to personnel. The principal would have veto power, but if his decisions were contrary to the wishes of the team he would have to explain himself, and if he became an obstructionist, the cadre could take its grievances to the top: the superintendent's assistant in charge of SBM (Petruziello, eventually) or to me if necessary. I monitored everything, so that meant it was usually me.

On matters that might involve policy change, of course, any SBM proposal would have to clear the school board itself. For example, when they were up and moving, one elementary school wanted to do away with assistant principals, another wanted to phase out its Spanish instructor and bring in Berlitz. Those were policy changes (which the board approved). So checks and balances were in place, but not to the point of stifling originality or action. The first checkpoint was the most important — cadres had to answer to themselves. This was possible because they represented all the factions and therefore could make decisions on a democratic basis.

Schools were allowed to decide for themselves about going SBM. To do so would require a two-thirds vote of the teachers, with the principal's sign-off. In New York, for various reasons related to governance structures unique to the city, we made it 75 percent of the teachers and parents and the principal's sign-off, *and* the district superintendent's.

In Miami, we didn't give the district managers veto power. I kept it for the superintendent (Britton, then me), on the SBM committee's recommendation.

As D-day drew closer, we held a series of workshops on Miami Beach for the schools who were interested. We encouraged them to make their official proposals as inventive as they dared — to "dream a little." Not every meeting went smoothly. I sometimes found myself speaking out against administrators who were sitting right there: "Forget what these guys want! They're worried about losing turf!" I know I made some of them uncomfortable. They were always adjusting their ties.

I don't know what I expected, but I would have been satisfied if ten or twelve schools submitted proposals. We got fifty-seven. Some of the entries were tentative to the extreme, reflecting a suspicion of mine that school leaders often don't know their own limits in being able to do things within the system. Most of the proposals were good, some were great.

To process so many, however, I had to create teams of union people and administrators, and we locked ourselves into a hotel for a weekend to make the final selections. We didn't tell them which schools they were evaluating, only that thirty-three would be chosen — eight from each of the four districts, plus one. There was no magic to the number; it just seemed like a manageable figure. Our intention was to keep the thirty-three intact and nurture them through a four-year pilot program, then reevaluate after that.

But the good word spread, and the idea took off much faster than we anticipated. Too fast, actually. I never intended for every school in Miami to be SBM. I do now, for New York City, because the governance issues are totally different, and SBM in its "second phase" is quicker to get through governance problems and on to matters of substance. But I didn't then. I felt it would work only when you were sure you had the right people combined in the effort and that it was never implemented just because the superintendent or the chancellor ordered it.

We were quickly pressured to open up the roster for another fifty schools. By the time I was gone in 1990, three years later, Miami had 155 of its 273 schools on SBM, with a wide range of results directly correspondent, I think, to the degree of commitment. We should have been more deliberate. In some cases, we learned later, the faculties voted it in over the principals' objections, a situation made to order for problems. In New York, I've tried to make sure that won't happen. We already have more than two hundred in the fold and expect half the schools, or about five hundred, to be on SBM by the end of the 1993–94 school year. And as I said, at Tom Sobol's urging after a review of our results, the state has decreed that every school district must have a site-based management program in place by 1996.

We knew at the beginning in Miami that with no history to draw from, we would be flying by the seat of our pants. To change the way schools operate meant adding and discarding as we went along. We didn't have all the answers. We *still* don't have all the answers. But we're learning by our mistakes.

For example, when we were establishing cadres at the schools, we didn't say specifically that parents *had* to be included. It was an assumption, because to be open to ideas and local scrutiny, a cadre needs to be totally representative. But when we started evaluating we found that some schools left parents off. We went back and fixed it, with a mandate. In New York, I didn't include the "supervisors" (department heads) in the mix that would vote on whether a school would become SBM. Unlike Miami, New York department heads are counted as part of the administration instead of the teachers group. I thought the principals would speak for the supervisors. The supervisors convinced us otherwise. We made a change.

Even when we finally got started, not everybody appreciated the scope of what we were doing. For all our efforts to sensitize the Dade County School Board, and for all the encouragement it gave us, not all its seven members were comfortable with this plunge into uncharted waters. Janet McAliley, who now chairs the Dade board, is a very bright woman, but she gave me fits on SBM. She didn't understand that it wasn't a cure-all, it was just a better way to do things.

But, oh, how exciting the start-up was. The tendency with SBM is to let the horses run, let the schools find their own limits, and in those first months it was like turning Patton loose on the Western front. When we had our first weekend meeting of all the thirty-three cadres about two months later, I went from group to group listening to the experiences, and I *knew* it was working. The place was alive with ideas. It made my hair stand on end.

With their new freedom, schools changed textbooks, created smaller classes, eliminated redundant jobs so that funds could be diverted to more crucial areas or to extracurricular activities. Four schools wound up eliminating an assistant principal's job, to put the roughly $40,000 that saved to other uses. Teachers in some departments gave up their free period every day so that they could reduce their class sizes and better help their students. About sixty schools, many of them in the inner city, where "distinctions" over clothes can get violent, went to uniforms. About that same number offered classes on Saturday. Drew Elementary opened up a Saturday mentoring program.

Palmetto Elementary School in the affluent Kendall area arranged to have its "unsatisfactory" language program restructured to hire Berlitz teachers to accelerate the learning of Spanish. South Miami Junior High, which had a magnet program for artistically talented students, cut eight "redundant" teachers and hired outside instructors to teach music and dance on an hourly basis. Hialeah High created a night school — not for adults, but for kids who had to work. Killian High started a night high school for dropouts.

Some schools created schools within schools, where teachers would advance right along with their students from, say, the ninth grade on through the twelfth. Some modified their report card distribution to require a regular dialogue with parents. One elementary school cut out the pay supplements some teachers were getting for extra duties and used the money to hire a teacher/monitor to be on hand at 7 A.M. for working parents who needed to drop off their children early. At Sunset High, teachers were permitted to shorten class periods to 45 minutes to create a 35-minute "extra period" to work one-on-one with students who had academic or personal problems.

One of the more radical ideas involved combining some administrative and teaching duties and creating new pay scales at the schools. At Nautilus Junior High, the cadre phased out an assistant principal and gave the counseling duties to two faculty members on a split schedule, with a $1,200 increase in salary for each. Horace Mann Junior High put curriculum development in the hands of several teachers, with bonuses of $3,500 apiece. But the involvement transcended money considerations. Teachers *wanted* to be reinvigorated, and parents duly noted the results. In the Palmetto area, the signs of a new vitality in the public schools resulted in scores of students returning to their ranks from private schools.

Time magazine chronicled the successes at William Jennings Bryan Elementary. Principal Nora Brandt's cadre found ways to fund a "Bryan Pride" campaign that began with a new paint job for the aging building and an elaborate "reading emphasis" program that included monthly bus trips to the Dade County Public Library for four hundred of its children. Brandt's cadre was relatively small: she as the elected head, two parents, and seven teachers. They put their proposals to the faculty for a monthly vote. Brandt said she was surprised to find that ideas they wouldn't have gotten much enthusiasm for if they'd tried to shove them down the faculty's throat got voted in without a hassle. Teachers, in turn, reveled in their new freedom to come up with better ways to run their classes.

But did we have problems? Of course we did.

Limited resources, combined with overly ambitious goals, are always a problem when you are trying to flesh out your dreams. Schools could not exceed their budgets with their innovations (if you robbed from Peter, you had to pay Paul), and with the national money crunch in education generally inhibiting programs anyway, there were bound to be frustrations. When the Dade system had to go through more budget cuts in 1990, ideas that could have taken off had to be retooled or dropped.

Some principals, especially those who had been on the job a long time, experienced "authority" cramps — mostly a matter of relinquishing control, of operating as team managers instead of autocrats. Others adapted well. Lawrence Feldman of Palmetto Elementary told the New York *Times* that although still involved in all the key matters of hiring and policy-making and curriculum, he'd become more of a "coach, advisor and counselor" than a supreme leader, and although he knew it would likely be his wagon if the school wound up $5,000 short after some project, he said he "liked" his new role. "People are starting to trust each other," he said.

Some schools tried to play games with the process. Some handpicked the parents for the cadres, and when we got complaints, we had to make them start over. One principal handpicked the entire management team — and was charged with unfair labor practices by the union.

Some of our ideas took us into mine fields. The all-male class (for at-risk black kids) that was proposed at Pine Villa Elementary had to be scrapped when the federal Office of Civil Rights said we could be in violation of discrimination laws. In the first round of changes, we allowed Chapman Elementary to move its two Spanish courses — one for kids wanting Spanish as a second language, the other for Latinos looking to maintain their native language proficiency — to after-school hours to relieve some of the overcrowding. Since classes weren't mandatory, we thought that the six hundred kids who availed themselves of the program would be happy to stay after school from 3 to 4. We were wrong. The next year we had a 50 percent drop-off in enrollment for those courses. Chapman went back to a regular schedule, and I rejected three other schools who proposed the same after-hours arrangement.

Crucial to the whole SBM operation was the data we collected and drew from. I can't emphasize enough the need for good data. Hialeah got its nighttime high school when information indicated that the reason the school had such a high dropout rate was because so many of the low-income Hispanic families in the area needed their kids to work to help with finances. So curriculum times were made flexible to allow for night school or for kids to come to class in the mid-morning if they'd worked late the night before.

Evaluations of each new program were crucial. An evaluation told a school what a business audit would tell a company: what was working and what wasn't. I'm not a professional evaluator, so I set up a strategy to include outside help, with 40 percent of the surveys done in-house and 60 by contract with, say, the University of Miami's research department.

I had three hard rules:

1. We evaluated everything — every component of SBM had to be examined. That's not usually done, but in the learning stages we needed the closest scrutiny possible, even if it meant added expense.

2. Once the whole process was evaluated, it would be *validated* by an outside consultant, someone with national credibility. We used the Rand Corporation.

3. The split would always be 40–60, with the in-house evaluation team (most big-city school systems now have one) handling items that had no need to be taken elsewhere, such as whether attendance figures, or reading scores, or parental involvement, or teacher grievances, were up or down. Those comparisons are easy to gather.

But if the question is: Has there been *meaningful* parental participation? or, How do you evaluate your reading program? those are tougher. You need an expert to make those determinations.

I wanted a total evaluation because what we were doing was revolutionary and I knew there'd be a whole body of critics out there itching to take potshots. Moreover, there is so much money involved in big-city school budgets that I didn't want to open us up to any suggestion that we might be letting the foxes tend the henhouse. I wanted it clear that we were keeping a close watch on everything, and had no secrets.

In all areas, we had both formative and summative evaluations, summative being the final evaluation. You need both. If you're looking to increase the number of Haitian graduates, for example, you have to know each year how it's working, not after four years. The role of the Rand Corporation in this case was to say, "These are the things you should be looking for. These are the samplings you need."

The news of our successes spread quickly. We became a lightning rod for other school districts, inquiring and sending representatives to check us out. The commissioner of education in Hawaii and some of his principals paid us a call, and asked me to return the favor (I never got the chance). As our credits multiplied, people were coming and going all the time. Our own teachers and principals and staff literally criss-crossed the country making SBM presentations, preaching the word. Pat Tornillo went to London to talk with school superintendents there.

Albert Shanker, president of the American Federation of Teachers, said we did things "schools across the country haven't even thought about yet." From within our own fired-up ranks, the creative juices flowed, and new voices joined the chorus. Teachers who had never been heard from before were being quizzed on how *they* would do things. They said, "I'm glad you finally asked!"

But on that point I should stress the obvious: you can't put something as potentially volatile as SBM control into the hands of people willy-nilly. True to the criticisms of the last several decades, there are more than a few principals and teachers out there who need to be replaced, not recharged. There are more than a few who are not looking for more responsibility, but for less, if any at all. And not every good teacher wants to be challenged; some would rather play it safe, put in their hours and go home. And many principals would rather cling to their control than share it.

And some schools, for those reasons and others, need a wholesale housecleaning in personnel before they're given too much say in their operation. There were schools in Miami that I thought would never, ever make it to SBM. Schools that I would have just as soon closed down than save. Little River Elementary was one of them.

Little River is in the depressed heart of what has become a Haitian refugee enclave in Miami's northwest section. When I first toured the school as superintendent, I was convinced nothing short of radical surgery could turn it around. More than sixty years old, and looking it, Little River was virtually comatose: low self-esteem throughout the staff, no parental support, a "nasty" principal. Teachers looked at the world through broken windows and cleaned animal excrement off the back porches of their classrooms each morning before school. Crises in operations occurred daily.

I wasn't even considering Little River becoming "school-base managed" because there was no responsible leadership in evidence. I threatened a "complete overhaul," from the principal down. My threat made headlines. The teachers at the school demanded a hearing.

I went there on a Friday afternoon with Pat Tornillo, and we met with the faculty in the cafeteria. They applauded my being the first superintendent to come to their school, but after that when any subject was raised they cheered Pat, the union leader, and booed hell out of me, the guy who was trying to do them in. But the more I heard the more I realized how much they'd suffered. A lot of hostility emerged.

We stayed until 6 o'clock. They were very upset, but what they wanted more than anything else was another chance. They knew, however, they needed new leadership, because when I was walking out they shook my hand and slipped me notes: "We haven't had new books in three years." "The principal still hasn't ordered playground equipment." They were afraid to speak up. My hand got big with notes.

I finally agreed to convert Little River to School-Based Management and hired to run it a fresh young face I'd seen emerging through a special internship program I'd started for aspiring principals.

Fred Zerlin is a theatrical little man with steel-rimmed glasses and a large, tinny voice. When I made him principal of Little River, he went out and bought a new car, and when he drove it up to the school for the first time, he said he thought seriously of trading it in.

"It was scary," Zerlin said of the school, "and it was filthy. The floors were blacker than the bottom of my coffee cup. I still don't know why the health department hadn't closed the cafeteria."

That summer Zerlin and the Little River cadre arranged for the students to eat out on the playground, and with freedom to operate, they went about converting the sow's ear into a silk purse. Twenty-five teachers were replaced. SBM budget shifting allowed for a new teachers lounge (with telephones) and the classrooms to be painted. New books were purchased. Grass and shrubs and hanging plants, and $40,000 worth of playground equipment, materialized on what had been a Sahara of raw sand and weeds.

The immigrant Haitian kids, many unable to speak English, got hugs and pats on the cheek from Zerlin and the newly invigorated teachers, and "Super Kid" stickers and buttons for almost any achievement, including keeping off the new grass. "They were starved for love," said Zerlin. The students also got a 24-unit computer lab and field trips to nearby parks, and on weekends Zerlin and members of the cadre roamed the neighborhood, spreading the word and reminding parents that it was *their* school, too, and when it was mistreated or vandalized, it was *their* loss.

Later, Zerlin showed me through the halls and classrooms at Little River. He pointed out floors you could eat off. When we went into the rooms, he drew cheers. "Look at this school," he said, sweeping his hand across a view from the front lawn. "Does this look like the inner city to you?"

That June, Little River scored heady victories in a number of scholastic competitions with thirty-two area schools. Its scholars won first-place awards in oral and writing contests, and its achievement averages were shown to have gone up in every category except reading.

Zerlin sent me the clips. He pointed out the accomplishments, and how proud I should be.

I wrote him back. I said, "What about those reading scores?"

A major positive we realized about SBM was how in most cases other initiatives tied into it to result in more good reasons to applaud. We pushed through as a "program enhancement" the package that increased Dade teachers' salaries 28 percent over three years, to an average higher than New York City's. Our efforts to "professionalize" teachers, to return teaching to the level of respect it once enjoyed by paying competitive wages and improving the workplace, helped infuse the system with the promise of a greater ingenuity in the educational process.

The numbers in our Dade Partners program ballooned as enthusiasm in the business community grew. Although the figures were to pale next to the generosity toward schools I was to find in New York, the giving from the business community and through foundations reached $8 million annually in Miami. The secret of shaking it loose? More often than not, by taking that one crucial first step people are always so reluctant to take: by asking. Once we started asking, we didn't stop. We were good learners. When the Rockefeller Foundation said it would give us $375,000 a year for three years if *we* raised $450,000 a year, we said, "Tell us who to talk to." We raised the $450,000.

And within the growing number of innovations, we ran with the idea for satellite schools.

I don't know how it got started exactly. We were always hatching something at staff meetings. But it was on my mind when we were at a goals conference with Miami business leaders at the Ocean Reef Club on Key Largo in the summer of 1987, my first year as superintendent. I kept hearing these corporate types complaining about our schools, so I challenged them with the concept.

I told them to put up or shut up. I said if any of them would agree to provide an adequate facility at the work site, we'd provide the rest. Then they could say they not only had given education a boost, but had given parents in their own work force some necessary peace of mind. For them, it could translate into greater productivity. For us, millions of dollars saved on construction costs.

Somebody listened. Specifically, Kirk Landon of the American Bankers Insurance Group. In the fall of 1987, American Bankers, with a thousand employees in south Dade County, opened the first satellite school: a $350,000 classroom for grades K through 2 and an adjoining day-care center. A second satellite was opened on the north campus of Miami-Dade Community College the following spring, and in November that year, a $750,000 state-of-the-art classroom/day-care center was dedicated on the grounds of Miami International Airport.

Kirk Landon heralded the results at American Bankers: a drastically reduced absentee and tardiness rate among employees with children in the school and day-care center. Teachers in the school, of course, had the same to say about their students. Pat Tornillo, the union president, said his original doubts about the concept kept getting shot down. Those who argued that satellite schools were "elitist" hadn't stopped to realize that the sons of company executives would be learning right alongside the daughters of secretaries and baggage handlers. Civil rights activists concerned about racial balance hadn't stopped to think that the workplace is always more integrated than the neighborhood. It's the law. The government does the policing for you.

When we dedicated the satellite at Miami International, Tornillo was there. "I'm still looking for the flaws, Joe," he said from the podium. "I can't find any. You're frustrating the hell out of me."

A young man in a work shirt with a company name sewn on the pocket cornered me right after the ceremony. He practically glowed with gratitude. He said he was a single parent of two boys, ages four and six, both enrolled at the school and the day-care center. He had tried busing and found it a "terrible experience, having them so far away, wondering what might happen." He'd had some "bad times" at private child-care centers, one where the director had been indicted for drug trafficking, another where there had been allegations of teacher-child sexual abuse.

He said, "I was going to quit my job because I couldn't take it anymore. Now if there's an emergency, I'm two minutes away. We drive in together and we talk, and we drive home and we talk, and I can even eat lunch with them if I want. You saved our lives."

Before I left Miami, eleven more applications for satellites crossed my desk, including one at the Doral Industrial Park complex adjacent to the Doral Golf and Country Club, where the parent company, Lennar Builders, wanted to put in a full elementary school, K through 6. Anything beyond second grade requires a library and ten acres of playground to meet the state's physical education requirements. Lennar was going to donate the land.

Remember the caveat, however: reform works only when people work at it, and not everybody who is "for" education is willing to do that. Joe Tekerman, my point man for the satellites, was so strong an advocate that he and the vice president of American Bankers, Phil Sharkey, were invited to school districts around the country (Texas, St. Louis, Washington, Chicago) to sing their praises.

But the politics of education work their ill in Miami as effectively as anyplace else. Tekerman was a "Fernandez man," and when I left he was transferred out of the superintendent's office to the Office of Information Technology ("Elba," Tekerman called it), and for that and reasons I can only characterize as an active indifference, the satellite program stalled. The three that we started still thrive, but no new ones have been built.

Anyway, the general heady sense of improving the lot of Dade County's teachers and moving forward prompted a surprising early success in areas I didn't expect to be affected so quickly, and I can't help thinking that the SBM influence deserves much of the credit. Dade's dropout rate plunged from 30 to 24 percent. Reducing the dropout rate goes hand in glove with increasing the graduation rate, and with the quality of skills that implies. And that, in turn, ties in to having more kids in special honors classes, and to giving them better opportunities for study and for taking advanced placement tests, and so forth.

The reading and math scores stayed constant, but I knew that wasn't going to change for a while because Miami was still absorbing an unnaturally heavy influx of refugees and immigrants and the assimilation of non-English-speaking children was sure to depress academic averages, for years even. Holding their own, in that context, was practically a victory.

The record $980 million bond referendum for modernizing Miami's schools couldn't be separated from the SBM influence, either, for the same reasons and for the same common goal: the prospect of a better education for the children. When you improve facilities and have good teachers operating in a healthier environment for learning, you most certainly will have greater success in the classroom.

If you'd asked me then, even in the rush of success, if I had any misgivings about SBM, I'd have said no, but with a qualifier or two. I knew soon enough that some of the schools did not have compatible cadres. And that if a principal went sour on the idea, he was certainly in a position to sabotage it, or at least make it suffer. And if a cadre has to work around a principal to get the job done, that's not good, either, nor is it truly an SBM model.

But as it turned out, I could count on the fingers of one hand the times we knew of where a principal had to overrule a cadre on a school issue, or we got complaints of a principal being heavy-handed. The process, for the most part, seemed to breed harmony, with pretty clear lines of responsibility for making it work. If a cadre at an all-black school was dumb enough to invite a speaker from the Ku Klux Klan to a testimonial dinner, the principal would surely have to step in. But that's not the fault of SBM, it's the fault of a flaky cadre. Or if the principal were to push for scheduling examinations on a high holy day, it's not the SBM's fault, it's the flaky principal's.

It is nevertheless true that some good faculties and some dedicated principals might not have opted for SBM at all. They might still have preferred a more structured school arrangement or to keep going with whatever was working. But you'd be surprised what we found in some of these cases. In Miami, the grade school that for years has been recognized as the best of the best is Pinecrest Elementary in the Kendall area, a "non-SBM" school. Its principal is an old friend of mine, Bonnie Wheatley. Her husband, Russ, one of my oldest, dearest friends in education, had been my principal when I was on the faculty at Miami Lakes.

Bonnie doesn't run an "official" SBM school, which is to say it was never declared such. She'll tell you that the only declaration to a cause at Pinecrest is the one that says "we *will* improve student performance," and the results speak for themselves. When you've got a school where the community is breaking down the doors to get in, and teachers are breaking down doors to teach there, the bottom line is that it's working, and no titles are necessary. We get hung up on titles.

But at Pinecrest, Bonnie Wheatley doesn't make a major decision at any time without input from faculty and parents. She gets them involved in all substantive issues. If there's a boundary discussion, she brings them in. If they've got to decide on a bilingual program, she brings them in. She's a perfect model of an SBM principal: firm but nonthreatening, and quick to include the faculty and parents. Pinecrest is virtually an SBM school.

A lingering complaint I still hear from nonbelievers in Miami about SBM is that it calls for "too much paperwork" and "too many meetings," and that despite everything, the principal still has too much to say. Some of that, I tell them politely, is hooey. If you're running an SBM school correctly, there shouldn't be more paperwork, there should be less. If there's more, it's because you're making it for yourself. In Miami, we even had a "paperwork reduction" task force that came up with ways to trim the load at all schools, SBM or otherwise. But less paperwork is an SBM priority.

As for meetings, a lot depends on how well they're structured and how closely a group is made to stick to an agenda. Teachers meet usually once a week anyway so some schools expanded their regular meetings to include SBM discussions. The feedback I got was that with time to grow as a team came an increased ability to find more effective lines of communication. Business could be conducted with greater dispatch — less time, less turmoil, less minutiae. A lot of meetings wander aimlessly when an agenda isn't followed, but that's true of any group, from fraternity row to Capitol Hill.

However, weighing the facts and thrashing things out is what democratic action is all about, and if you're not prepared to do that, you've got the wrong game plan. When an SBM school is experiencing growing pains, the pains will need to be addressed. During the early stages that will surely add to the time requirements. It's also true that a school might elect too large a management team (one cadre in Miami had thirty-two members), and the sheer weight of people "having their say" will slow it down. But a cadre mustn't be too small, either, because then it risks becoming a star chamber.

It boils down to finding your own comfort level on things like numbers — by testing what works best at your school for its own peculiar needs. I've always been loath to say, "This is exactly how you do it: you'll need x number of parents, x number of teachers, etc., etc." Too many want that — to have the whole plan neatly laid out in a booklet. That's not what SBM is supposed to be. It's supposed to be innovative, fluid, progressive.

As for principals being reluctant to turn in their swords, that's sure to happen occasionally, given the traditional relationship between principal and faculty. In Miami after I left, at a meeting of three hundred teachers (all union stewards), criticism of principals who had proved unwilling to accommodate power sharing at some SBM schools got big applause. There were complaints about a lack of communication and dwindling support at a number of schools. Certainly some of that can be blamed on the failure of principals to buy into the idea in the first place. It takes no special insight to see how that can happen.

But that's where accountability and help from the top are supposed to kick in. There are idiots at every level, and they have to be controlled or brought down. When a principal digs in his heels, somebody up there is obliged to step in. From the beginning it made sense to me that if we were going to ask all these people to take risks, we not only had to support them vigorously when they failed, but also had to encourage them to face up to it when they weren't acting responsibly. That's the way to make course corrections.

But School-Based Management is so free-form and open to initiatives, and unrestrained by a long list of rules and obligations, that it performs best in an atmosphere of unbridled enthusiasm, like a pitcher responding to a chattering infield or a reassuring coach. An involved, committed kind of encouragement.

And if you don't have somebody at the top who believes in what you're doing and is actively prodding it along, impetus can wane in a hurry. I have to think that much of the backsliding that occurred with SBM after I left Miami was due to the failure of leadership to keep the fires burning. Nurturing is vital through those early stages. If the cadres don't get the spiritual support they need from downtown, where is help going to come from when a breakdown occurs? If their key source of encouragement turns its back, disillusionment will not be far behind.

Dade has had three superintendents since 1990, none of whom had any real hand in SBM's origin or success, and if they didn't actively undermine the program, they all but disassociated themselves from it, and that can be just as damaging when the soldiers in the field look to the center for assurance.

Don't misunderstand. School-Based Management, once in place in a school (and in the *minds* of people), is virtually impossible to dislodge. Dr. William Renuart, a longtime star principal in the Dade system, said in a letter to the Miami *Herald* at the time: you can never go back, not when you've enjoyed the freedom to achieve that SBM allows. He said that even if Dade County killed every SBM program, those schools that have been operating under the plan would still operate that way. They might not have the latitude with the budget, they might lose some autonomy, but the synergism among faculty and administration and parents is impossible to kill outright.

As much as I regret having to say it, however, I know now that my leaving had a strong negative impact on SBM in Miami. I realize that some of it was natural. New leadership is not inclined to work hard to further the successes that may be credited to someone else, and by simply creating a void where power has been can get things *und*one. Renuart likened it to a plant that has been nourished to good health, and in full bloom is abruptly handed over to new caretakers — who then just stand aside and let it die. It's easy then to blame the system instead of the neglect.

I don't know everything that went on, but I do know that change exposes egos, and there exists now in the school operations in Miami the absurd mentality that if "Fernandez and his people" started it, we don't want any part. It's like feeling threatened by an ex-husband who is no longer around. How else could you explain the fact that three of SBM's main range-riders are no longer on the drive? Gerry Dreyfuss was sent back to his junior high principalship. Joe Tekerman was moved out of the main office to computer operations. Frank Petruziello, left alone to head up SBM and handle all the complaints, hung on for a while, but the fight was taken out of him. He wound up being rewarded elsewhere for his efforts: he became superintendent of the Houston school system.

That's one of the reasons I now say I should have cleaned house when I took the job. I kept Paul Bell in the loop as one of my deputies, although I thought he was a nonbeliever. Paul wielded a lot of influence — enough, in fact, to get him the superintendent's job eventually. I'm sure that his reluctance to support SBM was due to a troubled relationship we had during my last days in Miami.

When I knew I was going to New York, I called in my three deputies — Bell, Angie Welty, and Tee Greer — and told them my plans. I said if more than one of them wanted the job, I'd keep quiet and not support anyone. Greer said he had no interest, that he thought his time was past, but he'd gladly serve as interim superintendent until a new one was chosen, which he did. Paul Bell had repeatedly said he wasn't interested. Only Angie Welty wanted a shot at it, so I gladly promised her my support and came out publicly in her behalf.

Then Bell had a change of heart. He declared his candidacy, and when I told him the position that put me in, we had words. The last three months were very strained between us, and when he took over, it was clear he had no intention of doing the gung-ho things SBM needed to keep gaining altitude. As fate would have it, Bell died on the job a year later, and Octavio Visiedo, who had been in my cabinet and had become a big supporter of Bell after I left, got the job.

I wasn't sure if Visiedo would continue the fight, or if he could. He had no more than a limited knowledge of what SBM was all about. But he gave himself away not long after that when he was quoted as saying, "A lot of people believed that [School-Based Management] was the answer to education reform. I never believed that." A dismissal like that from the top can poison the well quicker than anything. Stories out of Miami quoted a number of principals and teachers who followed Visiedo's lead to say that SBM made their jobs "more difficult" — even while a 1991 study conceded that morale was up, the dropout rate down, and the environment "more collegial and less autocratic" in SBM schools.

What troubled me more, however, was what *wasn't* emphasized in the criticism: that fully two-thirds of the thirty-three principals who had originally signed on for School-Based Management and had gone through all that work to put the program in motion were not there anymore — having been promoted or transferred out. Couple that with the loss of key personnel at the top (Petruziello, et al.) and it had to affect progress. Fortunately, the Dade County School Board, which has avoided being decimated every election year and thus pretty much stays on course with programs, has stuck to its support of SBM. I'm with Bill Renuart in believing that not even hostile neglect from the superintendent, whoever he or she may be, can turn it back.

I am convinced, moreover, that the key to success for any major reform is momentum. When you dawdle, you not only risk going off track, you risk giving the naysayers a chance to catch their breath. On

that note, the biggest mistake chancellors or superintendents can make
when they have something vital to sell is not to hit the ground running.
That especially applies to their agenda when starting out on a new job,
but it is no less true for SBM.

I think that's obviously one of the reasons why some of the programs
we left in the care of our successors in Miami have suffered, and why in
New York City we were able to bring SBM along so much faster.
Because we certainly hit the ground running in New York, to the point
where people were telling us to please slow down, that we were going
too fast.

New York schools were in a much better position to move SBM along
than Miami's had been in terms of promoting substantive issues. In
New York, we had the roles of the teachers vis-à-vis the principals
clearly defined and an understanding of who would be responsible for
what already established up and down the line. We seemed to skip right
past the governance problems we had in Miami and moved directly into
implementation.

What also worked to our advantage in this "second phase" of SBM
was that in New York we trained up front; in Miami, we trained as we
went along, not really knowing any better. In New York I immediately
ordered a crash course for fifty people to prepare for being facilitators
at the schools that adopted SBM. I hoped that we would get close to
that many schools in the first call for recruits.

As it turned out, I underestimated the enthusiasm that Sandra Feldman, leader of the teachers union, and her people had built up for the
idea in advance of our coming. We wound up with 207 schools on SBM
in New York City at the end of the first full school year and had a
facilitator on the scene each time one kicked in. We couldn't have done
that in Miami. The New York business community was also a lot more
responsive. IBM loaned us twenty-five middle-management people to
work with the facilitators during the start-up period.

In Miami, we were some while learning how much and in what form
support from the central office should take. In New York, I had that
support ready before we put a single SBM on line. We wouldn't have
been able to ring in all those schools otherwise. In the case of about
thirty schools that were already following what was known as the Corridor Plan for feeder operations, faculty collaboration was in place,
making cooperation easier from the start. They didn't call it shared
decision making, but that's what it was.

New York schools going SBM had still another important advantage: decentralization throughout the system. In Miami, the one superintendent is beholden to one school board, with four district superintendents (or managers) beholden to him. In New York City, the chancellor has thirty-two district superintendents beholden not so much to him as they are to their own district boards. The chancellor has the ultimate authority to step in when there's an emergency, but on most substantive issues the districts make their own decisions. As a result, SBM schools can act on ideas or problems immediately, needing only the sign-off of their local superintendent.

Thirty of the thirty-two district superintendents bought in to SBM in New York. Some of the local boards, however, didn't follow suit. Some boards and superintendents are almost fanatical about relinquishing control, which, I've found, is often the source of the opportunism (and corruption) that plagues New York City schools. The thing that has really been a hindrance to immediate eye-catching results at SBM schools, however, is the terrible money crunch we've had to deal with for two straight budgets. Not just belt-tightening measures, but staggering, crippling, multimillion-dollar cuts in funding. Austerity of such magnitude limits your options and diverts your attention from reform.

But interestingly enough, a budget crunch actually accentuates the strength of SBM. Wholesale money problems virtually create the stimulus to find solutions through the redirection of funds and offer windows of opportunity to invent better ways to make do with what you've got. Despite the cuts, with strategic planning we were able to initiate a string of new programs through SBM, as varied as the schools are varied. Some schools in high-crime areas started crime-watch programs. One, in a particularly poor neighborhood, had four to five hundred parents at every SBM meeting and is now offering night classes to those parents. An administrator at the same school said he was getting as many as twenty or thirty parents a day volunteering to help out in the office and around the campus.

One comment I heard about SBM after I left Miami took me totally by surprise — that it was a kind of "cult" phenomenon, born of the strength of one man (me) as innovator, improviser, etc., and that it could make it only when such a man has the unflagging energy and the wherewithal to persist when others fall away. I don't know if that's flattering or not, but it simply isn't so. SBM is no more a cult than the democratic republic is a cult, and as much as I'd like to claim it, it isn't even "all mine."

But, for sure, when such a strategy is adopted, it had better have a leader who is willing to fight for it. To be there for it. To be willing to help create the right climate and then keep everything moving. No one can say I wasn't prepared to do that.

I will argue this about my "style," if you want to call it that. The downfall of many chancellors and superintendents who are supposed to be champions of education is that they don't stay on course. They vacillate. And when the inevitable happens, it's not just a problem for them and their job security, it's a problem for the people who work for them, and their agenda, and the community itself. Because it's not the amount of starch in a laundered shirt that they're deciding, it's the welfare of thousands of kids. The mixed signals they throw off when they aren't consistent result in *impeding* progress instead of accelerating it.

Sometimes it is, indeed, a matter of style, and a critical one. No one has a problem with the superintendent who says, "Look, we didn't think this thing through. We've got to reconsider our position," or, "Ladies and gentlemen, we screwed up. This isn't working." What causes havoc is when you advocate a course of action, go public, and then somewhere along the line (usually at the point where you get your last piece of "advice" from an influential board member) you change your position without letting your people know. Because in the meantime they will have been out there pushing the position you took originally, and they get embarrassed both ways. You aren't managing well — you aren't managing *at all* — if you do what the last board member who has your ear tells you to do. And if you've talked with seven board members, *nobody* knows where you stand.

My stance as a manager has always been this simple: there'll be no surprises. I demand the same of my staff. If I'm dealing with the board, I do my homework, base my case on the best information I have, and present it. And if anybody makes a better case, and I want to modify mine, I say so. But when I've reached a position (or made a decision), I stick with it. People appreciate that.

I expect the same kind of forthrightness from my own. I encourage individuals to give me their best thoughts, even if it means an argument. Under Johnny Jones I thrived on arguing the issues, and I think I helped the superintendents I worked for by speaking up when it was appropriate. I have gotten help in the same way from my people, some more vocally than others. Tom Cerra, who was my director of labor relations in Miami, was outspoken to the point of challenging — and I liked it. So were Joe Tekerman, Angie Welty, and Dick Hinds. They'd jump in even if they knew it meant a fuss.

Others never quite got there. I'd be hoping they would, that they'd screw up their courage and say, "Fernandez, on this one you're an asshole!" but they wouldn't. I've found that the "man in charge" can be a terrible intimidator, without even trying.

I keep on my desk a rather conspicuous glass paperweight, shaped like a globe, with a butterfly suspended inside. You can't miss it if you're at my desk. One of my senior staff members — call him "Fred" — came into my office one day for a meeting with a small group, and we reached a point where I needed to get the personnel director on the phone. When I did, I switched to a conference call so everybody in the room could hear. Fred was talking, and I don't know what possessed me — the old class cutup from Bishop DuBois High, I suppose — but I took the butterfly weight and put it in front of him and said, "Here, talk into this so he can hear you better."

And Fred did. He talked right into the paperweight, thinking, I can only guess, that it was some far-out new telephone. Now, Fred is a bright guy, with a PhD, and I like him. But that shows how you can rattle people with a little authority. I really wasn't trying to embarrass him, and if I did, I'm sorry. But we *did* get a laugh out of it.

A Tekerman, on the other hand, would have said, "Talk into a paperweight? *Me?* You gotta be kidding. *You* talk into it." And *I* wouldn't have, either. But Fred did.

The upshot is that I prefer the combative to the wary. I think you get much more out of it when you have staffers who aren't afraid to ruffle your feathers. I have that kind of relationship in New York with Jim Vlasto, my media relations director. We fight like alley cats, swearing and yelling at one another. When we're really going at it, you can see people around the office cringing and closing their doors, or my secretary will come and close mine. It's wild, but productive.

In all modesty, I didn't have a single major disappointment in the two years I was superintendent in Miami. Considering all we tried to do, that's probably a miracle, but I just can't think of anything that you could truly call a "failure." Part of that was due to the wonderful rapport I had with Pat Tornillo, the union leader (who took a lot more chances than I did), but I was also blessed with a progressive school board, with veteran members like Holmes Braddock, Bob Renick, Paul Cejas, Janet McAliley, Mickey Krop, and Bill Turner, who made you feel they always had the best interests of the schools as their priority. They never turned me down on anything important.

That symbiosis made it easy to push ideas and play off one another's strengths. We got along. We worked well together. Unanimous votes of approval of a plan don't happen by accident. Our three-year union contract forging those pay raises was unprecedented, but I think it was bought unanimously because we presented a strong case that it was a program-enhancement issue, not a salary issue. I believe we generated a better sense of mission throughout the system with that approach.

We took steps that no other school district in the country had taken, because the board was always able to see the reasons for them and then act. I don't know of another school board anywhere that classified all principals at one level, as we did then. The board grasped the idea, and ran with it. With that kind of synergism, and the strong ties we developed with the teachers through Pat Tornillo, the sky was the limit in Miami. Janet McAliley, looking back, said it was hard to believe we could accomplish so much in just two years.

How much of that should be credited to my own stubborn determination to outwork everybody else I'm not prepared to even guess. I am, and was then, a 7 A.M. to 7 P.M. guy. It was not unusual for me to make twenty or thirty telephone calls *before* I got to the office in the morning, using the one thing Leonard Britton left me that I appreciated: a car phone. I enjoy people, and I love repartee, and I like to kid around and needle the Joe Tekermans and Jim Vlastos of the world, but I'm totally results oriented, so I guess I'd probably go nuts if I wasn't trying to accomplish something.

The whirlwind that I created around myself used to worry Holmes and some of the other board members. They were always telling me to slow down, to take time off, to go check my blood pressure. Bill Turner used to beg me to "leave at two o'clock at least one day a week. You're gonna kill yourself."

I won't pretend that this dedication to the job has been a life-long attribute. The truth is, my best efforts as a youngster and a young man were expended on ways to get *out* of things. In basic training, as a seventeen-year-old, I noticed that if you walked around with a clipboard you could get out of almost anything. It was like a status symbol: you looked like you were up to something. Guys would be getting duty orders, and I'd be walking around with my little clipboard. No one bothered me.

Much of that had to be the pleasure of "beating the system," however, because even then I had a strong work ethic and a take-charge attitude that was undoubtedly a carryover from boyhood: *I* wanted to be the one who decided what games we played, and *I* wanted to be the one who picked the teams. Even in the Air Force, before I attained any rank, I'd see something going wrong in my squad and I'd take over: "The reason we're screwing up is that we're not doing so-and-so."

How much of that translates into dedication, and how much of it is just a matter of liking to run things, is hard to say. Either way, it's in my blood.

As a classroom teacher, and then a principal, and then an assistant superintendent, I was always a stickler for getting things done on time and impatient for results. When I became deputy superintendent, I put together an executive training program we called LEO (for Leadership Experience Opportunity) as an ingredient in the professionalization of principals and teachers, and I'd advise LEO candidates always to go the extra mile: "Put yourself in a position to be thought of as the most valuable person in the school so that when you're not there, everyone wishes you were."

Nowadays, of course, my time on the job is extended by meetings and other external influences: dealing with editorial boards, dealing with advocacy groups, dealing with the business community, etc. In a high-pressure, high-profile position, I look for "quiet" periods when I can catch up on routine things (mail, messages, reports and journals to review, etc.), and that means early in the morning or late in the evening, when I can be alone or can meet with my senior staff. It still translates into a 12-hour day.

The downside for a leader with that kind of commitment is that he is inclined to expect it of everyone around him, forgetting they have lives of their own. That's not realistic. Tekerman used to say, "You've got my undivided attention from Monday through Friday, but the weekends belong to me." With time, I have tried to be more tolerant, and I do think I've mellowed — not slowed, mellowed. And I'm probably more philosophical about such things.

Certainly, enough crises have come and gone to give me what I think is a healthy attitude about pressure. I have come to realize that no matter how controversial an issue, or how painful it might be to get through, it's really just a small thing in God's master plan. Just one little thing compared with a whole universe of problems and difficulties. Like the old college coach said before the big game: "Don't take this so seriously, fellows. Nine hundred million Chinese won't even know you played."

All those controversial, anxiety-ridden episodes like the condom issue will pass. They always do. Tomorrow there'll be a different problem for another time frame. So I say to myself, Don't let this thing take you down. The attitude serves me well. I can't imagine any reasonable goal being unachievable, and I won't tolerate having people around me who are predispositionally despairing. "Oh, how will we ever do this . . . Oh, we'll never finish on time." That drives me crazy.

I try to have staff people who think along those same positive lines: "Here's the problem, what are the options, how can we get it done?" I'm tough on them in that regard, I admit it. But they know I do it to make them better and to make good things happen. In all cases I encourage give-and-take. The worst thing a risk-taker can do is surround himself with yes-people. There's real danger in having *too* much compatibility. Imagine being in a meeting and hearing somebody say, "We need a program that will advocate sterilizing young people so that we can eliminate teenage pregnancies" — and having no one jump up to challenge it!

In Miami, I needed all the input I could get, because there was never a time that we didn't have a lot going on, and never a time when we didn't have to hack our way through fields of red tape. When you've got all those balls in the air, if you don't have help keeping them up, and you start to lose one, you risk dropping everything. You need talented people willing to work, not bureaucrats who take three months to make a lunch date.

So it was important to me to have a conscientious Dick Hinds heading up the budget — advising, correcting, finding ways. Dick had been a teacher and a one-time seminarian and had gotten his doctorate in school finance. And it was important to have a Tom Cerra heading up labor relations. I doubt we'd have gotten SBM going without Tom. Following Gavin O'Brien, he took the job to an even greater sophistication by tying in the legislative aspects. Cerra is one of the few administrators I know who understands the *politics* of education, who knows how to influence legislative decisions to benefit school programs. People who say politics and education are oil and water don't understand modern education.

And, of course, it was absolutely vital that I had Pat Tornillo, who recognized that even as you cling to the hard-won tenets of a good union contract, for reform to work you have to be willing to compromise. Thanks to Pat, when we went to contract to make SBM (and other ideas) go, I didn't have to give up a single facet of the plan because of union rules.

We got waivers on seniority, waivers on salaries, waivers on teaching after-school clubs and sports. We got waivers that allowed for merit pay for teachers and merit pay across the board (i.e., bonuses for teachers, administrators, and custodians) at some schools. Unions traditionally balk at merit pay because of the implications: there hasn't been an evaluation system yet devised that was totally apolitical.

I happen to be for merit pay, if there's some integrity to it and the pay is justified on an ongoing basis. The merit teacher can't be a flash in the pan who happens to do a great lesson the one day he or she is observed. And a good evaluation tool has to be used to identify candidates. In Miami, we had what we called the Teacher Assessment Development System (TADS), based on the premise that observers would be there to help, not "catch" teachers, and evaluations would conclude with a written prescription for improvement. In New York, we got something similar going for the first time in 1991 when we named from each borough our top five elementary, junior high, and high school teachers, and the top five principals at each level. They were given a "well done" — and $10,000 apiece.

Anyway, as SBM and our reforms accelerated in Miami, Pat Tornillo removed his traditional union combat helmet and put on the robes of conciliation and cooperation, and if he hadn't been so popular and so entrenched as a leader, I doubt he could have gotten away with all he did. But he wanted what we wanted: professionalization for Dade's teachers and the confirmation of School-Based Management. He knew, too, that down deep my thinking was grass-roots. That I was basically a teacher at heart.

Pat put issues on the table that ordinarily would kill a union (or a union chief). He helped push for differentiated staffing — paying teachers according to what they're worth based on what they do in the school. He pushed for merit pay and merit schools. He pushed some of our totally radical ideas, one of which bubbled to the surface during a teacher shortage: to waive the requirement that teachers be graduated from teachers colleges and open up the field for, say, retiring (but still young) members of the armed forces or returning Peace Corps volunteers, via alternative certification.

I take full responsibility for the Peace Corps idea. It seemed so, well, *idealistic*. What better people to recruit than those who had been

willing to endure hardships, willing to deal with the lowest of the
lower class, and at the same time were bilingual? How appropriate for
Miami. Indeed, why *not* use Peace Corps workers on their return to
America?

So we did, through a device we invented called the Teacher Recruitment Incentive Program, which we got funded by the American Can
Company. The full scope of the plan was that we'd bring in professionals from other fields (business, journalism, whatever), let them
teach four periods a day while they got their teacher's training at the
University of Miami, get them certified the first year, and, at no cost to
them, have them earn their master's the second.

And as a first experiment, we brought in this one Peace Corps veteran from Guatemala, who'd been in the jungles for two years with the
insurgents — eating raw snakes, fighting malaria and hepatitis, getting shot at.

And we stuck him in one of our toughest inner-city high schools.

And he lasted one semester.

He said, "I'm going back to Guatemala where it's safe."

Small setbacks notwithstanding, we kept generating one new
scheme after another. We were moving so fast on so many of them that
when any of our people ran into delays, I'd tell them, as a rule of
thumb, "Find a way. Don't break any laws, but don't give me any crap
about not being able to do it because of this or that 'regulation.' Go to
the governing body that created the obstacle. Talk to the county, the
state, the feds, whatever. And if you can't get a positive response, find
another way."

When we were working with American Bankers for that first satellite school, we got challenged from the opening bell. The bureaucrats
said we couldn't get the portable classroom there in time . . . we
couldn't get hooked up to the water . . . we couldn't get the landscaping done. They said we shouldn't be putting the school there in the
first place because it was "too close to a high school." That we wouldn't
have any parking. That we needed full-time security.

They threw up all the roadblocks, and we zipped past every one. We
completed the satellite in two months, and if we broke every rule in the
book doing it, who could complain? We got our portable, got the
plumbing and accessories, started the kindergarten class, then added
grade one, and when the new building was completed for us by American Bankers the following year, we were coasting.

The level of cooperation on such projects *outside* the bureaucracy, and the mutual interest all around, were exhilarating. We created a consortium with eleven other districts around the nation to exchange ideas and weigh the evidence, and initiated a compact with universities and colleges for the purpose of talking with each other about improving teacher training (instead of talking *about* each other separately, which is the way it's usually done).

During those two years you couldn't pick up an education journal or publication anywhere without reading about Miami. I had to carve an extra hour or so out of every day to meet with the groups that came in to see us: from China, Japan, Australia, England — even New York City, with a delegation of principals and teachers headed up by the late chancellor Richard Green.

It was more than enough to turn our heads, but I knew to keep mine straight because no matter how successful you are, sometimes the bureaucracy is going to win, and sometimes your ideas will run out of juice. One I had when I was associate superintendent was to require buses to run more routes than one a day. We were in another money crunch in Miami, and it seemed logical to me that a bus that picks up elementary school kids before 7 and has done its route by 2:30 could certainly run another route, if we could only vary the school starting times by grades.

I sold my idea to Britton, to some district leaders, to a parent group, and I put it to the school board — which gave it one whiff and dismissed it by a 7–0 vote. The board correctly argued that the last thing we wanted was different starting and finishing times for schools in the same district, with high school kids getting out early and going over to the junior high and harassing younger kids, and parents with more than one child upset over time differences, etc. I told the board, "Well, I accomplished one thing. I got you guys to vote unanimously."

But we won so many more than we lost, that there was no time to dwell on the negatives. There developed an enthusiasm for originality and change that was contagious. You got the feeling that people could hardly *wait* to get to work. When the pay increases were established, a battle cry was sounded. "Professionalization is now a reality in Miami. In Miami, it works. The future is now!"

Sometimes, when our enthusiasm got too far ahead of us, the future came on a little too quickly and "find a way" had to be adjusted to "save your rear." The mayor of Bal Harbour in northern Dade and Rosie Feinberg, a member of our board, went to Drew Elementary one afternoon and without alerting us held a press conference in which they promised parents that if the kids in the fifth grade finished high school they would make sure they got college scholarships. In effect, copying Eugene Lang's "I Have a Dream" formula.

Unfortunately, the mayor didn't have the money to cover his offer. And the board member shouldn't have allowed herself to be swept up by the rhetoric without checking with the staff first, because we had no funds available for such a program, either. They made the promise and walked, and we were stuck with finding a way to bail them out.

We came up with one. We put together what we called the Superintendent's Scholarship Ball, for which we sold tables and dressed everything up to look like a grand ball — and on the big night we raised almost a quarter of a million dollars. To keep it neat, we channeled the money through the College Assistance Program (CAP), a nonprofit group with a national umbrella, and let them handle the administration. Holmes Braddock was on the CAP board and acted in our behalf.

It was another example of what could be done if you reached out. Because of our success with Drew, we were able to do the same thing for other schools. And to supplement the funding, we took another cooperative step. At the time, I was being asked to speak at conferences and seminars around the country, as were others on the staff and from among the key players in the system. Honorariums were usually two or three thousand dollars a pop, sometimes five. We made it a policy that those fees would be donated to the scholarship fund. With that and the scholarship balls, a steady stream of revenue flowed in. Hundreds of kids benefited.

Realizing we might have stumbled on a good thing, we put the office's imprimatur on other schemes. We held a Superintendent's Awards Dinner to fete high school valedictorians and salutatorians. We formed a Superintendent's Council of thirty-two community leaders to critique the various new programs. We held Superintendent's Forums at each of the twenty-four high schools that were the hub of the feeder operations and invited in groups from the elementary and junior high schools that fed them. We included parents, teachers, administrators, and all "interested parties," and threw them open to Q & A.

Any decent proposal whose primary motive was the benefit of school kids got a shot. We started a program to give students credit for performing community service — cleanup work, house painting, etc. — and inaugurated "community report cards" for parents and concerned citizens to use to grade their local schools. We also held impromptu "press conferences" at the schools, patterned after those you see on television where everybody shouts at the President or the new football coach and nobody gets a straight answer. In this case, the man in the hot seat was me. The kids loved it. The press conferences got so big some of the schools televised them through their media departments.

To encourage young people to go into the teaching profession, we put a Future Educators of America chapter in every school, even at the elementary level. Dade's FEA chapter became the largest of its kind in the country. To the same end, we created the Dade Academy of the Teaching Arts and gave teachers who were interested nine-week mini-sabbaticals to take part. We pumped new life into the LEO program in an effort to coax more minorities — blacks, women, Hispanics — into the mainstream to become principals and upper-level administrators.

LEO instructed future principals on budgets, scheduling and curriculum problems, and other textbook items, but also on conflict resolution and all the other gut-check items that make big-city schools so much more difficult to run today. We interviewed the candidates in my office, and trained thirty or forty LEOs at a time. They took classes for five months, then served a five-month internship, and then did a summer stint in the central office before taking over at a school.

I was alert to their capabilities, so when a standing principal was leaving a school, I'd check the list of finalists (if there was one) and recommend a LEO "grad," even if he or she wasn't as experienced as other candidates. It drove the administrative association crazy. "You can't do that, we need experienced people in there!" I said, "You mean those experienced people who keep fouling up our schools?" Most of our LEOs were crackerjacks, and the program got such good reviews that the state of Florida picked up on it and got it going in other districts.

Funding was a constant nag. A lot of our money we got through grants (that $8 million a year), and we had to be especially creative to get it, because there aren't many foundations in Dade County. Most of what we applied for, besides the big private foundation grants, was state and federal money. I went after every buck I knew to be out there — every grant that was remotely applicable. I went over the foundation letters myself, and when I saw one that looked attainable I'd check our "grants office" to find out who on the staff had applied for it. If they hadn't, I wanted to know why. And if they couldn't convince me that it took more staff time than the grant was worth to go for it, I gave them some good personal reasons to try harder next time.

Meanwhile, "find a way" became more than a slogan, it became a way of life. No need was too small or too far-out. On one occasion, I got a call from one of the parent activists at Fienberg-Fisher Elementary on Miami Beach, the school where the movie *Porky's* was filmed. She was livid. "Fernandez, what kind of schools are you guys running down there?"

"Calm down," I said. "What's going on?"

"We've got men using the girls' bathrooms!"

"What?"

"Transvestites! They refuse to use the boys' bathroom. Our parents are up in arms."

"You're putting me on."

"Come see for yourself. They're doing it, all right."

I did, and they were. Big guys, too, dressed like women and wearing lipstick and rouge. They were Mariel (Cuba) boatlift refugees in a bilingual class, taking courses in English as a second language. It was during regular school hours, so the kids were there to see it all, in a manner of speaking.

The transvestites were organized, however, and they demanded "their right" to use the bathroom. I couldn't get the two sides together even to talk about it. The parents didn't want to be seen with "those perverts." So I put them into two separate rooms and discussed it with them a group at a time. When I got to the *Marielitos*, I resorted to my best broken Spanish, and we finally resolved the problem by rescheduling the bilingual classes for the evening hours — when no one else was around.

Some of our ideas never quite made it to the runway. One that Pat Tornillo and I called The Great Career Ladder would have given master teachers a large stipend to be at our beck and call for assignments at troubled schools, where they'd be sent to handle major scholastic and behavioral problems. We planned to put whole teams together for that purpose. (I hesitate to call them SWAT teams, but that's the general idea.) If I were still there, we'd have gotten that one going, because it was part of our next level of professionalization. I intend to make it happen in New York.

At one point I wanted to require Miami principals to teach a class a year, just to keep their hand in. I had tried that when I was principal at Central; I taught a first-period math class on the "teaching principal" model, originated, as I recall, by Sonya Hernandez in San Antonio when she was Hispanic Teacher of the Year and had gone on to become a principal. But when I did it, more often than not I had to excuse myself from class to run down a principal's problem. My day was just too busy. But I still considered it a good idea.

I think principals should be made to remember every now and again what it's like in the classroom, especially in SBM schools, where so much is happening and intramural give-and-take is important. Principals tend to forget the simplest things — that they interrupt classes too frequently with PA announcements and that when they indiscriminately pass along things for the teachers to do, the added load can weigh a teacher down. Principals and administrators — and superintendents and chancellors — need to feel the impact of the paperwork they create.

But I've pretty much decided that the only way this kind of intermittent involvement will work is if you make provisions so that the class doesn't lose continuity. I tried to require administrators in the district and the superintendent's offices to teach four days a year, but that didn't work, either. The teachers-for-a-day too often went in unprepared, and their classroom appearances were mostly rap sessions. The regular teachers complained that they were left with too much damage control. So I reduced the requirement to two times a year, then dropped it entirely. There wasn't enough return on the investment.

Of all the things we did, I suppose the most far-reaching for Dade County was the record $980 million bond issue for capital construction — for building 49 new schools and renovating 260 more over a seven-year period. To put wheels under that one, I dusted off a dissertation I'd done for my doctorate on dealing with propositions on tax limitations — in other words, how to beat the taxing procedures when you need construction money.

Among other things, my dissertation outlined how to circumvent broad-based tax limits like Proposition 13 by shifting the gain on a school-by-school basis; how to make a building program work by offering, in detail, what impact a bond referendum would make on individual districts, and how by going at it from that angle your district would get, specifically (and as an example), a new elementary school, or five new classrooms for the junior high, or a new gymnasium for the high school.

The bond referendum was crucial. Dade desperately needed new schools and to renovate old ones. The work should have been done years before. As it turned out, once we convinced the board of the route to take (there had been some agitation for a special election, but that would have cost us $500,000 up front) and got word that the referendum was on the ballot, we had a very small time frame to work with:

sixty days. Barely two months, from January to March 1988, to convince the community it should burden itself with almost a billion dollars in new taxes.

Quickly, we got some surveys done to determine where our strengths were, and built our battle plan on those findings. First indicators showed that the Cuban community would vote us down overwhelmingly. Our hope was to make that up through other constituency groups: senior citizens, the whites, the blacks. We concentrated our salesmanship on those. We didn't *say* we were doing that, not on the record, but that's what we did. Two Hispanic members of the school board picked up on it and criticized our strategy. They wanted to change the game plan, but it was already in my hands and I wouldn't allow it.

Thank God we didn't. If we'd diffused our energies and spent more time in the Hispanic community, we'd have eaten up valuable time. As it was, our staff and the business people we briefed to help us out made eleven hundred speeches in those two months. I made almost three hundred myself, sometimes as many as five a day.

We got some strong resistance from black leaders who didn't want *any* new taxes for *any*thing. They'd been burned before when promises were made on bond issues — promises for new jobs that never materialized and community improvements that were never made. Athalie Range, a powerful black civic leader who had been a city commissioner, wouldn't support us, but at least agreed to hold her tongue. A black former city manager, Howard Gary, came out in favor, however, and his was an important endorsement. We still had to hustle like mad in the black community. When we took our first poll, it showed the blacks were split 50–50. We figured we needed 80 percent. We kept working.

The poll showed Hispanics would vote us down, 70–30. With the small effort we made in Little Havana, we still gained about ten points there. The Catholic church didn't support us at all. I met with the archbishop at his residence on the bay to get a letter of support, but instead of recognizing the good the bond would do for *all* the kids of Dade County, he tried to bully me into helping the Catholic schools in particular. He wanted us to provide bus transportation in return for his endorsement — virtually a blackmail.

I told him it wasn't possible. "We can't use public funds to help private schools." Furthermore, I said, "What does one thing have to do with the other?"

So we didn't get the Catholic endorsement.

It came down to the wire. When a late sampling of the electorate indicated that Miami's senior citizens were opposed to the referendum and that victory could ride on their vote, we moved in their direction.

Senior citizens in Florida are organized, and they vote. In one condo group alone on Miami Beach there were 4,500 registered voters, the largest precinct in Dade County. Whenever a group met, I made it a point to have someone there or to be there myself. It was wild, because older people don't like being treated like discards and can get pretty testy. At one meeting I was on the dais and couldn't help but overhear two men at a front table. One must have had hearing problems because his voice boomed.

"WHO IS THIS GUY?" (I'd already been introduced.)

"He's the superintendent," said his companion.

The first man cupped his hand to his ear.

"THE *WHAT*?"

"The superintendent!"

"OH, YES. THE SUPERINTENDENT. OF WHICH BUILDING?"

I finally arranged to have breakfast with about a hundred of their leaders. They're like ward bosses, the way they control voting blocs. I didn't give them any baloney. I told them how much the bond issue meant to education in Miami, but that I knew they had the least to gain from it — more like *nothing* to gain, aside from the satisfaction of taking a stand. We talked, and then I put them on buses and took them to North Miami Elementary School and let the kids love them to death.

They were lined up with flowers when the condo leaders disembarked, blinking in the sun. They sang for them, they entertained them, they took them to lunch. Later, we offered all senior citizens in Miami a gold card to allow them to eat in our cafeterias and attend school functions anywhere in the county. By the time they got back on the buses, they were family.

When the big day finally came, the senior citizens voted 72 percent in our favor. We got 92 percent of the black vote.

And in what many considered the most important election in Dade County history, the bond issue carried, 52 percent to 48.

When I think about it now, and compare what we're facing in New York City, I have to admit that I was living an educator's dream in Miami. Everything we did for two and a half years seemed to catch a favorable light. Not everybody loved us, of course. I know some principals and more than a few administrators who felt the whip of my criticism (or my actions) and hated the ground I walked on. I was called "a martinet," and worse. I had óne critic, an academic gadfly at Florida International University, whom the media would go to regularly to "get the other side" on an issue. He could be counted on to put me down in colorful terms. (At one point, he called me the "Joe Stalin of Dade County schools." Imagine.) He practically made knocking my efforts his life's work.

But by and large I had good relations with the Miami press, just as I now have with most of the media in New York. I think part of that has to do with my insistence that we be wide open with everything we do. That we have no hidden agendas. And that as leaders in a free society we be accessible to the media. No subject should be off-limits, no question too sensitive. This isn't the Kremlin, this is schools.

Over the years I've allowed media people to get as close as they wanted, to the point of having some of them over to the house for a swim or to play racquetball, and maybe to stick around for some chicken and yellow rice. Sometimes you get a clearer line of communication (and fewer misquotes) when you know each other better. And when I felt we wouldn't get sandbagged, and could trust their discretion, I've also let some of them sit in on the most private meetings of our staff, even with potentially explosive issues on the table.

I had a writer from a national magazine sitting right there at a cabinet meeting in Miami when we had our only real brush with scandal during my superintendency.

We were going over the findings of an eight-month investigation into the school board's former finance director. There had been rumors of improprieties, and worse. I'd reviewed the procedures, conducted an audit, and found some major flaws. One in particular was shocking: it allowed the transfer of huge sums from the board's bank to private accounts in other banks, using nothing more than the telephone. We tested it out, and did it ourselves: moved a million dollars with a single call. It was that easy.

About that time, I happened to spot a book on the director's desk — all about Swiss bank accounts. Something like that happens and your mind goes crazy. I began to think, This guy's going to Brazil!

Instead of keeping it quiet, I summoned our in-house investigators, and when that didn't turn up anything, I called in the state attorney's office and intensified the investigation. I kept thinking about Johnny

Jones and how easy it is for these things to spin out of control. I wasn't about to get burned again.

And to everyone's satisfaction, no wrongdoing was found. No improprieties, no shortages. Nothing except loopholes that needed closing. The director, who had been reassigned during the investigation (and passed a lie detector test), was brought in, dusted off, and sent to another department, with a collective sigh of relief.

I suppose that in the end, though, what will mark those two and a half years as Dade superintendent for me was none of the sensational things, but all those wonderful memories of how close we got to the people: to the schools, the kids, the teachers, the families. Things you can't hang on a wall, but live forever in your heart.

I'll never forget a distress call I got my second year as superintendent, from somebody at Central High who remembered my days as principal there. I'd been asked to speak at the Central graduation ceremonies that year, but I was told not to expect a happy crowd. The kids' enthusiasm for graduation had been dampened when the money they had laid out for their yearbooks was stolen.

I told Joe Tekerman, "We've got to get a yearbook for those kids." A few phone calls later we had pulled together $5,000 in donations for a quick fix. Tek got a former University of Miami basketball player and friend of ours, Wayne Beckner, who produced yearbooks and class rings, to put together the Central book for cost. And the night of the graduation, the three of us — Beckner, Tekerman, and I — brought the books to the school in the trunks of our cars and passed them out. They weren't true yearbooks, mostly just pictures, but the seniors had their memories between hard covers.

That Christmas, we put together a drive for clothes and gifts for the migrant children of south Dade County. Burt Arnold, who was in charge of our parent programs in Miami, was responsible. He had told me about all the migrant kids who had moved in around Homestead and the Redlands, how bleak their Christmas would be. Burt has one of the biggest hearts for kids I've ever known.

We called in a few people, and Alex Bromir marshaled in other area schools to donate things — second-hand toys, clothing, etc. Some businesses got involved, making donations. Harry Smith, the CEO at Barnett Bank, and his wife got involved, giving their time and money. Our hope was that we'd be able to accumulate six or seven bags of toys to pass out at the three migrant camps. We got almost five *truck*loads, and I showed up in a baggy Santa Claus suit that Burt found for the distribution. We moved our little caravan from camp to camp and kept giving out gifts and toys and clothes until there were no more kids to give them to.

If you're a hands-on leader, those things are going to keep happening to you, and unless your heart is no bigger than your nose, you'll be touched by them. More important, the people you serve, mainly the kids and their parents, will be touched. I think it's imperative that those people who depend on you to make their lives better through education know not only that you're there, but that you genuinely care. It ties everything together.

Of course, other good things may come your way then, too. In 1989, my contract with the Dade school board was extended, and my pay was raised to an unheard-of (for me) $155,000 a year, or about thirty times more than I made my first year as a Dade County teacher so long before.

At that point, I saw no real downside to anything that was happening. Lily and I were living, if not in luxury, certainly in a comfortable house in a nice section of town, and our four kids, now young adults, were well on their way to making us proud. I won't say the world was our oyster, but at least we were in a position to enjoy the stone crabs at Joe's when we wanted them.

For a redeemed dropout from Spanish Harlem, life couldn't have been much better.

I mean, you'd have to be a fool to give up something like that.

So now let me tell you how a fool wound up in New York City.

PART VI

CONTRARY TO WHAT might have been believed, I never harbored a secret wish to leave the superintendency of the Dade County school system for the chancellorship of the schools of New York City — "advancing," as it were, from the fourth-largest system to the largest. Even when it became known that I was being courted to that end, I was more bemused than bewitched.

Ego alone, I admit, would have led me to mentally play out the scenario: the one-time high school dropout and gang member returning in triumph to the city of his birth. But we're talking about a time several light-years removed from those days and that old neighborhood, and a man several notches advanced from youthful naïveté. I mean, I didn't have to go back to Spanish Harlem to know I preferred Suniland. My boyhood buddy Johnny Thornton came to Miami to visit us in the '80s. He couldn't believe I had a swimming pool in my backyard. He said, "Where do you play stickball?"

And as much of a dreamer as I like to be when it comes to school renewal, when the task is at hand I'm much more into hard realities. And the realities told me this: I already had the job I wanted. It was paying off not only in terms of making the schools of Miami better, and making our efforts a flash point of educational reform, but I had just signed a new contract that would have moved my salary to $200,000 in four years. Lily and I had bought a little family hideaway on the Florida Keys for weekends, and with health, pension, and other benefits, I was as secure in life as I thought it necessary to be.

Moreover, I knew enough about the New York school system from my own memories and the knowledge accumulated by frequent visits and conferences, and a regular interplay with Great City Schools leadership, to believe that no one person could turn it around, no matter how large or justified his ego. Not in a hurry, anyway. And not ever without a clear-cut mandate.

Actually, no. *More* than a mandate. He'd have to be given an unprecedented latitude and cooperation during the reconstruction period and be reasonably assured an unprecedented benediction from all those legions of critics in the union halls and editorial rooms who inevitably descend on change-makers in New York City, and more often than not bring them down — and that still wouldn't get him past the biggest hurdles: the politics of the schools in the city and state, and the disabling battles they go through over funding.

Reforming *any* school district is more than a one-man job, of course. But New York is so much more than "any school district." The sheer size of it is awesome: more than a thousand schools, and just shy of a million students, and close to 120,000 employees, and a $7 billion budget (larger than twenty-six *state* budgets). A corporate monolith. Ironically, what was to have (and should have) made it better, the decentralization of the system in 1968 after a particularly bitter teachers strike, only served to make it worse and was probably the main reason for its moribund condition.

Decentralization created what was essentially a two-headed monster: one, the thirty-two districts where community boards were given almost total control of the elementary and middle schools (and in far too many cases took advantage of that autonomy to create, in the worst New York City tradition, their own corrupt little fiefdoms, complete with cronyism and nepotism, and a depressing sense of mismanagement); and, two, the more-than-five-thousand-man central bureaucracy headquartered at 110 Livingston Street in Brooklyn, where the seven-member Board of Education, made up of appointees from each of the five boroughs and two from the mayor's office, held policy-making sway over the system and its titular leader, the chancellor.

Critical to understanding both my reluctance to take the job and the events that occurred after I did is an appreciation for the chancellor's place in this arrangement. The chancellor implements the budget, with all that implies; he has direct control over the 124 high schools and the citywide special education programs involving 125,000 kids and has an overseer's limited power over the thirty-two district boards. How much power he can exert to correct mistakes in the districts and bring about reform is just enough in doubt to make it imperative that he have a strong working relationship with his boss, the school board — the Board of Education.

Pivotal to everything is that relationship. A board's job is to make policy; a chancellor's is to administer that policy and make all personnel decisions. A progressive board, like the one that hired me (and was virtually dissolved six months later, to my everlasting regret), is a must if reform is to work. If a board is divided or, for whatever reason, digs in its heels and in defiance of the guidelines tries to micromanage the system — i.e., crosses over the line from policymaker to administrator — it can virtually emasculate the chancellor. That or make his job such a misery he'll want out. I will show you how that works.

(But please don't get me wrong here. A school board is as necessary to a good school system as the Congress is to the running of the republic and must never be a rubber stamp. Even in the best of worlds, chancellors and superintendents should not expect to get their way all the time. In Miami, where I had a progressive board, I made my recommendations for measures and presented my case, and the board decided yes or no. It was then my job to follow through. You know it's working when the board doesn't question your intentions or integrity, gives you clear signals on its position, and is not recidivistic.)

As for the New York City schools themselves, and the crucible they operate in, well, you could easily make the case that everything in New York that is bad — the lawlessness, the drugs, the violence, the inner-city blight, the broken families, the civic malaise, the huge fiscal deficits, the political gridlock — all of it affects the schools in one way or another. And just as the city's wonderful cultural treasures and exciting creativity make it so appealing, so do all its failures, in the light of so much scrutiny, seem more magnified. And ominous.

Even from afar, it was evident that the schools were tarred by that same brush. They were caught in a system *New York* magazine called "corrupt and crumbling," one that for years had been paralyzed by a routine incompetence. When you talk about New York schools, you're not talking about taking them into the twenty-first century, you're talking about bringing them into the *twentieth* century. In 1989, when the state singled out its forty-three most troubled schools, thirty-nine were in New York City.

Half the kids in the system did not read up to their grade level. Sixty percent of the high school kids failed at least one subject every semester. More than a quarter took five years to graduate, and upward of 30 percent did not graduate at all — a dropout rate of almost one-third the total enrollment. Close to 60 percent of that enrollment was poor enough to qualify for food subsidies. Ten percent spoke little or no English.

The overcrowding that helps spawn such statistics was shown to be almost punitive. No high school should have more than a thousand students. (Our New Visions schools will be limited to five to seven hundred.) George Washington High in Washington Heights had an enrollment of forty-four hundred — larger than many colleges and universities. The entire system was more than ninety-five thousand seats short of being able to accommodate all its students. Kids were being instructed in broom closets, on stages, in bathrooms, in hallways, on make-do desks out in the school yard.

Mostly, that kind of overcrowding translates into the need for emergency relief: for whole schools to be built. But it was also a matter of schools being so rundown, and buildings being so dangerously dilapidated, that not all the available space was being used. Entire floors in some buildings were boarded up because of leaking ceilings or critical disrepair. There had accumulated over a fifteen-year period a $500 million backlog of maintenance orders throughout the system — a total of forty-three thousand repair jobs waiting to be done.

Part of that neglect was the legacy of the big recession that hit New York in the mid-'70s. The system let fourteen thousand teachers go at the time, and the number of tradespeople — electricians, plumbers, painters — was cut from sixteen hundred to three hundred. Those forces were gradually brought back up, but in 1991, as we agonized over maintenance needs that will reach $1 billion by the end of 1993, the system still had only eight hundred tradespeople to do all the work. Miami has that many for fewer than one-third the number of schools.

And Miami's schools, though also in need of wholesale upgrading, generally are much newer. Half the school buildings in New York City are more than fifty years old. More than 350 still have coal-burning furnaces, which means they each have to hire a fireman and a stoker to keep them warm in the winter. And at the other extreme, the biggest summer school program in the country annually is being housed in NYC schools that have no air-conditioning.

No help in any of this — in fact, the most negative factor of all — is what can only be described as the adversarial relationship between the city, headed up by the present mayor, David Dinkins, and the state, presently led by Governor Mario Cuomo, over a series of interlocking funding formulas that invariably put the city's schools in the middle — and disadvantaged. New York City schools do not have their own taxing base; they are dependent on state and city taxes. They get the worst of both worlds.

Meanwhile, the system had chewed up chancellors and spat them out like tobacco juice. In rapid-fire order, New York went through six chancellors in twelve years. The last, Richard Green, had died in office after an asthma attack in May 1989. A thoroughly decent man with great dignity, Green had come from Minneapolis, where his low-key approach worked wonders. In New York, taking over what Robert Hochstein of the Carnegie Foundation for the Advancement of Teaching calls "the toughest job in American education," Green started slowly with a self-imposed hundred-day observation period, couldn't get his agenda moving, and never knew what hit him. He died fourteen months later.

Enter Joseph A. Fernandez, and the key question he had to ask himself: why *wouldn't* a compulsive crusader leap at the chance to clean up such a compelling mess? I can only tell you what this crusader felt. That the New York job was a dead end. A task that could pin you down and cover you over, unless . . . Unless (1) you moved so quickly at the start that change would be in place before the reactionaries could muster a counteroffensive, and (2) you were given a rock-hard commitment from all those in positions of influence to support your agenda: the mayor, the editorial boards of the major newspapers, the unions, the state, and so forth. Even then you'd probably still be done in by the odds.

I also knew that the peddler's public has a very short memory. What they love you for today they'll despise you for tomorrow if you don't measure up to what *they* think progress should be.

And that's the Achilles' heel of school reform movements. Too many people who get caught up in them don't really understand that the things you're trying to produce — better schools, better students, higher scholastic achievement — won't happen until the groundwork is firmly laid. That in order to improve academic performance you must first revitalize the workplace: make it better and safer for kids and a more conducive environment for the good teachers you must attract. Academic reform begins with administrative reform and facilities reform. The good grades and the higher achievement and the lower dropout rates come afterward. It's a process. If you get impressive statistical results in any of those areas immediately, chances are it's a fluke.

All that considered, and even while there was speculation that New York had me on its short list after Green's death, the job was farthest from my thinking when I was approached for it in July 1989. I told Joe Tekerman when I got the call, "The only way I'd ever take it is if they make me an offer I can't refuse." Meaning an offer that would be cradled in the promise that I'd be given the authority I needed to beat the odds and enough material benefits to make it right for my family. Lily, for sure, was not eager to move back to New York. She'd learned to enjoy life without an overcoat and living it on an acre where the grass and trees were perpetually green.

Stan Litow made the first call. A public-policy advocate who for years had been one of the NYC schools' toughest critics, Litow was point man for the school board's search committee and acted in tandem with Robert F. Wagner, Jr., the board's president and son of a former mayor. I agreed to talk with them in person a week later in Washington, where I was speaking at a teachers conference. I liked them both from the start — Litow for his knowledge of the system (from a position as devil's advocate), Bobby Wagner for his idealistic but solid belief in education and what I sensed was a cooperative nature that augured well for coalition efforts.

Best of all, they both embraced the idea that School-Based Management would serve well for the future of New York's schools. But I hedged. I had just signed that new contract, and SBM in Miami was really still only a baby — *my* baby. I couldn't desert it now. Litow said, "Just don't say no. Give us a chance to work on some things."

I agreed to go to the next step: to meet secretly with Litow's full committee in New York. Stan said later that after that first meeting in Washington he told Wagner, "Fernandez is the guy. Let's do the deal now and go poll the board members."

Actually, the search committee was still talking with candidates from Portland, Oregon, Memphis, and Pittsburgh, and I was still pretty sure I didn't want to be included, or even mentioned. But somebody at 110 Livingston leaked my name to the *Times* — Wagner said whoever did it was trying to sabotage the deal — and when the story broke prematurely that I was to meet with the committee, I immediately canceled my trip to New York and all but announced I wasn't interested. I had Tekerman handle all calls from Litow, and on August 10, I sent a memo to my own Dade board, which was now looking to be reassured: "I intend to remain your superintendent . . . ."

Litow was on the phone to Tekerman four times a day from that point. Tek held him off with any excuse he could think up ("Joe's fishing on the Keys"), but between the two of us, we started a list of demands that would almost surely kill a deal. A kind of "they-can't-possibly-agree-to-this" list. Six days later, having decided it was ridiculous, I called Litow and said, "Stan, the timing just isn't right." He said, "Don't say that. You might not ever get this chance again. If you say yes, you can write your own ticket." I let him talk me into a "showdown" meeting in Miami with Wagner.

We met privately at the hotel in Miami International Airport. Pat Tornillo made the arrangement. I gave them my preliminary list of conditions. More than anything else, I said, I wanted assurance that not only would the board accept my game plan in principle, but would not object when I started firing people. I said, "I need to know I'll be able to really clean house if I have to." Furthermore, I said, my salary and various benefits would have to reflect the 27 percent cost-of-living difference between Miami and New York City, and I would insist on letting the Dade board decide how much time it needed for me to stay on the job before leaving.

They agreed to put the deal before the committee, with no announcements. I especially didn't want any publicity at that point because the Koch-Dinkins mayoral race was heating up and I didn't want to get caught in the position of being some kind of Hispanic pawn in NYC politics. The election primary was on September 12. On September 15, I declared myself a candidate for the chancellorship, making it official, and on the nineteenth, with plane tickets under the names Smith and Jones, Tekerman and I flew to New York to meet with the search committee.

Litow sneaked us up on the freight elevator at the back of the Equitable Building for the meeting. It went well. The committee voted unanimously to recommend I be offered the job. I then met with the board, the offer was made, and I accepted. Then Stan hustled us back downstairs and to our hotel.

Contract negotiations on the nitty-gritty items then began by long-distance telephone. Litow orchestrated, even while he vacationed on a Navajo Indian reservation in Nevada. Mainly I let Tekerman handle my end, half thinking (and, I guess, half hoping) that with each new clause we'd reach a point where somebody would say, "No deal." Because deep down I was still thinking, I can't do this.

But as big-league ballplayers and big-time corporate CEOs will tell you, no demand is too far out anymore. Tek kept adding to the list, and we went back and forth. At one point, I said, "I want a quarter of a million dollars in salary." They came back and said, "We can't give you $250,000, but we can give you $195,000 and make up the difference in the following ways . . ." I almost felt guilty. I said fine and gave them a slightly lower figure to work with.

The final four-year package, negotiated by my attorney, Barry Craig, came to $230,000 a year and included a car and chauffeur, $113,500 for my unused Florida sick leave, $213,000 in pension benefits, a $5,500-a-year premium for life insurance, a $10,000 annual expense account for official entertaining, $14,250 to offset higher New York taxes, and a chancellor's residence that would be provided but owned by the city. Now, if you think of all that as outrageous compensation, I would agree, except that it would be nothing compared to what a fellow can get for hitting .250 for the Mets, and I like to think schools are more important.

Meanwhile, the prospect of the move had made the press, turning the wheeling and dealing into a circus. The New York media, famous for their resourcefulness, wouldn't leave us alone. They parked outside my house and never stopped digging. The Miami media got in the chase, too, mainly with loaded questions about my "finishing the job" there.

That was the sticky part. When I got back from New York and told the Dade school board what I had decided, I wasn't prepared for the emotion I felt about leaving. These were my friends, and we'd gone through a lot together. I couldn't help choking up. Several board members were clearly upset, too, but not in the same way. They were upset that I was pulling out. Holmes Braddock called it a matter of ego: "Joe's got a big one." Privately he wished me well, but I think he felt betrayed.

Much later (*too* much later), Mickey Krop tried to find a way to get the board to match the offer, even though I didn't think it possible, or even advisable, considering how soon this was happening after my new Dade contract. To tell you the truth, at that point I felt any hint that I might consider staying would be unseemly. But Mickey came to me at the eleventh hour and said, "Whatever you're getting in New York, I'm gonna try to get for you here."

He went back and quietly worked on some of the board members. I know about it because Bill Turner called me. Turner and I were very close. He said, "Joe, do you wanta stay?"

I said, "Bill, I think we've passed the point of no return. Bridges have been burned. Either way I'm gonna be criticized, but I don't want to pit one side against the other. I'm leaving."

I still had so much ambivalence. I was just over two years into my superintendency. We'd pushed through the bond issue for school construction and were in good financial shape. In fact, I left my successors with a $45 million reserve that got them past the next school year. But I really *didn't* think I'd finished what I had set out to do. Besides that, it meant Lily and I would be leaving our grown children, all established in Miami, and a life-style we really enjoyed.

On the other hand, New York did represent a bigger challenge, and I certainly have an ego about those things. When it was put to me the good we could do on such a broad front, I told myself, "You know, New York was your home. It's where you were born. You should do it. After all, it doesn't have to be forever." I knew I'd never go back to being Miami's superintendent, but who was to say we wouldn't retire to South Florida? To that end, Lily and I decided to keep our place on the Keys.

But I have to admit that if Mickey Krop's effort at the end had come a little sooner, and given me a last good reason to say no to New York, I probably would never have left Miami. Looking back now, I might even be tempted to say I *should* have stayed. I won't, though, because that would give my critics in each place too easy an opening to agree. Or disagree.

It has been said that the success of most revolutions is decided in the first ninety days. Ours had a ninety-day head start. In effect, we started *before* we started.

The New York City Board of Education made my selection official on the Wednesday after our Monday meeting in New York. On Thursday, I had Stan Litow begin putting a transition plan in place there while I was phasing out in Miami. The Dade board asked me to stay through December. I agreed, but Litow and I made arrangements for me to spend the weekends in New York for briefings and meetings preparatory to a January 1, 1990, takeover.

From September to January, I participated in 162 meetings. I'd come into New York on a Thursday night or a Friday, stay until Sunday night, and in between, at any and all hours, meet with every conceivable member of my new constituency: politicians, business people, union leaders, reporters, editors, councilmen, parent groups, the heads of advocacy groups, the arts groups — a long list Litow carefully assembled. I met with the outgoing mayor, Ed Koch, and the mayor-to-be David Dinkins. I met with all the editorial boards, some more than once, and all the daily beat reporters. For each group, I outlined my legislative agenda, my management agenda, my budget agenda, and answered questions.

I'd start at 7 o'clock in the morning, sometimes with two and three breakfast meetings in a row, and go until late in the evening. It wasn't unusual to make twenty-five meetings on a weekend. If it was scheduled, I was there. I didn't back out of anything. Litow laid the groundwork by having briefing memos prepared so that I had a line on the people I'd be dealing with and the issues they were involved in or likely to want to talk about. During the week, Litow and my executive assistant in Miami, Connie Kostyra, burned up the fax lines with letters and memos, some for me to get a reading on, others for Stan to review and help determine a response.

I was briefed on everything from the disposition of the Board of Estimates to who the "trusted" players were in the mayor's office. In meetings with union leaders and editorial boards, I laid out my hopes for an SBM blitz and hammered at it almost daily in interviews with the press.

I told them all up front: "You're going to either love me or hate me, because I'm going to stir hell out of this pot."

I convinced Litow to stay on as my deputy chancellor (he said it would be his first experience "on the other side") and hired Jim Vlasto as my director for media relations. A veteran New York PR man, Vlasto once handled the press for Governor Hugh Carey. I got Connie Kostyra to come to New York with me as my executive assistant. I tried to get Tekerman, too, but Joe said he'd "already been to New York." Being such good friends, we kept in touch almost daily afterward, and I worked on him pretty good, but I couldn't change his mind. He said he didn't want to risk losing his tan.

There was a marked contrast between my January inauguration and that of Richard Green two years before. Green's was virtually a coronation. All the Board of Education members wore robes, and presidents of colleges came in wearing their colors, and a choir sang. It was very impressive. On my coronation day, I came in to 110 Livingston at 7 A.M., sat down at my desk, and went to work. The headlines said: "Fernandez Takes Over Without Fanfare."

I also took over without hesitation. I didn't need a hundred days to get "acclimated," I was more interested in giving potential allies a hundred good reasons to follow my lead — or chase my footsteps, because I intended to be moving out. I didn't want *any* day to go by unused. As far as I was concerned, that beginning period represented a critical window of opportunity that I wouldn't get again.

The enormity of the job, or the thought that it was undoable, never really entered my mind again. I was too busy putting in place a capable staff and identifying the immediate problems. From the beginning we were all so wrapped up in dealing with the issues that we didn't have time to be "overwhelmed." I knew I had to cope with the existing structure, and that it was put in place by law, and that I might have to get the law to make some of the changes we needed, but I didn't think that was impossible, either.

I had two basic priorities for what I thought was necessary for a more effective governance of the system: (1) the ability to have input into the selection of the thirty-two district superintendents and (2) the ability to intercede whenever things went wrong (or were already wrong) anywhere.

That's the short answer for it, of course, but at the beginning everything else spun from those two things, including some of the really touchy issues that I was primed to take on from day one: abolishing "building tenure" for principals, that absurd practice peculiar to New York that awarded a principal with five years on the job permanent station at his school (and made it almost impossible to get rid of or reassign a *bad* principal), and disbanding the archaic Board of Examiners, the scandal-marred licensing agency that complicated the hiring of teachers and administrators.

With input into the selection of district superintendents, and the ability to intercede, and given my jurisdiction over the high schools, I thought I'd pretty much have all the clout I needed to make corrections wherever and whenever I saw fit. All the other things I needed I knew I could get because I'd been there before. I knew from experience, for example, that you *can* get public opinion on your side, and you *can* get the editorial boards on your side, and that's crucial, because those are your tools to force legislatures and advocacy groups and unions to respond favorably.

I wouldn't have gotten building tenure eliminated so quickly (if at all) had we not had the pressure put on by editorials and the public at large. Not that people are always so willing to pick up on a cause, but one contingent alone, in East Brooklyn, delivered more than four thousand letters supporting my agenda. Legislators respond to things like that, just as they respond to the pointed editorial in the *Times* or the critical essay in the *Post*.

Never underestimate the power of the printing press. While still mayor, Ed Koch said he'd build a statue in my honor if we got rid of the Board of Examiners and building tenure for principals. He should have, but not to honor me, to honor the editorial writers who rallied to those campaigns. When we were losing momentum in our drive to unseat the examiners, I went back to some editorial boards three and four times to stoke their support. They reacted (referring to my opponents as "the chancellor's handcuffs" in one case and to the examiners as "dead wood" in another). When Brooklyn Democrat Mel Miller, the speaker of the state assembly, made negative remarks about my "presuming" legislative help, *Newsday* castigated him for not joining the battle against the "arrogant, self-serving, deeply entrenched principals' union and the archaic agency that licenses teachers." I couldn't have said it better myself.

But those were things accomplished through efforts expended more or less behind the scenes. What made the headlines at the beginning were the things we did in the open.

The pattern was set on the very first day. I arrived at 110 Livingston to find the windows of my office so filthy you could write your name on them and the carpet littered with wire clippings from a computer hookup that evidently had just been installed the day before. I asked a secretary to call the custodian to tidy things up a bit.

Now, I admit that I'm a fanatic about clean schools, up to and including odor-free restrooms and graffiti-free walls. I feel that the cleanliness-neatness factor is a first order of business in creating a proper environment. I've fired principals who couldn't keep their schools shipshape, and you would think, along that line, that if anybody in the world could see the advantages in such a position it would be school custodians.

But New York City spends more to get less in custodial services than any metropolitan school system in America. Our custodians' average salary is a whopping $58,000 — $20,000 more than teachers, $18,000 more than cops, $16,000 more than firemen. Their pay is on a par with that of our principals. And despite that, their contract is loaded with things they *won't* do. Such as mop the cafeteria floors more than once a week or the school floors more than once a year.

Or move furniture.

Or do almost anything a principal might ask, even if it's only to hang a picture.

Or — the most asinine of all — paint any outside wall above a point ten feet from the ground. You have to visit a school for yourself to see how ridiculous that looks: new paint to a certain level, then dirty old paint and graffiti above that.

I didn't know all this at the time, however. When I asked for help cleaning up my office, the secretary came back and said, "The custodian says he only vacuums every third day."

I said, "Get him up here!"

We had it out. I told him to look at the mess in my office. I told him to look at the windows. (You had to look *at* them because you couldn't look *through* them.) He said, "Well, we're only supposed to clean the windows once a year. It's in our contract."

I said, "Knowing that and seeing the results firsthand are two different things."

I called the union chief. I said, "This doesn't make sense. You guys get so much bad press, and here you've got a new chancellor, first day on the job, and I can't even get a dirty carpet swept. Wouldn't it be smart to get these things done, even if it's not in the contract?"

He said, "You're right." And he did.

But the episode made headlines, and it didn't end there.

When I looked around the system, I found that schools with dirty floors and messy windows were more the rule than the exception. I found broken toilets and water fountains going unrepaired, broken glass going months without being replaced, the residue of roaches and vermin everywhere. Falling plaster, peeling paint, leaking ceilings. They were $500 million behind in maintenance work orders.

I examined the contract with Union Local 891. It was one of the worst I'd ever seen. The union had gained concessions that worked against the very schools its members were supposed to serve. They literally had a license to steal. They got exorbitant fees for opening the schools early or after 6 P.M. or on weekends. They were allowed to use school board money to buy things (computer systems, fax machines, office furniture, refrigerators) that, after a period of time (usually three to five years), they could keep for themselves. Even Jeeps. We found 164 janitors driving Jeeps the board had all but paid for, and immediately put a stop order on the practice.

Under a grandfather clause, but in violation of a ban imposed in 1988, some two hundred custodians had spouses on the payroll. One, at a junior high school in Sheepshead Bay, was known as "Sabbatical Sal." He was surrounded by paid relatives: sons, nephews, and — listed as a "handyman" — his wife. Sal was making $62,300 a year. According to records, he spent $490 of city funds to buy his school a lawn edger-trimmer and another $119 to repair a lawn mower. What made this such an attention-grabber was that the school didn't have a lawn. Sal did.

In lieu of the expense it would have been to battle that absurd contract, we got Sabbatical Sal to "retire early." And after the study, I looked to take control of the cleaning and maintenance operations to see if we could do better by privatizing services and repairs and giving principals the final say in operations. A system that allows a custodian to tell a principal when he'll mop the cafeteria floor is simply not workable. Cafeteria floors should be mopped three times a day if necessary.

Institutionalized abuse isn't easily routed, however. We were at odds over the terms of a new, unsigned contract with the custodians (the International Union of Operating Engineers) for two years when, in July 1992, I finally hired private cleaning services to take over the operations at eleven schools that had custodial openings and lined up twenty-nine more for replacement in the fall. Under two-year contracts with the private firms, schools would be open from 7 A.M. to 10 P.M. on weekdays and 8 A.M. to noon on Saturdays, at no extra cost to the system. In fact, even with all that extra service we figured to *save* $80,000. Moreover, principals would have authority over the custodians and the power to terminate them at any time if their work was bad.

But the headlines made by my opening forays against dirty windows and messy floors were nothing compared to the reaction we got from the demolition derby we conducted in those first frenetic days: firing principals, putting superintendents and district boards on notice, purging redundant jobs at 110 Livingston, taking automobiles away from board officials, etc., etc.

If it all seemed draconian, you have to understand the frame of reference. I fired one tenured principal strictly because of her incompetence. That had *never been done before* in New York City, at least not in modern times. Principals had been fired, but not because they were lousy principals. Crazy.

Then there were the district boards, those bastions of "decentralization" that had become, for everybody to see, little more than throwbacks to the old political clubs where patronage and nepotism and out-and-out larceny ruled and the hell with what's right and what's responsible. Not all thirty-two of them, certainly, but far too many were being managed like Balkan states, playing "let's make a deal" on every issue, standing for nothing (certainly not integrity), and systematically stifling what little faith there was in the educational process. When Richard Green died in May 1989, a full third of their number had been under investigation, for everything from selling drugs to selling jobs.

In the weeks before I took over as chancellor, during the time I was commuting back and forth to New York on weekends, Coleman Genn, a fed-up thirty-two-year veteran of the system and superintendent of District 27 in Queens, secretly taped the wheeling and dealing of his board members as they filled high-paying positions with unqualified cronies and bragged how they were going to take down "the whole store." Genn said he believed that more than half the city's school districts were politically corrupt.

In my first month on the job, I had to order — not ask, order — a local board (District 9 in the Bronx) to fire a superintendent, Dr. Annie B. Wolinsky, for using $10,000 in special education funds to decorate her office with drapes and furniture. The purchases were concealed in false orders for stationery. That's theft, no matter how you coat it, and the local board was going to do nothing.

Board 9, in fact, had made an art form out of ignoring its sins. Just the week before, I had ordered Superintendent Wolinsky to dismiss a principal (William Green) who had hired a known child molester (Frank Carr) as a teacher. Carr had been charged with the crime in New Jersey, convicted of it in another instance in Connecticut, then was accused of molesting two more girls soon after taking over a junior high school in the Bronx. His sterling record, which included eight arrests, had passed right through the Board of Examiners.

District 9 also gave us, as a prime example of the idiocy of building tenure, the Matthew Barnwell case. An elementary school principal with a history of absenteeism and alcohol abuse, Barnwell was indicted in 1988 for cocaine possession. The district board that had ignored these facts was suspended for that and other malfeasances, including using and distributing drugs, stealing a piano, and extorting money from school employees. Three board members pleaded guilty to the criminal charges and the entire board was replaced in May 1989.

Barnwell, meanwhile, stayed on the payroll. Instead of demanding his dismissal, which chancellors were always loath to do because of building tenure, Chancellor Green suggested a show of compassion on

Barnwell's behalf. It was such a flagrant forswearing of responsibility that the whole district was up in arms. Barnwell was finally convicted in early 1990 and fired my third week on the job. At the same time, I had Wolinsky dismissed as the District 9 superintendent.

But even that wasn't the end of it. District 9 continued on its errant way. The board president pleaded guilty to charges that he had been the recipient of various bribes, including a cashmere coat, and had taken $18,000 in kickbacks from stationery suppliers. An office executive assistant and tutor was arrested on charges of sexual abuse and showing pornographic movies to two preteenage boys at his home. In an audit conducted by the Board of Education a year later, we found that the district had wasted or put at risk more than $2 million in funding that should have gone into direct services for the children. The report charged that thirteen senior district officials had mismanaged finances and programs, teachers and paraprofessionals had been overpaid, excessive vacation and sick leave money had been awarded — and twenty-one pieces of major equipment were missing.

All of that is shameful enough. Making it tragic was the fact that the district, in the Morrisania area of the South Bronx, is made up of thirty thousand mostly poor black and Hispanic kids who need every break they can get, not to be raked over by a bunch of grafters and virtually abandoned by their only hope, the educators. Dereliction of duty among the latter was commonplace. We found that even though two-thirds of the district's children were reading below grade level (only one other district had a worse record), the director of the reading program rarely showed up at the schools. Lacking in bare essentials — crayons, scissors, etc. — and undersupplied to the point where they had to pass textbooks from school to school like sacred tablets, teachers were so dispirited they didn't even bother to order the materials that *were* available.

The only thing the district seemed to have in numbing abundance was an in-your-face arrogance. One board vice president, George Palermo, showed up in the office of the superintendent brandishing a gun, for reasons said to involve a contract dispute, and told the superintendent's executive assistant, Brent Cutler, to "step outside and die like a man." No one was hurt, but Palermo was arrested, and I suspended him.

Several months later, Helaine Atlas, Brent Cutler's wife and a former acting principal in the district, named Palermo in a suit charging that he tried to extort $18,000 to have her appointed principal at a Fulton Avenue elementary school. Brent Cutler, in the same $1 million civil action, accused the board president, Carmelo Saez, with pressuring him to raise $23,000 for a drum and bugle corps that Saez directed (for a $35,000 stipend). Cutler claimed Saez threatened to fire him if he didn't come up with the money. Saez denied it.

The suit further charged that jobs were for sale in the district and that campaign contributors got preferential contracts. Three days after it was made public, nude photographs of Ms. Atlas, said to have been sent to Saez nine months previously to "entice him to offer Atlas the principalship of PS 4," were delivered to the *Post* by a Bronx official. Cutler said the well-timed "revelations" of his wife — in forty different poses — were typical of the "vicious" way these "gutter people" did business. Ms. Atlas said the photos were from a personal collection. She couldn't say how they got into such hostile hands.

By that time I had dismissed Palermo outright, and in May 1992 I suspended Saez when it was discovered he had used district money and personnel to produce a fund-raising videotape for his drum and bugle corps. Unrepentant to the end, Saez claimed that I was "out to get him all along." Meanwhile, a Board of Education investigative team I put together to monitor the district determined that Superintendent Edward Whitney, on the job less than a year after replacing Wolinsky, was without "clear goals" for turning his schools around, and recommended a wholesale replacement of all personnel in advisory positions.

I replaced Whitney with a bright new face who was later one of our Reliance Award winners for executive achievement, Felton (Buddy) Johnson, and got IBM to come in on the business side to help ramrod a full restructuring of the district's programs. But even with all the heat we put on, I couldn't claim that District 9's troubles are over. The sleaze runs deep. But it was at least a start.

Meanwhile, other district boards were doing their damnedest to be as spectacularly corrupt as 9. Boards 27 and 12 were on suspension, 27 because of the Genn disclosures, which had resulted in a trial (but only one conviction). Genn himself had gotten out, fearing, he said, for his life. Board 27, in the Queens area encompassing Howard Beach and the Rockaways, was seriously divided along racial lines. I had to suspend a white board member over charges she had sought to barter her vote for a black superintendent in return for the black board president's agreeing to step down in favor of a white.

I had to put a stop order on board 12 in the South Bronx when it tried to reappoint a district superintendent who was under local indictment for bribery. Late in 1991, I had to go back to 12, also serving (if

you can call it that) children from low-income families, to take over its
fiscal operations after it persisted in missing budget deadlines, failed to
pay its teachers on time, and was in danger of losing money for supplies
because of poor management. An auditor found teachers and supervisors padding their salaries with bogus jobs and claiming to have
worked on national holidays — and on days that *didn't exist*: February
30, February 31.

Board 12's "unholy mess," as the *Daily News* described it, reached an
artistic low in early '92 when a city councilwoman cast the deciding
vote on the local school board to have some of her campaign workers
named principals. Two of the new principals had no supervisory experience. One had been dismissed as a teacher for incompetence. I
blocked those and the appointment of six principals in all, and when I
was challenged, I threatened to replace all the board members if they
didn't follow my order to postpone appointments until various charges
(including anti-Semitism) against the selection process could be investigated.

I had to stop another board (13, in the Fort Greene section of
Brooklyn) from reappointing an elementary school principal who had
stolen $20,000 in welfare funds. The district refused to dismiss Bar-
bara Chandler-Goddard even though the superintendent ordered it
and City Council President Andrew Stein, getting to the heart of the
matter, called it a "terrible insult" to the children of the school knowing
their principal was a convicted thief.

District 32 in the Bushwick area of Brooklyn was found to have
misspent almost half a million dollars. The Board of Education's auditor general reported improper payroll charges, misreporting of finances, overpayments, questionable purchases, and expenditures for
goods and services lacking in documentation or receipts. I ordered in a
budget team to take over the district's finances.

As a first stab at flexing my right to block the appointment of unfit
superintendents, I moved against District 19 in the impoverished East
New York area when the auditor general revealed that board members
had leaned on the superintendent, Levander Lilly, to hire relatives,
friends, and political allies as a condition for renewing his contract.
Lilly, with a solid reputation as a drug counselor and three years on
the job as superintendent, had the parents on his side and refused to
play ball.

The local board responded by replacing him in favor of a junior
high principal, Felix Vasquez, who had a spotty record as an admin-

istrator but was "politically connected" (his sister was a Democratic district leader in Brooklyn). When the complaints poured in, I superseded the appointment and told the district to go back to the drawing board.

I then brought the embattled Lilly and the board president, Corina Grant, a Vasquez supporter, into my office to see if they could resolve their differences and work together to end the infighting in the district. Relations were so bad local police had to patrol the halls at board meetings to protect members from angry parents. With Lilly clearly having the edge in parental support, Grant relaxed the board's position and order was restored. Not peace, but order. Lilly was kept on as superintendent. Vasquez was not reappointed. He is now out of the system.

In District 17, the plundering took a bizarre, almost comic twist. The district's director of funded programs was a forty-one-year-old opportunist named Henriot Zephirin, whose job included buying books for the mostly immigrant children of the schools in the area. Among Zephirin's purchases was a 148-page reader called *Bilingue à l'Aise*, written in French and English by a first-time author from Haiti, Luc Edouard, whose awesome butchering of both languages made it clear he was in over his head. The book, among other things, advised that "earth" is pronounced "erfe" and conjugated the verb "chide" as "chide, chid, chidden," and "catch" as "catch, cought, cought."

This didn't deter Zephirin. He ordered eight thousand copies — for the one hundred (count 'em, one hundred) French-speaking children in the district. Author Edouard was paid $46,000 out of school funds. Then, he told authorities, he was ordered to return $11,000 to Zephirin. In cash. In a parking lot.

A background check on Zephirin's work for District 17 revealed similar "arrangements." He had once purchased two thousand English-language copies of *The Red Badge of Courage* for four hundred district students who did not speak English. When two of the district's federally funded programs needed evaluation, District 17 hired a firm called GMP to do the evaluations. G, M, P are the initials of Gerard M. Paret — the cousin of the director of funded programs, the ubiquitous Henriot Zephirin. The two reports totaled twenty-one pages, or about five thousand words. For that, cousin Paret was paid $30,000, or $6 a word, a fee that would make him the envy of any freelance writer in America. But Paret said he didn't get to keep it all. He said $21,000 was kicked back to — why, of course — Henriot Zephirin.

Zephirin was indicted. William Kunstler, the celebrated defense attorney, defended him, claiming the moneys Zephirin kept putting himself into position for were "loans." But even such a brilliant courtroom light as Kunstler wasn't enough to render a Brooklyn State Supreme Court jury blind. It convicted Zephirin of grand larceny, falsifying documents, and defrauding the government.

Now, stop right here and consider the ramifications of all these things. If we were talking about any other enterprise, they would still be shocking stories. If this were the exploitation of a dockworkers union or a savings and loan, it would be disgusting enough. But these were *schools*. This was the *education of children* that was being ravaged. What could be more damaging, or more reprehensible? Or more indicative of a school system gone terribly wrong?

So if you are among those who wondered why I felt the need to take the offensive immediately against the brigands in educators' robes who routinely despoil New York City's schools, keep that in mind.

If you wonder why I am so impatient with bureaucrats and mayors and city councils and governors and school boards who let these things grow into a massive contamination, keep that in mind.

When schools are treated like a vassal state, education becomes a by-product, not a priority.

To be sure, in taking on the districts I was going against the proud heart of New York's "decentralized" system. Which may seem at first blush a major contradiction because, despite the implications, and what was charged by some critics, I was then and am now *for* decentralization. I shouldn't have to prove it, but obviously School-Based Management epitomizes decentralization, and I'm certainly for SBM.

No, the measures I took against the district boards were a contradiction only if you could say decentralization in New York City stood for responsible leadership and meaningful distribution of power, and not a means of getting greedy fingers into the till or perpetuating a dismal status quo. What I wanted from the districts wasn't more authority over them, it was accountability. Centralized or decentralized, no authority is good if it is not accountable. Neither School-Based Management nor any other grass-roots reform based on bottom-up governance will work if the supervisory power is in the wrong hands.

Which is why I pushed from the start for legislative action to change certain governance flaws in the New York system (e.g., building tenure and the Board of Examiners). The business of who's running what, and how good a job they were doing, had to be addressed. But I certainly wasn't spoiling to go to war with the district boards; I wasn't foaming at the mouth to rout out errant superintendents and principals. I would have preferred to come in under a flag of peace and get right into scholastic renewal instead of occupying my time with police work. But to play the game right, the playing field has to be level, and in New York from district to district it was a moonscape.

I was challenged on the decentralization issue over and over that first year, but critics kept missing the point. New York City didn't have decentralization. It had a tyranny of local dominions. Too many districts were using decentralization the way the South once used states rights laws to keep a legal boot on the neck of desegregation. And lest we forget, the federal government had to put its own heavy foot down to make integration work — to make those reluctant states "accountable."

So going in I made up my mind I would attack bad governance whenever and wherever I saw it, and if it meant finding out exactly how much clout the chancellor had for what he needed to do, all the better. Just before I took over, the acting chancellor ordered a new principal to replace one who had gotten in with dubious credentials at an elementary school in Bedford-Stuyvesant. The principal refused to leave the school.

Asked my opinion of the case, I said, "If that happens when I'm chancellor, I'll have the principal removed bodily." I said I'd have done the same to the junior high principal in Sunset Park who had ordered teachers not to fail too many students and actually changed some kids' grades to boost her school's academic standing. I said she wouldn't have seen another sunrise on the New York City payroll.

Yes, I was throwing down the gauntlet. Yes, I knew it would be picked up, eagerly in some quarters.

So I formed a watchdog committee — a monitoring office — to keep tabs on the community boards and report directly to me. I said if I found schools or districts that had gone astray and wouldn't straighten up after being placed on notice, I would take them over until they did. I said I had no desire to run them, but I would not allow them to be run any way but correctly and honestly. I vowed to do the same with the high schools.

Although challenges to the district boards' authority were rare to the point of being unique, I felt my jurisdictional prerogatives were clear. The chancellor's job description calls for him to "set minimum educational standards" for the districts and to enforce them. I interpret that as a responsibility to review and challenge an appointment or a performance, individually or collectively, and to monitor courses of action and step in whenever needed.

Since the lines weren't clear as to what might happen if a chancellor took "interpretive" action, I decided I'd *make* them clear by aggressively stepping over when I thought the situation demanded it. If it meant going to court over jurisdictional disputes, so be it.

In fact, I *wanted* to be sued, or at least challenged, in these gray areas. I wanted to get as much light into the dark corners of the system as I could. I felt that if we went to court we could establish case law as a basis for future decisions. In other words, we'd have to do it only once. And I thought we'd win most cases because it didn't make good political sense for a court to decide a civil dispute in favor of mismanagement of public schools.

Some of the local boards did, indeed, dig in, and I was sued often that first year — sometimes personally, sometimes as agent for the Board of Education. Actually, I've been sued often *every* year. In New York, everybody sues, and in school board matters I naturally would be named, so I don't take it personally. I'm protected. Lawsuits tend to buzz around the office like honeybees anyway, and for about the same reason: a search for sugar over a violated contract or a botched collection. Mostly they're nuisance suits that tend to languish in piles on the "pending" list.

But when they impact on my decisions, I get involved. The only real legal setback we had the first six months came over a directive — Circular 37 — I'd issued in January on this very issue, the supervision of the district boards. I knew Circular 37 would rile defenders of the status quo because it sought to establish a clearer basis for the chancellor to act in the selection of district superintendents by declaring his right to evaluate and reject nominees. Ten school boards took us to court over it, and in July a New York State Supreme Court judge in Queens ruled that Circular 37 was invalid. He found that the directive usurped the local board's power to hire.

But it was only a glancing blow, not a knockout. And we gained more than we lost. In his "sympathetic" (to me) ruling, the judge put into legal terms for the first time the chancellor's right to reject superintendents who do not meet the minimum education standards he has set, and that it was his right alone to set those standards. That was really all the scouring power I needed to rid the system of bad superintendents, but it also meant I would have to do so only *after* their local boards had picked them for the job and sought to install them.

My preference would be to screen out weak candidates beforehand, even if it meant using the local board's own hiring guidelines, just to make the procedure more accountable. Why let a poor superintendent get through the selection process in the first place? We're talking about individuals who are paid more than $100,000 a year as the chief educational official in a community of twenty-five to thirty schools. They're responsible for the education of as many as thirty thousand children and a budget of $150 million. If I had the obligation to guarantee that they adhere to minimum educational standards, I felt I should have the right to ensure that initial evaluations be made to fulfill that guarantee. So I appealed the decisions.

The chancellor's chief counsel, Larry Becker, advised me well on these cases. Of the suits that mattered, we won all but a couple, and I haven't necessarily given up on those. At this writing, School Board 12 is challenging the authority I used to supersede its fiscal operations. The State Supreme Court will hear the appeal. Three former members of Board 27 filed a federal suit alleging I had violated their constitutional rights by refusing them reinstatement after the board was dissolved in the wake of the Genn revelations. My position was that their names weren't on the new list provided by a screening committee of parents I commissioned to represent the district's sixteen schools, so they couldn't be considered.

Community School Board 24 sued over my directive to give parents and teachers a say in the hiring of principals and assistant principals. I had invoked our Circular 30 plan, which called for the beginning of the selection process to be put in the hands of a two-teacher, six-parent screening committee — to advertise for candidates, interview them, and hand them up to the superintendent for the board's final vote. Given its history of patronage, I didn't want Board 24 to be able to choose from its own list of candidates. The board sued on the grounds that I was shutting it out of the first stage of selection. Well, of course I was. That was the whole idea. The judge sided with me, and refused the injunction. Larry Becker was warned to expect an appeal, but one didn't come.

It should be pretty obvious at this point that I wouldn't have had to go to these lengths with a school system that was doing its job. Everywhere you looked there was some kind of operational eyesore. But I have to say that the impression I got those first weeks on the job was that New York just didn't know any better. It had suffered through such a long night of failure with its schools that it was virtually blind to what many of us from *outside* the loop already knew: that it was a system without a working philosophy or a true educational agenda.

Everything New York school leadership did was reactive. Programs were started or needs identified not by a strategic plan (New York schools didn't have one) but because somebody came in and complained or screamed it out in a speech or an editorial. There was no concept, no identification of the few major needs that a course of action could be tied to.

It was a system run by a downtown bureaucracy that was generally regarded as "Fat City." The main office, known as "The Livingston Hilton," was a place where people worked without purposeful leadership or esprit de corps. On my first visit there, it was embarrassing to find that employees couldn't name fellow workers from floor to floor — or even on the same floor! Their administration was a slow, sloppy operation that had a reputation for never delivering anything (or getting back to anybody) on time, never writing anything down, never coming up with a new idea, never offering a proposal. Just sitting around twiddling its thumbs while the schools went to hell.

Nobody could tell you what they stood for because they didn't know. What they *did* know was that "you can't do that." Whenever you wanted to try something, that's what you got. "You can't take on the principals." "You can't take on the district boards." "You can't take on the unions." "You can't take on the black lobby, or the Hispanics, or the white teachers, or the Board of Examiners." "You can't take on the legislature, or the mayor, or decentralization."

So people did exactly that: nothing. Strangled by the bureaucracy. Saying, over and over, "This is a job that can't be done." Talk of a leaner, meaner management, with techniques that would bring it up to date and a sophisticated political agenda that would be willing to take on any and all special interests, was, in the words of one skeptical columnist in January 1990, "no more than wishful thinking."

The utter wackiness of a system working against itself could be seen immediately, in the littlest of things. On that first day, after venting my anger at the custodians, I asked one of the secretaries for some yellow highlighter pens. I use them all the time going through material and have come to think of them as indispensable items. She came back with the news: "I'll have to order some, because we're out. Purchasing says it'll take a month to get them."

Now, consider the implications. If they were treating *me* this way, and I was the man in charge, what was going on everywhere else?

I made a point of this to the media that flocked in for everything we did that first month or so, and almost immediately got reacquainted with something New Yorkers are instinctively aware of about New York. That people who live elsewhere may knock it, and may not always understand it, but they're very much tuned in to what goes on there. In the mail the next few days I must have gotten the equivalent of three crates of yellow highlighter pens, from all over the country, including Miami. Enough to last me at least until my contract expires. The standing joke was that this must be the way Fernandez intends to resolve shortages: complain about what you're out of, then wait for the stuff to pour in through the mails.

Actually, we didn't wait for anything. When the bell rang for day one, we were already off the stool and into the middle of the ring, swinging away. We literally cleaned house at 110 Livingston, from the paint on the walls and the clutter in the halls to the redundant personnel behind the desks.

In my previous visits there I had never thought the school board building looked very professional. Not because it was so old — the 1926 neo-Italianate architecture actually gave it some charm — but because like too many of the people inside, it reflected a general lack of pride. The elevators didn't always work, the offices were dirty and disorganized.

I went to war on all the junk that had accumulated, and had my own offices on the tenth floor stripped of everything and repainted. For that leaner, meaner look, we shoved the huge oak conference table the previous chancellor had used against the wall in my office in favor of a more functional model we dug out of storage and had refinished. We swapped the bulky armchairs for chairs *without* arms to get more people around the table, and to accommodate the steady stream of confreres and combatants opened up a nice, unpretentious waiting area where you could sit and read professional magazines while waiting your shot at the chancellor.

I announced that all departments in the building would be open for business by 7:30 A.M., and if I called personnel or transportation or operations at 7:31, I better get an answer. No more 9 o'clock scholars. I said I expected them to look and act the way professionals should when running the most prominent school district in the country: no more sneakers, no more personalized cards and letterheads.

I said we all worked for the same school board, we were on that team, and there would be only one letterhead. I told them to keep their desks neat and watch their phone etiquette (New Yorkers tend to use the telephone like a jackhammer), and I even sent around a directive on improving letter-writing technique when I saw how sloppy and ungrammatical the simplest correspondence was going out. There couldn't be a shabbier reflection on an educational institution.

But streamlining the work force was the battle I had to win quickly, because it meant putting people in the street and nobody likes the taste of that. There was no avoiding it, however. I'd had six months to study the organizational structure of 110 Livingston, with all its duplication of effort and piddling, no-point jobs, and I knew major cuts were imperative. The Board of Education's main office was a monument to waste, both in its numbers and its methodology.

Every bureau had its own budget people, its own evaluation people, its own personnel people. I said, "From now on, there'll be one centralized operation for each of those functions."

All the chancellor's deputies had any number of assistants. I said, "From now on, you each get one."

The chancellor before me had twelve special assistants. I said I would make do with three.

In my meetings with Stan Litow and Bobby Wagner, Jr., beforehand, I'd gotten a pretty good idea where the cuts should be made, so in preparation for the downsizing I got the acting chancellor to order a freeze on all jobs and salaries before I took over on January 2. I requested resignations from three hundred employees and accepted fifty I knew were expendable on the very first day. I also took fourteen leased automobiles away from Board of Education officials who had no good reason to have them. Sometimes that kind of thing — slicing into perks — can cause as many hard feelings as outright dismissals, but it also sends the correct message when you want people to know there are limits.

There's no way, of course, to avoid hard feelings when you're reorganizing, unless you don't make the tough personnel decisions you should. I'd tried to get away with that in Miami and had to live with the consequences of having senior staffers who weren't committed to my reforms hunkered down in positions of authority. In that first round of cuts at 110 Livingston, we fired 218 people. Two of them were chancellor's deputies, with all their assistants, so I couldn't have been any closer to the bleeding.

In the end, we wound up reducing the fat of Fat City by more than a thousand employees: from around 4,800 (which actually represented

5,259 job lines on the payroll) to 3,590. We eliminated fourteen entire departments. Besides the streamlining that accomplished, it also meant a savings of $34 million a year for administration. I had to laugh to myself at the irony. About that same time, the press got hold of the "extravagant" $1 million house the board had purchased on my behalf (again, to be owned by the city, not by me) and made it sound as if we were taking milk from starving babies.

As for my own staff, I had it mostly in place in December, tailored for the needs, and I lucked out with some truly great choices. Getting Stan Litow to come on as deputy chancellor for operations, my second in command, was my best move. No one knows more about the flaws in the New York City school system than Stan. He had been its most persistent critic, authoring more than forty critical reviews on school operations for Interface, the political action group, and I knew from our first discussions how incisive a thinker he is. What I didn't know was how hard he works. In Miami I never had anybody who consistently beat me into the office or stayed later. Stan does both.

Joe Saccente and Jim Vlasto were shoulder to shoulder with Stan at the point of attack in those first hectic months. Saccente was one of the three-hundred-plus I had asked resignations from in December, but as soon as I met him I knew I wouldn't be accepting his. He had served seven chancellors in twenty years on the job, and everyone I spoke with had good things to say about him. I said, "Joe, you're going to be in charge of district operations. I want us to monitor every move they make. What do you need?"

Joe Saccente didn't need much. Like Joe Tekerman, he has a gift for working with people, and like me he is an ex-math teacher with the savvy to have made it up through the ranks. When he retired at the end of the '92 school year (I moved the talented Burt Sacks into his job as "chief executive for monitoring and school improvement"), the *Times* said that nobody moved through the labyrinth at 110 Livingston better than Joe.

I interviewed about fifty people for the jobs closest to me. Jim Vlasto I kid a lot, but he's a crack press secretary with no fear of being overworked and no chance of being outtalked. He has some blind spots, especially with "lesser" media and some of the minority papers that I'm particularly sensitive to, but I yell at him enough to keep that from being a problem. He and Litow, of course, were "outsiders," as was Robin Willner, whom I brought in from Interface to be my executive director of strategic planning, research, and development.

The insiders I kept on or moved into key positions on the cabinet included Lenny Hellenbrand as budget director, Tom Ryan as head of human resources and labor relations, and Jim Coney in an enhanced role as auditor general, reporting directly to me.

All of them were first-rate. Robin Willner's chief task was to assemble the data base and coordinate the production of the system's first strategic plan, something I insisted we'd have to have when I took the job. It was ludicrous that New York City never had one. What Robin put together, with input all around, is a road map of ways and means to take the program smartly into the next century. No large school system should be without a strategic plan. Robin's is exceptional. I compare it with what Angie Welty and I pieced together in those hectic after-hours in Miami years ago, and it's like moving from the stone age to the space age.

I kept Larry Becker as my counsel, by good accident. I wanted a minority in the office, but I couldn't find the right person for the job, so I kept stalling, and Larry, who's white, kept proving himself a brilliant attorney. His strength is that he can adjust his approach to the law to fit the management style. The chancellor who is a careful administrator needs a careful attorney. If he wants to rattle cages, he needs an aggressive one. Larry Becker had been reading the law from a conservative viewpoint, reflecting the chancellors he worked for. I wanted him to be broader with his strokes, to help me use my powers as much as I could. He turned out to be a master at aggressive litigation and worked especially well with Joe Saccente putting the pressure on the districts.

Some of the people I selected didn't turn out. Some I put in key positions have been good but not top-notch. I went on recommendations and their work records, and they're OK, but their big problem is they're still geared to the old days and the old ways, with no sense of urgency for the task at hand.

I did some hiring based on ethnicity, too, which has to be a consideration today, and was glad to get Amina Abdur-Rahman as deputy for external programs and community affairs. Amina had taught in the street academies for high school dropouts and went on to direct the New York City Urban League's education programs before becoming education adviser to David Dinkins when he was Manhattan borough president. I made Amina the ranking black member of my cabinet, a key player in dealings with the black community and black advocacy groups. She filled the bill.

How important is an "ethnic consideration"? As an educator, I would always object to the idea that you hire *anybody* on the basis of color or origin. But the hard reality today is that you need input, and you need empathy, and you need interplay in the multi-ethnic big-city schools of America, especially when so many black and Hispanic kids are at academic risk, and if it takes special considerations in hiring to make the connection, you should do it. A necessary evil for the times we live in, perhaps, but necessary nonetheless.

You need look no further than the top positions of school management in our biggest cities to see the importance we now place on having a "minority presence" (and minority successes) in the leadership of institutions that serve large, turbulent inner cities — where minorities *are* the majority. On the day I took over in New York, the superintendent of schools in Los Angeles was a Mexican-American, the superintendents in Chicago and Philadelphia were black, and my eventual replacement in Miami was a Cuban-American. All seemed to be eminently qualified. With me as New York's chancellor (a Latino in name if not in communicative skills) it meant the five largest school districts in the country were run by "minorities."

You could certainly make a case that this wouldn't be a good thing if it meant selections were being made on any criterion other than merit. But I submit that the elevation of qualified minority leadership is important to encourage and recognize, and is justified on the grounds that it *is* necessary. The superintendent of schools in Washington, D.C., with the constituency being what it is in the capital city, will now almost surely always be black, and ought to be. A white superintendent would have to be exceptional to get and hold the job, given the problems peculiar to that system. I don't see bias in that at all.

But I admit that such "practical" considerations are fraught with potential peril. The dilemma is a beaut: we must sometimes make personnel decisions based on racial or ethnic grounds — but without appearing to be biased! How's that for a fine line to walk? I like to think that at the very top, where we are exposed to so much interpretation of motives, we will be fair enough and responsible enough to walk it intelligently. The difficulty comes when we have to make those positive personnel decisions (hiring people) and the negative ones (firing people) down through the ranks *without* caving in to special interests or pressures.

One factor is inevitable. Constituencies, ethnic or otherwise, will always try to get as much as possible out of you for themselves, even at the expense of fair play. It's as natural as breathing. You must deal with it as you would any other special interest. And the best way I've found to do so is to make a stand at the very beginning: my hiring and firing privilege will be sacrosanct. I haven't had any lasting problems with it in New York because I made it clear when I came on that I wouldn't play games with personnel.

As a matter of fact, in all the years I've been running schools, I've never had anything like an outright attempt to coerce me on personnel decisions. Not even a pressure ploy — "If you don't do this, I'll make sure your contract doesn't get extended." Oh, I've had attempts to manipulate me, usually with painfully transparent logic ("You better not assign this principal to so-and-so high school, Joe. That's a very orthodox community and he'd have a hard time there. Now *this* guy could do the job"), but usually it was somebody on the school board watching out for his own and it was easy to sympathize without submitting. I had a standard line: "Well, if he becomes a finalist, I'll look into it"; then I'd do what I thought was right for the school in question.

The key is to be consistent, and that includes making sure that every decision on school personnel will be based on the good of the children. What I've found in dealing with ethnic groups and minorities generally is that if you make that a tenet of faith, and they see you are consistently fair, you won't have to worry about being "influenced."

Actually, I think we have advanced far enough in human relations in this country to where you seldom get heat anymore for bending over backward to hire qualified blacks or Hispanics. The temperature usually goes up only when you have to fire them. That's why it was so ironic in those first wild days in January that whenever I had to lower the boom in the schools, it was always on the head of a minority. If I'd been a white Anglo-Saxon Protestant, I would probably have been run out of town.

On my second day on the job, I had to fire a principal, Sonia Rivera, whose school, Eastern District High, was in chaos. I had to suspend the head of the city's special education programs, Waldemar (Bill) Rojas, for drunk driving. I had to order the removal of William Green, the principal in the sexual abuse case. I had to fire Matthew Barnwell, the principal arrested for crack. I had to order another district to fire Principal Chandler-Goddard. All were black or Hispanic, or both.

(I admit you get paranoid about it after a while. When I finally had to discipline superintendent Annie Wolinsky, I thought, At last!

Someone who's not black or Hispanic. My relief was diminished when I saw her. She was black. Waldemar Rojas eventually became one of our success stories. After attending Alcoholics Anonymous he was reinstated and I recommended his promotion to executive director of special ed. He kept impressing people, all the way to San Francisco, where he is now superintendent of schools.)

The tough one was the first, Sonia Rivera. As I said, no principal had ever been fired in New York City because of incompetence. In Ms. Rivera's case, I had an initial sympathy born of my own experience: that minority principals usually get the worst jobs, at the toughest schools. Plus, people liked her. Even knowing how ineffective she'd been, I'd have preferred to just pull Rivera out for a while and retrain her, but there wasn't time. There'd been three riots in a period of two weeks, and it was clear she was part of the problem. I think she might have been overwhelmed by the whole thing. Several meetings were held with leaders in her community, and she didn't even show.

What cinched it for me, however, was that Eastern District High, although a beautiful facility, with artificial turf athletic fields and all kinds of physical pluses, simply wasn't being utilized: no varsity sports teams in place to use the field (and rally the student body), no urgency to get academic programs in high gear. You'd go into the lab classes or the shop classes and find brand-new equipment still in boxes. The music facilities weren't being used. Nobody was scheduled in those classes except special education kids. And the school was eleven years old!

When I fired her, Rivera took it very hard. She complained that the kids just weren't interested, that there were outside agitators, that the community was bitterly split between black and Latino factions. Undoubtedly this was true. But I couldn't see her ever resolving those problems, not with all the others she was doing nothing about. I went to the school to judge for myself, and it was evident that I had done the right thing. Rivera was simply unable to hold things together.

As it turned out, I was roundly criticized by Latino groups in the area who had followed the controversy through the aftermath of the riots. Representatives of a coalition came to see me, and although a few indicated their support, others strongly implied that I would have been "afraid" to have "done that" to a black or a white principal.

Connie Kostyra says that it is at times like this that I tend to lose my sophisticated veneer and revert to type — meaning, I suppose, Joseph the Terrible. I will admit I got very upset, and if I counted to ten it was by fives.

I said, "Let's get this straight right now. If I have to base everything I do in this town on what ethnic group I might offend, you better petition the school board and tell them they've hired the wrong guy. I'm going to be just as hard on Latinos as I am on anyone else — but no harder. Come back a year from now and tell me if it isn't so."

Then I got it from the other side. My policy is to meet with any complaining group or faction willing to talk through an issue, but when I met later with a delegation of black militants headed up by a popular activist named Sonny Carson, who reportedly had been egging on the black kids at Eastern District High, the delegation started right off on a sour note: with demands.

I said, "Hold it right there! What is this 'demand' stuff? I'm here to try to work with you. If you want that, fine. But don't come in here telling me you 'demand' this or 'demand' that. I don't operate that way." It was a very hot meeting.

Sonia Rivera appealed her dismissal, but I was upheld, and she eventually settled with us. I put her in for retraining under three of my best principals and had her go through the program (as one of our first "students") at the Professional Development Center we created for that purpose at Bank Street College. The way it works, a principal is earmarked by a superintendent (or the chancellor) as "lacking," for want of a better term, and then is evaluated by an audit team that bases its recommendation on class test scores, grievances, control, parental involvement in the school, etc., etc. — a whole list of things.

It then becomes the principal's choice to accept retraining or not. We've now tapped more than 160 for the program at Bank Street. Some take the path of least resistance and retire, others submit to it and profit enough to get back on line or maybe discover that although they still are principal material, they would be better suited for a different level of education. In Sonia Rivera's case, we decided she needed a school where the stress wasn't on such a grand scale. When she became eligible for assignment the following year, we placed her at South Bronx High, a smaller, less volatile facility, where she has done a good job. Unfortunately, even with improvements a lasting peace hasn't come to Eastern District High. After a knifing incident in the fall of '92, parents led a rowdy boycott for improved safety measures. My firing of Sonia Rivera was recalled in a critical light. But it was something I still feel I had to do, as quickly as possible.

My modus operandi in every case like that had always been to deal with the party in question face to face, after making sure I was on firm ground. (You don't fire *anybody* as a knee-jerk reaction anymore, not when a harsh word can bring on a lawsuit, so you should know the answers before you ask the questions.) In New York, however, the very size of the system creates too many personnel problems for me to deal with them all personally. And even though firing or transferring tenured principals was a new experience for the city's schools, I knew that once we started cracking down there was bound to be a staggering case load.

I knew this even before I got acquainted with the procedures and the documentation we needed for taking action. In Miami we established a process for retraining that was much simpler, because I had more authority over principals and a contractual agreement with the teachers union to take appropriate action when we saw fit. It was not uncommon for us to pull twenty Dade principals and two hundred or so teachers for prescriptive retraining every year. They might not have liked the idea, but it was best for the schools, and therefore the kids, and it beat getting fired. In New York, even without the hands-on involvement I prefer, we dismissed more teachers and administrators in my first six months than had been let go in the previous five years. There was a 90 percent increase in case action; 193 individuals were brought up on charges.

I'm not proud of that. Nobody in his right mind should get any pleasure in seeing teachers and principals go down in flames. By the same token, we weren't conducting a witch hunt, either, so it tells you the conditions we were dealing with. It had to be done, and when it was done it sent a tremor through the system: "We are now going to demand more of you. Better get ready."

Most of those dismissals weren't made public, partly because they are hidden in the record as "personnel action" and partly because newsmen don't get exercised about fired teachers the way they do fired principals. It was the principals and their union, of course, that I had challenged on the building tenure issue. Firing Sonia Rivera was the first shot in that short war (short in that no one expected us to win it so quickly, if at all). The fact that it happened my second day on the job also served as a portent for the principals union: that this particular chancellor would not tolerate poor leadership in New York City schools, no matter how long it had been in place.

How much difference can a strong, committed principal make? All the difference in the world, given the need and the circumstance. An exceptionally strong principal can turn a school around almost single-handedly. I don't say I did that in my brief time as principal at Central High in inner-city Miami, but I certainly knew the gratification of making a difference. In New York, Frank Mickens, the "principal in the bow tie," has earned a national reputation for the gutsy, pride-inducing changes he made at Boys & Girls High, transforming a predominantly black school from a pariah to the pride of Bedford-Stuyvesant.

A twenty-four-year veteran of the system, but a maverick with a reputation as an abrasive, no-holds-barred disciplinarian, Mickens told me I'd learn to like him because he would remind me of me — a twelve-hour-a-day man with a passion for getting things done. He was right on both counts. In six years at Boys & Girls High, Frank converted a combat zone into a sanctuary. He routed dissidents and reclaimed dropouts. He pushed dress codes and Saturday classes, and roamed the halls preaching the twin gospels of discipline and academic achievement. The school's graduation rate soared, and so did the numbers who went on to college — even to colleges named Cornell and Colgate and Columbia.

Some people compare Mickens with New Jersey principal Joe Clark, who patrolled the halls of his school, too, but with a baseball bat. Frank does it barehanded, with guts and guile. I take no credit for his success. He had made his mark before I got there, and when I found out his methods, I had to think that some of the things he demanded would cause a riot in other schools — no gold teeth, no goatees, jewelry "minimums," shirts and ties for seniors, etc. — but the parents of Bedford-Stuyvesant loved him and the community rallied to the cause. That's the thing I liked most: his ability to get all that support for his programs. He is so good at it that I offered him a job in my office as an administrative assistant superintendent, to work with middle and senior high schools.

The point I'm trying to make is that you cannot minimize the importance of a good principal to a school, or the jeopardy a school is in when it has a *bad* principal. Bobby Wagner told me in October 1989, when I made my first reconnaissance trip to New York, that the protection building tenure gave bad principals had seriously impaired the system. He said that the majority of New York's principals were "mediocre" and a significant number — as many as 25 percent — were "incompetent." He said that openly, not just to me.

And when, on that very first weekend, I announced I would be gunning to bring down building tenure, and pointedly called it the most absurd thing I'd ever heard of, I knew I'd get a rise out of the principals and their union leaders. I *wanted* one. Because that was another battle I not only had to win but had to keep in the open, so that city and state administrators and the media could see for themselves how arrogant the union had become in resisting change for almost twenty years.

I said building tenure was absurd. "Why should the kids suffer because of incompetent principals?"

I said if I didn't get satisfaction from the union, I'd seek legislation in Albany, and immediately started laying the groundwork to do exactly that.

I had to because Donald Singer, the president of the union (officially, the Council of Supervisors and Administrators), and his lieutenants had already dug in on the issue. When my selection was first announced, they had verbally trashed School-Based Management as an inappropriate concept for New York schools (no power sharing with teachers and parents for them), and they had declared that in New York "we don't fire principals." They were right about that, but what they meant was that in Miami I had fired or transferred forty-eight principals in two years, and that scared hell out of them.

So when my selection was first announced, Singer issued a press release all but daring me to take on the "property right" of tenure. I doubt the CSA expected the reaction it got from the media. The *News*'s Bob Herbert called the release a "sleazy document" and said what he knew about "the Great God Tenure" was that it "stomped all over excellence" in New York schools. Hear hear. *Newsday* said Singer was "strutting like a schoolyard bully" and told him to prepare his union "to live in a world where principals are accountable."

The facts spoke for themselves. A principal qualified for tenure in five years and thenceforth could be removed from the school where he was stationed only by an impossibly complicated procedure of disciplinary charges and hearings. Of those who qualified (about fifty a year) an average of only one was denied tenure, and since 1978 no tenured principal had been fired or transferred. Despite years of complaints against the practice, and an annual call to switch over to the renewable contracts common to all big-city school systems, building tenure hung on.

But its days were now numbered. The tide of opinion and current events was on my side. As the newspapers played up the tensions growing between Singer's union and me, I was blessed with a series of good examples of why tenure was so bad. I had the unqualified elementary school teacher in Bedford-Stuyvesant who refused to be dismissed by the acting chancellor. I had Ms. Rivera, well into her fateful last days at Eastern District High. And I had the principal of Junior High 136 in Brooklyn, Gida Cavicchia, who was found to have established a "pass-fail" quota system in which she ordered teachers to pass failing students so that 75 percent of the student body would advance whether they deserved to or not (a charge for which I later suspended her, and she retired rather than fight). I couldn't have asked for riper evidence.

To Singer's credit, when the first wave of negative reaction to the union's stand coursed through the media, he began softening his position. Neither one of us really wanted to close the door on negotiations. On the contrary, I wanted Singer on my side, not only to see the need to make principals accountable, but to forge a common bond in support of School-Based Management. I felt that his fears were unfounded and could be resolved if properly addressed. (When it comes to SBM's curative powers, I am an eternal optimist.)

We met for the first time on a chilly morning that October, he and two of his lieutenants in business suits and me in blue jeans and a pullover, sitting around a little table in the park across from the United Nations Plaza Hotel, where I was staying. The setting was at my insistence, to stress the informality of the occasion, and the meeting was cordial, but I could have picked a better day to be outside. I told Singer of my legislative agenda, making no bones about my intentions, and he told me of his concerns that SBM might be a threat to the jobs of assistant principals and administrators. He kept citing stories about Miami schools dropping assistant principals and using the money for other things. I said the stories were exaggerated. I invited him to come to Dade County and see for himself.

A few weeks later, he brought a delegation of CSA officials to Miami to do just that and, ostensibly, to go the next mile in talking out our differences. At the start, it went well. But when his people went out to visit our SBM schools, Joe Tekerman got calls from two of our principals saying that one of Singer's deputies was asking loaded questions and trying to put a negative slant on everything we were doing. They said, "These guys from the CSA aren't here to learn, they're here to pick us apart."

I felt like I'd been sucker-punched. I told Tekerman, "Get them back in here!"

I brought the whole group into my conference room, Singer included, and spoke my piece. "Let's get a few things settled right now.

The issue of whether or not I'm going to be chancellor in New York is not up to you. That deal is done. And it's not a matter of whether you like me or not. You don't have to. But it *is* a matter of our getting along for the benefit of the schools of New York. I don't think you're going about it in a productive way."

And I zeroed in: "Here you've come into my home, at my invitation, and used my schools to push your own selfish aims. You've come in here on the pretense of learning about School-Based Management, and then done your damnedest to hurt it! If that's the way you do things in New York, you've got a rude awakening coming. My course is already set. You guys have no choice, it's been decided. You better make up your minds. You're going to have to work with me or move over."

That may have cleared the air once and for all, but I wasn't as cocksure as I sounded. New York City is very much a union town, and any time you try to forge major change with one union, you better check the pulse of the others. The CSA represents forty-five hundred supervisors and administrators. To get them to agree to give up building tenure, I needed the other unions to see why, and to be willing to go against the CSA's position. I had already started working on that, meeting with various union leaders, hoping to isolate the CSA. They didn't totally buy in, but agreed at least to remain silent if and when I tried to get the necessary legislation passed in Albany.

I knew in December I was winning. The editorial writers were bombing away at tenure, and Singer was making conciliatory statements, I think realizing how destructive a bruising legislative battle could be. It didn't hurt, either, that he was being reminded of this by the legislators themselves, who began pushing for an accord once I took over in January and started making a regular pitch in Albany for bipartisan support of my agenda. I knew then that getting the other unions to take a walk on tenure had been pivotal, because both sides of the legislature asked the same question: "How do the unions feel?"

At that point *I* felt I had support all around, although you can never be sure with unions or legislators. Having support pledged beforehand is one thing, getting it after the pressure builds is another. But by then it was a moot point. The full weight of all that opposition was lying heavy on the principals. Singer kept a token resistance going, but the rhetoric wasn't as fierce and it began to take on the odor of desperation. In February we got a complaint that they had resorted to using kids at a Queens elementary school. The principal and the parents association reportedly had promised pizza parties to help push a citywide letter-writing campaign organized by the CSA. The charge was denied, but it made headlines negative to the union.

The final breakthrough came in March. Singer and I were not only on better terms by then but had completed two months of behind-the-scenes discussions. The culmination was a three-page agreement that gave the chancellor the right (1) to remove incompetent principals from their schools (within the bounds of a reasonable hearing) and (2) to move principals from one school to another against their will — the first time the chancellor had had that right since 1975. It was the death knell for tenure.

Both Singer and I hailed the agreement as a victory "for the system." I said (and meant it) that Singer had "never lost sight of the fact that educating our children is the No. 1 priority."

Legislation followed, with the CSA's staff working with us to help make it go smoothly in Albany. The Republican-controlled senate, which had long held out on the issue, went along with the assembly, and the following month, Governor Cuomo signed the legislation into law. Almost simultaneously I suspended Gida Cavicchia, the principal with the magical ability to turn failing grades into passing students. Two weeks later, she announced her plans to "retire." In June, we announced *our* plans to remove fifteen to twenty more "lagging" principals and put them up for retraining.

By the end of June, we had also won the war to abolish the Board of Examiners. For that, credit must go where it is due: to the legislators in Albany, who not only put up with my nagging (I walked their halls almost weekly for five months), but stood up to be counted; to the editorial boards of the city's newspapers who now seemed as committed to school reform as I was (the *News* alone wrote more than twenty supportive editorials); and to the key players in education in the state cabinet who weren't afraid to take on issues potentially hazardous to their party's health.

I have been favored twice in my career by smart, stand-up education commissioners: Betty Castor in Florida, who some political experts predict will be that state's first female governor, and now Thomas Sobol in New York. Sobol hardly agrees with everything I say or do, and gives me loud, braying signals when he doesn't, but on the key issues where education is concerned, he's a rock. After watching our progress from afar, and then involving himself when the situation demanded, Sobol said he thought that much of what would affect the "story of our nation" in the years ahead was being written in New York's schools, and therefore "*everybody* has a stake in Fernandez's success."

What I knew about gaining the political support necessary to bring down the Board of Examiners I was learning fast.

What I knew about the Board of Examiners was what Sobol and, it seemed, everybody else in the free world knew but had been unable to do anything about: a redundant, outdated testing and certifying agency that had existed since time began (well, since 1898) but was now only a bureaucratic bottleneck to the hiring of good teachers. It had been originated to ensure that teachers were chosen on ability, not through politics or favoritism; it had degenerated into just the opposite, and a $6.5-million-a-year waste of taxpayers' money. It was also unique to New York City. (Why didn't that surprise me?)

The board's examinations — a confusion of 185 different tests for the various teaching jobs — had been made redundant long ago by the mandatory National Teachers Examinations, but they were kept in use for no discernible reason except the patronage they provided. They didn't attract good teachers to the system, they repelled them. The red tape and double testing led legions of prospects to throw up their hands and take their résumés elsewhere. The excessive payouts to active and retired principals, assistant principals, and college professors for administering the exams were an ongoing rip-off.

I helped my own cause on that particular point by printing a list of the people who were getting money from the examiners. It blew the lid off. Some who were already making high salaries were pulling down $20,000 and $30,000 extra as part-time examiners. The board's five-member ruling body compounded the arrogance by overspending everywhere else. In 1989 it was budgeted for $1.87 million to test teachers and supervisors (at $25 an hour), but it spent more than $3.1 million. And when there was a problem to be addressed, the board could usually be found in California or someplace attending a convention.

Elimination of the examiners had been tried in various ways in the past but had always crashed at the same turn. The assembly, which is Democratically controlled, would invariably agree to a change, but the Republican-controlled senate would balk and there'd be a standoff. Obviously, I had to push for more cooperation there, mainly in the personage of Republican James Donovan of Utica, the respected, long-time chairman of the Senate Education Committee. Donovan had been the chief defender of the system (from my perspective, an obstructionist) and had made remarks before I came that he wouldn't be changing his position just because of me.

To turn the vote, I was convinced I would have to neutralize Donovan and make an ally out of Mel Miller, the assembly speaker from Brooklyn and one of the most powerful politicians in the state. Miller had ridiculed my first calls for legislation as a cop-out for 110 Livingston's failure to do the job on its own in the past. He's an interesting guy, Miller: talks fast, fidgets, doesn't look you in the eye, but is very bright — one of the few legislators I've known who's a good enough numbers man to understand the budget. When I went in to see him, he chased his staff out, asked my staff to leave, and gave me his version of the view from Albany.

He said he wanted to help me understand the lay of the land. "This isn't like Florida, Joe," he said. "The only things that happen here are what I want to happen." I said I could understand that, "but that makes it very much like Florida, because the speaker there, and the president of the state senate, are the ones who wield all the power." We appreciated each other's grasp of the situation.

He had me meet with the New York City delegation he chairs, and we bantered for two hours, not about substantive issues, as I'd hoped, but about their individual district needs ("When is the gym floor at so-and-so high going to be finished?" "When is my school going to get painted?"). I scolded them a little. I said, "Here you have the chancellor in front of you with a major legislative agenda and you haven't asked a single question about that."

But the fact is that many of our state legislators across the country have direct ties to schools, and therefore a vested interest in their well-being. Miller's wife is on one of our district boards. After a while the obvious dawns on you: that when there is a familial involvement in the betterment of education you can get even cynical politicians excited. After the meeting, Miller's group, still thinking constituency, wanted to pose one-on-one for pictures with me for their local papers, so I stayed another hour. Anything for the cause.

I finally met with Donovan after a couple of postponements due to his illness. He was sick with cancer and taking chemotherapy. He had gone to Sarajevo in Yugoslavia, after the reported sightings of the Virgin Mary, and he told me how his personal rosary had changed color — to gold — while he was there. He showed it to me. He seemed truly humbled by the experience.

We had a good talk. There was no rancor. I told him the straight of it: I simply wanted to streamline the selection process so we could hire better teachers quicker, for the best of reasons: to improve our kids' chances in school.

Although I didn't expect him to make an about-face, I began to realize after that meeting and then others with Republican senators that the long, dogged defense of the Board of Examiners had already begun to flag.

After meeting with the delegates from New York City and getting their promise to lobby Donovan from the standpoint that the desired legislation would, after all, impact only New York City, not Utica or anywhere else, I was convinced I had bipartisan backing. The senator from Manhattan, Roy Goodman, said they had persuaded the senate majority leader, Ralph Marino, to support a bill to abolish the board. He said he thought Marino was convinced.

The growing weight of opposition to the Board of Examiners was too much for Donovan and his backers. In late June the legislative leaders of the assembly and senate — Miller and Marino — announced that terms for a cease-fire had been reached. The examiners would be scrapped at the end of the school year. We had swept aside one more major obstacle to school reform in New York City.

You say, sure, but wasn't that more a political victory than a scholastic one, and is that what running America's schools has come to? Political football? Yes, and yes. You can't separate politics from public education any more, even in small towns. You're dead if you try. You have to know the legislative issues and how they pertain; be a good lobbyist; call in the votes when you've earned them. Work through the front door if you can, but be prepared to go around back, too. Deal honestly with partisan issues as a nonpartisan, but deal.

And if you have to threaten (or take) legal action to get legislators to listen, do it, and then be prepared to accept a reasonable compromise. Chances are, if you sell your position properly, they'll give you something through the legislature. Maybe not all you want, but something.

By nature, I *am* political — more of a liberal than my conservative friends would prefer, and a Democrat by registration. But in all cases I'd gladly compromise any partisan stand in a minute if it meant doing better by our schools. I don't say that to sound noble, I say it because education to the educator today is too important for anything less. But you still can't separate yourself from politics, because that's where the power is.

So I walk the fine line, trying to keep all avenues open and being as *un*political as I can so that I won't start sounding like a candidate for something. I've been flattered when my name has come up in that light, but the truth of the matter is that it does more harm than good. I know I'd have an easier time with Mayor Dinkins if his staff weren't so paranoid about my looming in his future as an opponent — for a job I would want only if the alternative was a terminal case of shingles.

One thing you have to remember, though, and it's funny. Most politicians are worse than debutantes when it comes to the petty little jealousies and flights of ego that can foul you up. When I was beating my drum around Albany in those first weeks, I had Connie Kostyra work out a very careful schedule so that I could get in as much time as possible with the key people I had to see. Luncheon dates were the best for that.

But I picked up the paper one morning to read where Guy Velella, a Republican from the Bronx and one of the city's stronger voices in the senate, was upset that the chancellor "never called me, never came to see me, and here I am a member of the Education Committee." He said, "I think Mister Fernandez has an awful lot to learn about the way things work in Albany."

Well, there was no doubt about that. But if he'd taken the time to check his calendar, he'd have seen we had a date for lunch already scheduled for two days hence. At my request.

Meanwhile, Governor Cuomo had joined our efforts to eliminate the examiners at several key junctures, and accentuated his support eloquently in his state of the state address. We met two or three times during that period on various issues.

From our first meeting I got a big kick out of Cuomo: a smart, wonderfully persuasive, brilliantly articulate man. I was especially taken by his ability to push a point of view opposite to your own — while somehow making you feel he was serving *you* better for it.

We first talked for about half an hour at his office in the World Trade Center in New York City. Then in February I went to see him in Albany to try to get a commitment on my proposal to give the chancellor the right to screen candidates for district superintendent. I also wanted to discuss the Board of Examiners, and one other big item that I *really* wanted him to do something about — the terrible disparity between what the state gives New York City schools as our "fair share" of the school budget and what we are *supposed* to get according to the formula.

I had been quoted — accurately — as saying it might soon be necessary for New York City to take legal action against the governor (i.e., the state) to get what was due us: 37 percent of school funding based on comparative student numbers. We were getting 34 percent. It was a terrible disadvantage — a $400-million shortfall that translated into a per-pupil expenditure of $5,100 a year in NYC, compared, say, with $7,950 in Westchester County.

Cuomo actually brought it up, but offhandedly, like it just popped into his head. "Oh, by the way, I saw that article in the paper about you suing the state. That might not be a bad idea. Let me call my legal people on it." As if he could hardly wait to help me sue him.

He picked up the phone and was able to make immediate contact with the legal people he wanted. How convenient for us both. He put us on conference call and asked for their "expert" opinion on my prospects of winning such a suit. Surprise, surprise. They didn't think I had a chance. They said, "Naw, it's no good, chancellor. You'll just waste an awful lot of time and money."

I looked at Cuomo. He was still being sympathetic. "Let's not give up that quickly, though, Joe. Let's explore it."

I said, "Sure, governor. Fine."

That ended the meeting, but as I was going down in the elevator with my people and a couple of Cuomo's staff members, I was still getting pitched to, low and inside. One of his deputies said: "Do you know what'll happen if you sue? It could take years. And then what will be the result? What will the legislature do with you?"

I smiled. "Same thing they're doing now. Screwing us."

I really couldn't blame Cuomo too much, though. He has to work with that opposition-dominated senate, and when funding is on the line, you won't find politicians in Rye or Yonkers or Syracuse all that eager to redistribute dollars to New York City. We had the same problem in Miami. It took a suit filed by a South Florida consortium to finally get more equitable state funding for Dade's schools.

Lawsuits are always a crap shoot, of course, but after a while it becomes a question of what do you have to lose? In New Jersey, Texas, and Virginia, they forced reapportionment by suing, so you have to believe there's a good chance of winning a case based on equity.

And even if you don't win, you can create enough of a nuisance for the governor and the legislature to make them at least want to trade the next time around. To be sure, they could get vindictive about it and say, "Nuts to New York City," but so what? That's already happening. And on the other hand, they could say, "Look, can't we work something out?"

The bipartisan Salerno Commission authorized by the state several years ago dealt with the whole issue of equity for NYC school funding and made a series of recommendations to phase it in. The report was accepted by both houses and the governor, but it's been sitting there for three years and nothing has been realized.

Nevertheless, it tells you a lot, and leaves the state open to some leading questions. Why, for example, would it commission a special body to investigate the fairness issue if it didn't think something was wrong? And why would it "accept" the report's recommendations if it wasn't prepared to act on them? For that matter, why would the recommendations be made at all?

So my advice to my friend the governor is to keep his lawyers near the telephone.

With the realization that in New York I was going to have to give as much time to battles over budgets and governance issues as to the implementing of programs came another, sadder reality: that my direct involvement in the schools themselves — the joy of popping unannounced into classrooms, of jawing with kids and parents and teachers, and seeing for myself how ideas and innovations were going down — those days were as good as over. Not over completely, certainly; I would never allow that. But sharply diminished. There just weren't enough hours in the day.

On my very first morning at 110 Livingston, after one of those blue-lip cold showers that recalled my youth in Harlem (except in this case it was due to only a *temporary* loss of hot water in the apartment Lily and I were renting), I had made it a point to schedule a visit to an elementary school in the South Bronx area, where a reasonable facsimile of School-Based Management was already in place. The visit was to be symbolic in two ways: demonstrating my support for SBM, and exhibiting my good intentions to *be out there* as a hands-on administrator. Plans for the visit were announced beforehand and the media were alerted.

But I knew it wouldn't be the same when I walked out of the office to get in the car and was confronted by a group of gays from ACT-UP picketing the school board on behalf of "safer sex." Then when I got out of the car at PS 41 and joined Sandy Feldman, the president of the teachers union, we were immediately flanked by a whole array of reporters and cameramen there to capture — in the time-honored way of New York City journalism — every word and every twitch. In Miami for the same occasion we would have drawn a token force. This was a standing army, with full ordnance, and it was to remain pretty much intact for everything I did on the outside from then on.

Oh, but don't get me wrong. I enjoyed it. I made the rounds of PS 41 that morning to the *click* of cameras and the *wrrrr* of videos, and generally made myself a willing photo opportunity, posing at the appropriate places and conducting interviews on the fly. I chatted with teachers (*click*) and hefted kindergartners for hugs (*wrrrr*), and got around behind the cafeteria line, where the school was serving free breakfasts to needy children through its Head Start program, and ladled out French toast and syrup (*click, wrrrr*).

The principal took me into a number of classrooms, where we joked with teachers and played with Lego blocks with preschoolers, and I had a couple of those wonderful Art Linkletter–type conversations you have only with guileless little children. One told me in a loud voice that his mother had had a "sleep-over party" New Year's eve, and the highlight of the weekend was when his cousin got drunk. Mama would have brained him.

But while I will always think it's important for the top man or woman in a school district to know the schools, and to visit and make a presence felt if only to show concern about what's going on, I knew that day and in the months that followed that those appearances would no longer be productive. As "media events" they'd be more showcase than showdown, and more hectic than informative, and it would be a long time before I could leap up from my desk at the spur of the moment, call out to my New York version of Joe Tekerman to "bring the car around," and go visiting the school of my choice unannounced — and unprepared for.

I was convinced of the change one morning in late January when I was driving down the West Side Highway and spotted graffiti all over the wall of an elementary school that I had previously complained to about the problem (with what Tekerman calls my "best $100 anti-graffiti sermon"). I called the principal on my car phone and read her the riot act. She waited patiently for me to calm down and then explained that faculty cars blocked the wall during the weekdays, with no other place to park, and she couldn't get the painters to come on weekends. She was waiting for a time when a work order could coincide with an empty parking lot.

I should have known, of course, and kept my mouth shut.

I also learned on those madcap occasions when I ventured out or opened up our program to scrutiny that the squadrons of media people, the beat guys and the columnists and the regular TV correspondents who had an ongoing interest in education, were sometimes more competitive than they were consistent; that although they were as important to us as anything in dispensing the word on what we were trying to get done, some of them would play by different ground rules than the editorial boards.

Some seemed to operate under a credo that said, "When in doubt, go for it," and if you don't get the story quite right today, recoup and cover your mistakes tomorrow. I didn't lose any sleep over it, but I was *trying* to be high profile, to cooperate as best I could, and when they latched on to something and took a little "creative license," *I* was the one left with the damage control.

What made it so wacky was that they seemed to believe that with all my early successes (and headline-grabbing *ex*cesses, as one regular critic complained) I must certainly be using New York as a springboard to something bigger and better, as if this weren't already the biggest, toughest job going.

One morning on the *Good Morning America* show I was into the last minute of a six-minute interview when the host, almost as an afterthought, and as the very last question, asked: "You're now chancellor of the New York City school system. Where do you go from here? Have you thought about Secretary of Education?"

What a question. There I was, with my toes barely over the line into all the things we had to do in New York, and I'm hit with a hypothetical about how my *next* goal might be education's most important assignment.

I tried to be realistic, and appreciative, without sounding stupid. I said, "Well, first of all the seat's not open. It's occupied by a good man. But I'd be lying if I said that a superintendent or a chancellor who thinks he can make a difference in education in America wouldn't be interested in that job."

The interview ended, and from the studio I went almost directly to City Hall for a press conference with the mayor on the city's program for summer jobs. A bunch of dignitaries were there, including Laurence Tisch of CBS, who was chairing the jobs committee. I was there to represent the schools. It was an upbeat occasion because the committee had lined up some fifty-two thousand jobs for the kids — not all at entry-level wages, either, and many that could be kept during the school year. The program, which also gave lessons in dress and work etiquette, had proven to be excellent dropout prevention.

So I arrived to make my little pitch, and Mayor Dinkins, who likes to ad-lib at the end of an introduction, said something like, "And now here's *Doct*or Joe Fernandez, our schools chancellor. You know how hard it is to get a doctor to make calls, but he's here, and he's a *true* mathematician. *I* know because I used to be a math teacher and I've had to deal with him on the budget."

I got up for my couple of minutes, and the others took their turns, and then Dinkins opened the floor for questions.

A reporter raised her hand. "This question's for the chancellor." I stood up, and she said, "I understand you're putting out feelers for the Secretary of Education job."

Tilt.

I said, "No, I'm not, but I think I can tell you how that got started." And I did.

And as soon as I finished, the mayor jumped up and said, "All right, let's just limit the questions to the subject at hand. I'm sure Dr. Fernandez will be happy to stay afterward if you want to talk with him."

I said, "OK, but for just a little while. I've got to get to other things."

Jim Vlasto was waiting for me on the way out. He said, "There's a bunch of reporters who want to talk to you about that Secretary of Education business. You oughta say something."

So I did, as precisely as I could, explaining what had happened.

And the next day in the *Post* the headline read: "Fernandez Puts Out Feelers for Secretary of Education." A total creation which, for the next two or three weeks, I had to keep responding to. Every appearance I made would climax in a question from the floor that was always some variety of: "Are you going to be Secretary of Education?"

Considering the seriousness of all we had going on, it turned out to be more a diversion than a distraction. More like comic relief. And I admit that in the quiet hours, when I could shove everything else out of my mind, I had fun doing mental gymnastics with the scenario. Like any educator with an idea or two, I have my own beliefs on how the federal government should involve itself in the public schools.

But by then we had a line of initiatives a mile long and more than 190 schools poised to take the plunge into our School-Based Management start-up. We also had a three-hundred-pound gorilla in the parlor: the growing budget crisis that had all of New York City in its thrall and made every other emergency shrink in significance.

And then, on the first day of July 1990, almost out of nowhere, a twist of fate that turned out to be the worst blow of all for me: a

wholesale revamping of the Board of Education. I knew that some
change was inevitable when Koch was voted out and Dinkins in as
mayor the previous November, but the degree of the face-lift, the
character of the new board's makeup, was completely unexpected, and
I didn't see it coming. A new board, to all intents and purposes, meant
a new boss. And one, collectively, that almost overnight changed my
outlook from being totally confident in our course and totally happy in
my work — to neither.

I don't mean to sound dire. I am still *mostly* confident (it comes
naturally), and not yet *un*happy, so the scene needs to be given a little
more lighting.

From that first day in January 1990, through the summer toward the
beginning of the next school year in September, my staff and I — with
the blessing and encouragement of the standing board headed up by
Bobby Wagner, Jr. — did the equivalent of at least three years' work. We
set up what every big-city school system needs for an operating base: (1)
a program component (all the things we planned to change or do), (2) a
legislative component (our road map for dealing with city hall and Albany), and (3) a budgetary component. To say that they so occupied our
time that our minds were clouded to what was looming in July — the
changing of the guard at the Board of Ed — is to understate the case.

Our people worked without time off, without taking vacations. We
waded through all those traumatic dismissals and cost-cutting measures that *we* initiated, then plunged into the realities of the city's
overwhelming budget woes as they were directed toward the school
system. We made our budget in January for the 1990–91 school year,
and despite all our own belt-tightening measures, we were asked by the
Dinkins administration to absorb another $20 million in cuts . . . and
then $60 million . . . and then $190 million. Not realizing that it was
only going to get worse, we went about the business of "making do."

We found ways to save jobs and essential services without drastically
curtailing programs. We worked to keep class sizes down and the
teaching force intact, even as we cut more than seven thousand employees, mostly in administration. The teachers, assistant principals,
and principals we lost were primarily those who were eligible for early
retirement. We made do with less money for latchkey programs, textbooks, special art and music teachers, and supplies. We got teachers to
agree to a pay deferral that saved $41 million. In other words, we did
our part, not thinking of being "appreciated" for it, although no department in the city acted with greater responsibility or dispatch.

And even with that, we were full speed ahead into reform. We began laying the groundwork for satellite schools and a number of other pilot programs, started planning for a multicultural curriculum and implementation of a newer, tougher math and science regimen, and began work on the system's first strategic plan. We put out feelers through the business and college communities for more liaison support and went for a broader involvement in human and social services and a better formula for satisfying the growing needs of special education (for the learning disabled). To set the tone for greater accountability in the workplace, we recommended tough new drug-testing requirements for all job applicants but are still waiting for the go-ahead.

The downside as we plowed along was the realization that the systemic rot was so many layers deep that we could scarcely get through a week without uncovering another scandal — and with it the accompanying bleak headlines. Coleman Genn had gone public with his personal disclosures on the corruption, and the Gill Commission announced its baleful findings, indicting the whole system as being rife with patronage and hiring abuses and out of control fiscally.

In the schools themselves, I was so appalled by the violence — my worst nightmares were never as bad as the reality — that we immediately began pioneering ways to relieve the scourge, even to having the city designate special subway "student" cars, with guards, like troop trains in a war zone, for providing safe passage to and from school.

So it wasn't as if I was asleep at the switch when the change came in July. I even tried beforehand to put a good face on it, thinking it might turn out OK. The board I had found so easy to work with, the board that had hired me, was top-heavy with whites, five in all — Wagner, Dr. Irene Impellizzeri of Brooklyn, Edward Sadowsky of Queens, Stephen Franse of the Bronx, James Regan of Staten Island — plus one Hispanic, Amalia Betanzos, and one black, Dr. Gwendolyn Baker. Each of the five borough presidents gets to appoint a board member, and the mayor names two. Koch had appointed Wagner and Betanzos. Dinkins, then the Manhattan borough president, had appointed Gwen Baker. The terms of all seven were up on June 30, 1990.

So a lot was made of the need beforehand for a more "representative" board — meaning one that better reflected the ethnic mosaic of the city. I agreed. What I *didn't* want, however, although I didn't say it, was a board so inexperienced that it would not appreciate the crucial dividing line between its job to make policy and the chancellor's to carry it out (crossing the line being verboten), and the chancellor's responsibility — and his alone — to handle personnel decisions. Or, just as bad, a board that had such a confusion of sociopolitical motives that internal bickering and strife would become a way of life — an *unacceptable* way of life.

Which, of course, is exactly what I got.

But during the honeymoon period — those three months of preparation and six months of heady, steady progress — I thought we had gotten far enough ahead to handle the inch-along, scratch-and-claw marriage that now followed. The outgoing board had gone through a lot, including four chancellors in four years. I was the fourth, and we were galvanized from the start for a conspicuous team effort that captivated the city and set the tone for future efforts. As it turned out, if we hadn't put down such a firm foundation, and if it had been my fate to deal with the present board from the start, I probably would have been driven out (or driven crazy) in a month.

There are no great mysteries to the New York City Board of Education's political base. It's as simple as knowing where the boroughs are and where the mayor lives. New York City and Buffalo are the only two school districts in the state that are not independent, and I suspect it would require more than a legislative act to change that. Most of the nation's school boards *are* independent — meaning they operate from their own financial base, with tax assessment privileges, and are usually accountable only to state auditors (and to the voters who elect them).

But all New York City's school funding flows through the mayor's office, including that which derives from the state, so even though I'd prefer we be independent, I can't imagine any mayor giving up jurisdiction over a $6.9 billion enterprise, so I haven't even suggested it (yet). And as board members are appointed, that means they are *all* political. Elected boards can be politicized, too, of course, but with an appointed board you have no illusions as to where the loyalties lie.

In this arrangement, the mayor has many advantages, not only because he gets to pick two board members, but because he deals from a position of strength in city affairs. He has cards to play (e.g., "OK, you want that fire station we took out of the budget for your borough? Give me so-and-so on the school board, and you'll get your fire station"). I don't say Koch or Dinkins has done this exactly, but that's the way it works. And it's probably as it should be, because the mayor has to oversee the entire budget, and the schools are a huge part of that. As the overseer it's his responsibility to have good schools — and to his credit when they *are* good.

The new board, with each member named for four years at part-timer salaries of $15,000 a year (the chairman gets an extra $5,000), was made up of two blacks, two Hispanics, and three whites — on the surface a good mix. But there were only two holdovers, Dr. Impellizzeri, a ten-year board veteran and former teacher on leave as dean of teacher education at Brooklyn College, and Dr. Gwen Baker, the national executive director of the YWCA, USA. Dinkins, her champion, described Baker as a "superb" board member just before lobbying the new board successfully for her election as its chairman — a mistake.

Bobby Wagner had been a very strong president. His agenda was my agenda, in terms of what had to be done in the school system. He did his homework about legislation, was persuasive, astute. As the son of a former popular mayor, he had political clout. Gwen Baker had good intentions, but she couldn't generate the support Bobby had.

And what should have been a warning light for both of us (Baker and me) was that the five who had never served on a school board before, with no clear understanding of the subtle differences between policy-making and administration, came on as if cooperative effort and support of the programs in place were farthest from their minds. They were a mismatch from the start.

Taken individually, and apart from the board, the five were good people. One-on-one I liked them all. The whole just happened to be less than the sum of the parts. They were:

Westina Matthews, Dinkins's second appointee, a vice president for corporate contributions and community affairs at Merrill Lynch and also a former teacher;

Ninfa Segarra, from the Bronx, a lawyer and staff attorney for a Puerto Rican group who had formerly served as executive director of the city's Voter Assistance Commission under Koch. She had been bounced by Dinkins from that job and was said to be still miffed by it;

Dr. Luis Reyes, from the borough of Manhattan, a part-time college professor who had to quit his position as executive director of Aspira, an advocacy group for Hispanic students, to come on the board because it would have been a conflict;

Carol Gresser, a Queens housewife and leader of a number of parent associations during the years she spent putting her four kids through the public schools;

And Michael Petrides, representing Staten Island, the only Republican on the board, an engineering professor and dean of administration at the College of Staten Island. Petrides at one point had all five of his kids in public schools. Now only Segarra still had children in the system.

Being green in the operation wouldn't necessarily be a negative, of course, if there was a breaking-in period to allow for getting used to the line of authority that divides the board's responsibilities from the administration's. Nothing can bog you down quicker, or frustrate you more, than board members breaching that line. I had a few who liked to attempt crossings in Miami, but that was an elected board that had pretty much been in place for years (long enough for one member, Holmes Braddock, to have a school named after him), and they all knew how to tap-dance over the rules without frazzling the superintendent.

From day one I realized that the new board in New York wasn't going to have that kind of sophistication. All the signs were there for a bad marriage: the way members structured meetings; the way they postured in front of the TV cameras at board headquarters; the endless memos and time-consuming demands they put on staff to chase down niggling requests for information (I finally had to step in on that one); and an abysmal lack of control by the president.

Traditionally, the board met every other Wednesday. This one sometimes met twice a week, because the meetings weren't run well and nothing was ever done with dispatch. That meant time away from other tasks for the staff, and for me a lot of wheel-spinning. We'd never get through an agenda because they'd bog down on one or two items. Important things kept getting shoved aside. I commissioned a study on the school environment, dealing mainly with school safety, and got back an excellent report that included a series of recommendations to be implemented immediately and over the next five years. But I was delayed putting the report on the table at least four times.

The frustrations inevitably led to conflicts. I wasn't shy about telling them when to back off, and they weren't shy about testing me. When board members crossed over the line, trying to extend their jurisdiction into administration, I'd yell "whoa!" and that would start a whole new round of arguments.

There was constant friction all around — not just between them and me, but among themselves. They were frequently at odds with each other. And when it was evident to the rest of the board that Gwen Baker couldn't possibly get reelected (the presidency is voted on every year), there was even some blatant maneuvering to get in position to be her successor. Members did things deliberately to embarrass her, which in turn embarrassed the mayor.

From a practical standpoint, the worst part for me was this intramural strife, because it meant that the board was divided on almost every issue. A split board is the absolute pits for a chancellor or superintendent. Any time you're dealing with a 4–3 vote to decide things (instead of a 6–1 or 7–0, indicating a unanimity of purpose), you know you won't have a clear-cut mandate, which means there'll be sniping and backbiting over everything, even *after* the vote. Progress will then move only in fits and jerks. A prime example: seven months after they'd come on, we still hadn't put through a strategic plan. Without a strategic plan you don't have the agenda you need for years ahead, the contingencies in place for coping with economic trends and social and legal issues. We set about getting it done *despite* the board.

In all fairness, it was a difficult time to be overseeing the New York City schools. Every problem was exacerbated by the budget cuts, which hit the new board as soon as it took over. There was pressure from the mayor's office, from the borough presidents, from the unions.

But when every open meeting is a civil war, the academic and systemic advances you initiate get lost in the sound and fury. Things like the condom flap occupy more time than they should. We took more heat in 1992 with our "Children of the Rainbow" multicultural curriculum, which included a small segment (two pages out of 443) dealing with tolerance of "non-traditional" (including homosexual) family structures. My supporting opinion was that if we're ever going to get this country together, we have to deal with such biases early, even in the first grade. The board didn't buck me on that one, but by then *not* being at odds was an occasion. We had had one clash after another.

So each meeting got a little worse, and as tends to happen when there's board conflict, frustrations get taken out on the administration and individual relationships break down. At one time or another, every board member gave me some personal grief. The first words out of one member's mouth — his very first day on the board — were to criticize me for neglecting parents in my education package. He didn't know what he was talking about. Later, another said that it was the *children* I was neglecting, of all things. In a private, heated moment, she said, "You're not a chancellor for the children, you're a chancellor for the teachers!"

I should have laughed out loud, but I saw red, and said, "If you think like that, you ought to make a motion to fire me right now!" And at that moment I wished she had. She probably did, too.

Petrides, of course, had a virtual mandate to make trouble, being the only Republican on the board. He's a smart, savvy guy, too, and personally I like him a lot, even though our politics don't mesh. But he had no real allegiance to the mayor, and as far as his party was concerned, the more contentious he could be the better. I began to think of him as the board gadfly.

Some board members probed for weak spots in the dividing line and at one point talked about getting the board involved in the selection of principals. I told them the minute they tried I'd take the board to court. By law, the chancellor appoints principals, for good reason: it's his job to run the schools, and putting the right principals in place is vital to that.

The two things the new board soon got very good at was going off half-cocked on issues and leaking their objections and prejudices to the press, usually before it made any sense even from their standpoint to do so. Sometimes in the process they would blunder all over a good idea.

When we were entertaining the proposal to institute the Ujaama Institute, aimed at turning dysfunctional young black males away from what is now a national pattern of self-destruction, we were just putting plans together when somebody in the mayor's office expressed her "concern" about the civil rights implications of a mandated one-sex, one-race school.

I said that was not the intention at all, that this was to be a strictly "choice" alternative school for failures and dropouts, worked out through family contracts. We had gotten permission to use Medgar Evers College as a base of support and housing, and we were talking up the idea to state legislators for possible funding and the Aaron Diamond Foundation for a half-million-dollar grant, which would mean that the district wouldn't have to pay start-up costs.

"But forget all that for now," I said. "This thing is still very much in the planning stages. We'll address the civil rights issues when we come to them, *before* we present the full proposal to the board for discussion and approval."

But when the idea was prematurely leaked, all of a sudden everybody was on our case, calling for information and blasting our intentions (or embracing them, depending on how much they knew). Some compared it with an ill-fated Milwaukee plan for all-black, all-male inner-city academies, which was in the news at the time.

So Luis Reyes insisted it be put on the agenda for a board meeting to deal with it "in the open."

I said it was much too soon for that. I said no one really knew our plan because we *had* no plan, just a three-page concept we were working from and some feelers we'd put out to see what could happen. A hearing on it now, I said, could kill the idea while it was aborning.

The Ujaama school was put on the meeting agenda anyway. The board dutifully battled over the plan that wasn't a plan, and though the feedback was generally positive, it led to one complication after another. The press whacked at it and the ACLU bullied in with threats. The idea sprang leaks and took on water, and all but sank in the furor.

Six months later we finally had a plan to show, with a new structure, but with less enthusiasm all around than there'd have been if the board had done what it should have in the first place: said, "Go ahead with your planning, and at the appropriate time we'll put it on the agenda and examine it." That's the accepted approach. Shape an idea, talk it around as best you can, then present it for approval.

When we were constructing parameters for "warrantying" our high school graduates — giving employers guarantees that if the graduates didn't measure up we would take them back for retraining — I had a number of discussions with key people, including the chairman of the New York Regents, Fred Salerno, and told some of the media that we were developing a strategy. In this case I wanted to get their reaction, too. It made the news. The board immediately got upset. A couple of them said, "Why do we have to read about this plan in the papers?"

I said, "It's not a plan yet. We have a concept. We're just testing the waters on it. Every time I get an idea are we going to have to call a meeting and say we're thinking about something?"

Gwen Baker, although one of my biggest supporters and a lady I genuinely like, told me at one point that she wanted the board's affirmative action officer to report directly to me.

"Why would you want that?" I asked.

"That's how we did it in Michigan."

"That might be what the president of Michigan State University wants," I said, "but that's not what I want. I have an organization. The affirmative action officer reports to the human resource person, who reports to me. I'm not going to have to deal with another direct report."

"Well, the board wants it that way."

"Since when does the board decide on my organizational structuring? My job description calls for *me* to decide."

(Ironically, I did exactly what Gwen suggested later when we decided to put more emphasis on affirmative action.)

The nit-picking that was causing unconscionable delays in our drive for reform infuriated Stan Litow. He estimated that by just answering the board's questions and requests and attending the various and sundry "emergency" meetings cost my top assistants seven or eight working days a month. I got into a much-publicized hissing contest with Ninfa Segarra over her passion for memos. She kept the line glutted from the board's offices on the eleventh floor at 110 Livingston to our offices on the tenth until I finally challenged her on it and got her to ease off. One of her queries contained thirty-five questions, many of which were well beyond the pale.

There was no doubt in my mind that it was an adversarial board, and I'd never had that before. I'd had *adversaries* on issues or positions, but never as an institutionalized opposition. Especially troubling was that our differences not only made headlines, embarrassing to us all, but seemed to be couched in what I could only interpret as mean-spiritedness, an almost vindictive attitude.

I thus found myself bristling over the least little thing and making remarks that I had never felt the urge to make. At one point, Segarra, who happens to be a very bright young lady and a diligent (if somewhat overzealous) advocate, was called a "political prostitute" because of her turn-around on the condom issue. I had to think, sadly, how far we'd come from our first meetings when I thought of her as an ally.

But as much as I chafed personally over these breakdowns, I knew the real damage was being done to the board itself — to its stature as a responsible, functioning body. It was becoming chronically factionalized, not just on issues but as a working group of human beings charged with making decisions for a vital public institution, one that fairly demands harmony and good will. The members weren't dumb to what was happening. Michael Petrides told the *Times*'s chief education writer, Joseph Berger, that there was "a significant lack of trust" among board members. Others privately said a whole lot worse.

There were cross-currents of disrespect. Board members complained that other members didn't show enough interest and missed too many meetings. Others griped that some were *too* conscientious and had made board membership a full-time job. There were times when members didn't speak to one another. Michael Petrides, the most persistent opponent of my condom distribution plan, was openly at odds with Westina Matthews after Matthews switched her support for a parent opt-out clause that the board tried to saddle me with. A last-minute telephone call from Dinkins to Matthews had apparently done the trick, and Petrides and other board members didn't let her forget it.

The facade — what there was left of it — began to peel away when Gwen Baker stepped down as chairman and resigned from the Board of Education in July 1991. I have no doubt she would have been defeated had she declared again for president, but I think that factor was secondary to her own unhappiness with the way her term had gone.

Gwen was more a victim than a cause. She wasn't effective, it's true, but her support from the mayor's office had been conspicuously lacking. She was never put into position to deliver anything, although she'd been a mayoral appointee, and her trying to sway the board to the mayor's viewpoint all the time hurt more than helped her when the city didn't bend on the budget. She thus was virtually no good to either side.

Baker and I often shared concern for what was happening. More than a few times she said to me, "I don't know how you stand this," meaning all the Machiavellian undercurrents and byplay. Gwen could relate to my position as chancellor because as executive director of the YWCA she also had to deal with an active board. She said, "How can you put up with being micromanaged all the time?" I said I didn't intend to.

Much of Ninfa Segarra's apparent bitterness surfaced when she was shunted aside in her bid for the board chairmanship after Baker quit. Segarra obviously wanted it badly and had the votes until Mayor Dinkins introduced Baker's replacement on the board, and *his* choice for president, H. Carl McCall. At that point the members (except for Petrides) turned against her. Segarra went from heir apparent to also-ran overnight.

McCall came on with excellent credentials — a Dartmouth graduate, a former minister who had made his mark as a statesman in Harlem politics, a vice president for governmental relations for Citibank — and a reputation as a dynamic conciliator. He also knew more than a little bit about pressure, being one of six children of a Boston welfare family. So I doubt it fazed him much when the board's vote on his chairmanship wasn't unanimous, even on the last ballot, when tradition calls for a token show of unanimity. Segarra and Petrides held out against him and then didn't stay afterward when photographers took pictures.

You could only wonder, then, how much conciliation McCall could achieve very quickly. Petrides and Segarra were probably two of the most magnetic members of the board, and in such a tenuous atmosphere, where a 4–3 vote often wins the day, they clearly were in a position to do a lot of damage (or good, depending on your point of view). But I have to say that Carl made a strong first impression, and in the eyes of one or two board members could thereafter do no wrong. He zeroed in immediately on what he correctly diagnosed as the biggest danger of all: the growing tension between the board and the chancellor.

Barely a month after he came on, in an effort to "clear the air," McCall took everybody on a retreat to a resort motel in Tarrytown, where we privately let our hair down and, afterward, publicly said all the right things about reconciliation. McCall called the "rumors" of our rift "misleading and exaggerated." *I* said I welcomed a "new beginning" and praised him for stepping smartly into the breach. And Nick Chiles of *Newsday* came right behind us in print to praise Carl for the best trick of all, a giddy new experience at 110 Livingston: a 10-minute board meeting! We *all* applauded that one.

Unfortunately, the good feelings didn't last long, partly because the animosity ran so deep and partly because of the one issue that kept crowding back into the picture, the issue that was probably the biggest factor in our alienation in the first place: my condom availability plan. Introduced on Gwen Baker's watch, it had gone through a rocky passage with the new board, despite strong supporting voices in the health community and the press. For unconvinced board members the decision could not be allowed to pass peacefully into compliance.

Some history is in order. The condom strategy first began to take shape when I was evaluating the system's in-place programs and discovered that the three-year-old HIV-AIDS Advisory Council had a very spotty game plan and was getting nowhere through the schools' mandated health curriculum. Some schools offered no AIDS awareness instruction at all, despite State Department of Education requirements.

So I got the Academy of Medicine, a reputable city organization, to do a pro bono review of our entire health program. Its report said our AIDS instruction was outdated, and so was the key element in it: the assumption that simply warning kids was good enough indoctrination against the plague. According to the available data, more and more teenagers were having sex, and more and more were coming down with the HIV virus. The estimates that shocked everybody were that 50 to 80 percent of our 261,000 high school students were sexually active and that as many as 29 percent of all AIDS patients in the city may have been infected in their teens. Preaching abstinence alone clearly wasn't working. Considering the numbers who were putting themselves at risk, there was compelling reason to go to step two: protection.

I met with members of the HIV-AIDS Advisory Council — as the first chancellor to do so, I think I surprised them; they'd pretty much been ignored for three years — and right in the middle of our meeting they asked if I would support making condoms available to high schoolers. I said I'd need a lot more information before I did that, but I'd try to help get it.

So in the following weeks we expanded the council to include a parent, a student, and at least one AIDS carrier. We gathered the data, and later, after I announced my intentions, held hearings. The testimony we got was awesome. I challenge anyone to listen to kids who have the AIDS virus or have lost friends or relatives to it without being profoundly moved. Their stories break your heart.

My course, I thought, was clear. The school system has a moral responsibility to its children. Its children were dying, and although many would die no matter what we did, if we did nothing the numbers could be apocalyptic. Somebody had to take a position of leadership, so why not the schools? At an open meeting, I advised the school board that I was going to come in with a "condom availability" plan.

Reaction was about what you'd expect if you compounded several times over the response you get when a dentist's drill strikes an exposed nerve. The media leaped at us with questions and tried to find out who on the board would be for it and who against. Some board members, I'm sure, were caught off guard. Gwen Baker had voted against even health clinics years before, but I think the logic in the need for action impressed her and when asked to comment, she said, "I have no problem with making condoms available. I think it's not a matter of whether we do it, but *how* we do it."

Ninfa Segarra said two of her relatives had died of AIDS, so she supported me "fully." Luis Reyes, although once a brother in the Catholic order, was in favor, and so was Westina Matthews. Michael Petrides, a Catholic, went ballistic in his opposition, as I thought he would. So did Irene Impellizzeri, who once voted against sex education in the schools. Carol Gresser, a suburban housewife in an all-white community, at first seemed persuaded, but then backed off a bit on the grounds that it wasn't a school's given function, so I didn't trust her vote.

At the very worst, however, we felt we had a 4–3 edge. An advantage, but not to rest easy on.

Across the city, arguments over the plan heated up as the ranks of the opposition rallied, primarily around the Catholic archdiocese and John Cardinal O'Connor. I'd hoped it would not become a "religious issue," or even a "right-or-wrong issue," just a "health crisis issue," but that was wishful thinking. The Catholic church (again, my church) has more to say about New York City's politics and policies than it should, and the only real outside voice that concerned me was O'Connor's.

Although many conservative groups, including the United Parents Association, came out in our favor, the church was adamantly opposed from the start and never wavered. It rallied its forces to a counter-attack, scheduling public hearings, conducting letter-writing campaigns, leading the charge on the school board. For five sessions in a row the only thing that got addressed at board meetings was the condoms issue as hit squads came in to challenge the sanity of what we were doing. Bishop Thomas Daily of Brooklyn called the plan "an affront to parents."

Ironically, they never mentioned the health question. It was always the "moral" question, or the "you're-taking-away-the-parents'-responsibility" question, or the "you're-going-to-make-the-kids-promiscuous" question.

The "abstinence first" question kept coming up, and I was sympathetic to that to an extent. But I explained that our curriculum had always stressed abstinence from premarital sex and while it would continue to, based on the "values" of the nuclear family unit and the Judeo-Christian ethic, the new program would also say that if you're going to take a chance outside of marriage, you had better be responsible — to yourself, to your loved ones — and use protection. But even then, not to be misled. Because like the condoms themselves, protection was not foolproof. It was still risky business.

Nevertheless, the personal attacks on me by opposing columnists and my friends on the lunatic fringe grew to almost comic proportions. I was a political cartoonist's dream: "King Condom Fernandez," sex-meister. One guy got up at a board meeting and accused me and the board of being Nazis, of promoting sterilization rather than AIDS prevention. I had people come up to me at breakfast in restaurants, wanting to argue the issue. One man stopped me going into my house in Brooklyn Heights. I said, "Call me at the office." He said, "I wanta talk to you *now*." We talked.

Opponents on the board, led by Michael Petrides, kept delaying the vote. At one point Petrides said we should wait until the war in the

Persian Gulf was over, although I never understood what the war had to do with it. Then, in executive session, Carol Gresser opened up the "parent opt-out" provision, a proposal to give parents the right to block their kids from the program with a signed note. It was the most formidable argument we had to contend with.

I objected on the grounds that it was dangerously impractical. We wouldn't get many kids among that 80 percent to admit to their moms and dads they were "doing it" in order to get approval. I said I could understand parents who would be loath to give their OK, and fully expected some to storm the schools and say, "I won't allow my kid to be involved in this." By the same token, we had to address the problem for what it was: a life-and-death matter. The parent opt-out clause got a full airing before it was finally voted down.

Meanwhile, outside support for the plan spread. The statewide AIDS Advisory Committee endorsed it unanimously. According to a *Newsweek* poll, more than 60 percent of the people of New York were in favor. We got Mayor Dinkins to endorse the plan, but we had to *go* get him. He didn't volunteer. The endorsement I was hoping for was Governor Cuomo's, to help me neutralize the church. Cuomo is also Catholic. But he never said a word.

The church, when it realized it was losing the public relations war (almost every editorial board in the city supported the condom plan), came at us from other angles, not always letting the facts stand in the way of its arguments. I got a letter from one Harvard Medical School professor complaining that he resented the "inappropriate use of my research." It was being contended that AIDS was primarily a disease of homosexuals and lesbians, and the professor's research showed that simply was not the case in New York City. The most endangered group we had was black teenagers, followed by Latinos. But *all* the figures were too sketchy to draw those kinds of conclusions. Much of the damage already done wouldn't even be known for five or ten years because of the prolonged incubation period.

We were warned, too, that we'd be wide open for lawsuits when condom users turned up HIV-positive or got girlfriends pregnant. Our attorneys, with pro bono advice from the New York Bar Association plus legal opinions from the city's corporate counsel, said that wasn't a legitimate concern. Our position would be that we weren't distributing condoms as medicine, but as a product, with no guarantees they would work beyond what the manufacturers promised — which was virtually nothing.

To spike still another potential risk, we ruled that while requiring each of the 124 high schools to come up with an implementation strategy, no teacher, parent, or administrator would be forced to take part in the program.

After months of delays, the board finally approved the HIV-AIDS program with the condom availability component in February 1991 — on the very day the war in the Persian Gulf ended. Petrides must have known something.

But that didn't end *our* war. Far from it. The abstinence issue came up again in May 1992, with a new twist and a new twister: Ninfa Segarra, of all people — the woman with relatives who had died of AIDS, the representative whose district included the South Bronx, home of the nation's highest percentage of AIDS infection and the highest teen pregnancy rate in the state. Segarra voted with the previous minority for a 4–3 turnabout to levy an impossible restriction on the curriculum: that every class, every lecture, every written lesson or videotape involving AIDS must henceforth include a greater emphasis on abstinence than on any other preventative measure.

In short, this would require a virtual overhaul of already-approved curriculum materials and sabotage much of what we had in place. The resolution stressing abstinence went so far as to include a "loyalty pledge" that visiting speakers or organizations providing material on the subject would have to sign, and banned a film that had been used in school systems — including some parochial schools — around the country since 1987.

I made a plea to stop it, literally begging the board — and Ninfa and Carol Gresser in particular — to change their minds about taking so drastic a backward step. They voted it in anyway, again incurring the wrath of the media. (*Newsday* called the action "craven, reprehensible and dumb." The board definitely was getting a reputation with the editorialists of New York City.) Once more the watch was on for pending litigation.

Dr. Impellizzeri and Petrides had already hired a lawyer and sued me in Staten Island Supreme Court on the opt-out provision, contending that I was taking away the rights of parents. Impellizzeri petitioned the State Department of Education on the abstinence issue. The New York ACLU, expressing outrage over the new restrictions, threatened to sue the board on civil rights violations. Other factions were said to be "reviewing their options." I even started thinking about suing. I wasn't sure whom, but certainly *some*body. *C'est la guerre.*

This "new" board is not new any more, of course, and as our differences mount, questions arise about what an ideal board of education should be, especially with so many other superintendents in other areas complaining about the same kind of spirit-numbing jurisdictional conflict. The National School Boards Association, in a study released in March 1992, found that micromanaging by boards — infringing on matters that weren't their business and trying to push their own private causes — had led to constant turmoil and a high turnover rate among superintendents everywhere. On the average, my colleagues around the country were quitting or being replaced after only three years on the job.

Nevertheless, and this may surprise you, I really have few set views as to the makeup of that ideal school board. Whether it should be elected, and for how long. Or if it is appointed, who should do the appointing. Or how big it should be, or how much time it should be required to work, or whether it should be *full*-time. Despite everything that's happened I think either an elected or an appointed board can work if the members are properly motivated to the task (making schools better) and clearly understand their role: setting policy, approving budgets, approving or disapproving collective bargaining.

I have no objection, either, in New York that each borough president is allowed to select a board member. If you have an able borough president, he or she should be able to make a good enough choice. I do think that a full-time board is *not* the answer. Board members would be even more inclined to infringe on administration.

Mayor Dinkins came up with a breathtakingly transparent plan to strengthen his influence over the NYC board, suggesting it be pushed to eleven members so that he could have six appointments (and therefore a majority) instead of two. I actually can sympathize with Dinkins on that. In effect, it's his city to run, and since it would be to his eternal credit to have good schools, it hardly seems likely that he would undermine his chances with inferior appointees. My objection would be to the unwieldiness of a board the size of a football team. We have enough trouble getting through meetings with seven.

I've been asked over and over why school boards seem to be in the news more than, say, a university board of trustees or any of those "boards of directors" of foundations and corporations. The difference, quite simply, is night and day. Boards of trustees oversee, but you never hear them telling college presidents how to run the history department. Trustees and corporate boards don't meet as often, don't get involved in the nitty-gritty, and are far less likely to be swayed by politics. And, to be frank, these boards are usually of a higher level of sophistication.

School boards tend to be composed of grass-roots people, often much younger than their counterparts on university or corporate boards, and although this can be a good thing, it sometimes creates problems because of the narrow focus of the membership. Individual members are often one-item provocateurs, especially when boards are formed out of conflict, which is generally the way it happens. Someone gets in because of an issue or a scandal, or during a budget crisis, or via a desegregation problem, or a bilingual program dispute — all issues of conflict. That's why school boards are inclined to be more combative than corporate boards, and why new school boards almost always come in with a reform agenda.

Too, the corporate board's mission is strikingly simple: the bottom line (profit) rules. With a school board, there are a hundred goals and everything gets diffused. You get advocates on school boards instead of conciliators, with their own distinctive ideas about where the schools should be going. If when they talk about school systems it sounds as if they're speaking in one tongue, they're not. You look at the makeup of most school boards and you find major disparities in motivation and beliefs. Different strokes for different folks.

In the end, what makes a good school board is what makes a good ruling body of any kind. Quality, not quantity or mechanisms.

What does that mean, "quality"? It means you should elect (or appoint) board members who are not parochial on the issues, who have the interest of the whole system at heart and are not hung up on "the busing question" or the "integration question" or whatever hot topic might be getting attention at the moment. It would be good that they have some experience in the role differences between policy and implementation, but I don't think they necessarily need a background in education or even need be college graduates. I *do* think they should have (or have had) kids in public schools. I have a hard time appreciating the viewpoint of a board member who, like the Chevy salesman driving a Cadillac, has his kids enrolled in private schools.

Strictly from the superintendent's perspective, of course, I know that when you've got a quality board that's with you and willing to take chances, any goal is achievable. The sky's the limit. If you can move any agenda quickly, reform is possible anywhere, and will happen. I had that in Miami, and at the beginning in New York.

A split board, on the other hand, leaves you struggling on almost every issue. With the ground constantly shifting, every step is tentative. It becomes almost impossible to remain neutral in a battle over an issue or a proposal, and with each side trying to draw you into its camp, it means that any issue the chancellor tries to push through will be a tough issue.

I can muster some sympathy for the argument that says, "Well, let's just do away with all school boards. There's so much corruption, so many ways for them to go bad, why bother?" The side of me that wants to make *all* the decisions for my schools says, "Yes!" But that, obviously, is *not* the best way to go. You have to have checks and balances. And the board system, as a proven arbiter of school policy, is still the best system. There are boards that work very well, the way they were intended, so why should they be penalized because of the ones that fail?

As for my deteriorated relationship with this particular board, I finally decided to quit worrying about it. You can't gauge your profession or base your life's work on job security.

But I admit that it makes for an uncomfortable way to live. You get up every morning and you go in, and you know sooner or later you'll be squabbling over something. I enjoy a good row as much as the next man, but that kind of negative expectation takes its toll.

For me, it's a confidence factor. I need a board that will be responsive to needs and sympathetic to change if I'm going to do what has to be done. One of the reasons I came to New York in the first place was that I got a good feeling from the board. I had a list of things I said had to happen if they were serious about reform, and Bobby Wagner signed off on it. I was brought in on a reform agenda, with School-Based Management as my flagship. I'm still not sure if the majority of the new board believes in SBM — or even understands it.

And if they decide to switch to a no-reform policy, which is in their province to do, I'm cooked. I can't turn on them and say, "I'm gonna sue you because you don't agree to my reforms." I can't fight it, legally or otherwise. All I can do is complain.

But I will say honestly that I wouldn't have come to New York if it was to work for the board I have now.

And even with all the support I've enjoyed — with the city and its leadership rallying behind me — I am fully aware that a single misstep or controversy can turn that around very quickly. The condom fiasco couldn't do it because if the board fired me over that there'd have been a civil war. But there'll be causes for which I won't have wide support, only my own convictions to fall back on, and that will leave me vulnerable.

So I have a doomsday scenario that I envision, whereby I get so angry, so distraught, or get the board so upset, that we decide mutually to end the marriage. The truth is that in a job like this you reach a point where it's time to move on anyway. You begin to sense it when the conflicts start going off in series, like exploding firecrackers, and then it's usually a matter of time before something drastic happens, and heads roll.

Then, of course, comes the *real* downside. Once more it is education itself that suffers. Programs get discredited, or watered down, or shunted aside. Initiatives fade. Discouragement sets in. That hasn't happened yet for me because, despite the aggravations, we are still achieving, and that final big bang hasn't occurred. But when it does, I'll be gone.

Meanwhile, what do we have to show for three years on the cutting edge in New York City? And what do we have to look forward to?

I think it not immodest to say that we accomplished much more than even our most avid supporters dared hope for — but probably not enough to suit the detractors, and definitely not enough to suit me. It would not be inaccurate to say that we are a lot closer to making the whole thing work — but still far enough away that no celebrations are yet in order.

What was wrong with New York's schools didn't happen in three years. The failings and breakdowns accumulated over the decades. It will take longer than three years to make them whole again. But what we have seen and what we have learned, I think, are not only encouraging for us in New York but could help light the way for every big-city school system in America. The record speaks volumes.

As this is being written:

• School-Based Management is now a reality in 240 New York City schools — almost one-quarter of the total — with many more on deck, making ours the most ambitious school restructuring program in the country. With their newfound flexibility to involve parents and teachers in budget and scheduling decisions, individual schools have come up with ways to reduce class sizes, provide more intensive instruction in areas targeted for need, taught parents better ways to help their children, expanded tutorial services — and at one school, even built a greenhouse for a new horticulture program. The results have so impressed the state that SBM start-ups will be mandatory in every school district in New York by 1996.

• School attendance in New York City is the best it has been in twenty-five years, at a citywide high of 86.5 percent and over 90 percent in the elementary schools. From the beginning we made this a high priority — phoning parents, visiting homes, finding schools for the homeless, etc. — because (1) you obviously can't teach kids who aren't there, (2) a child in school is less likely to wind up a burden on the community (or a threat to it), and (3) schools get more state funding ($22 million more my first year) when attendance percentages are up. We have even provided some reluctant attendees with free eyeglasses (they couldn't see to do the work) and free dental and cosmetic surgery (they stayed home because they were embarrassed by their teeth or the size of their noses) to get them back to school.

• The dropout rate has plummeted to an under 7 percent annual rate, the lowest in school history. Los Angeles, by comparison, had a 16 percent dropout rate and Chicago 13.2 percent when that figure — for the 1991 school year — was announced in 1992. Not many years ago New York's inclusive dropout rate from the eighth to the twelfth grade was more than 40 percent; today it's 17.2 percent. We rewrote the program to fit SBM and focused on the thirty-two high schools with the worst dropout problems a prevention plan we called Project Achieve. Each school developed a strategy to involve parents, students, and the community, and encouraged even the hardest cases to stick around. Many did, even if it meant graduating in five years instead of four, and even if it meant at the legal age limit of twenty-one. You can't imagine what a good thing that is for the kids. And for the job market. And for the country.

• Math scores systemwide increased 5 percent, the largest one-year gain in more than twenty years, and were the best overall in six years in 1991. More than 60 percent of New York students tested at or above grade level in math. Reading standings did not advance as impressively, but thirty of the thirty-two school districts had improved scores, and for the first time in three years more than 50 percent of the total student population was reading at or above the national average. As I said earlier, when the budget cuts finally worked their ill in 1992, the scores settled back throughout the system, but we were encouraged that the best results were attained across the board at SBM schools.

• A new multicultural education program, to be fully phased in by 1996, has been instituted to provide educational materials that in a multi-ethnic society will broaden an understanding of what we're *all* about. We are reviewing and rewriting curricula from K through 12 to reflect contributions of every group. The need is a national one, particularly in inner cities, but ours will not cater to a single minority (studies won't be "Afro-centric" or "Latino-centric") but will mark contributions made by all races and ethnicities. The change is long overdue.

• Bilingual education in New York's schools now reaches all but one percent of those students with limited English proficiency (LEPs), most of whom are newly enrolled immigrants or children receiving English-as-a-second-language instruction. At a time when many big cities are overwhelmed by immigrant problems, including having to cope with illiteracy and every form of social maladjustment, that's vitally important. The figure was over 12 percent when we first came on. What we found was that a lot of districts had made no effort to get these kids into programs and were shamefully insensitive to their needs. When you consider that more than 100,000 new immigrant students from 108 different countries enrolled in New York City schools in the last three years, you realize how dumb that was. We cracked down.

• Special education — delivering services to students with extraordinary physical and mental needs — has been taken out of what was virtually a legal gridlock (the program was so messed up the courts were preparing to take it over) and been reinvigorated. State funding has been freed up, and a new effort is being made to identify problems early so that so many kids *don't* wind up permanently diverted into "special ed." The key is early intervention. We start working with them the moment they put foot in a pre-kindergarten class, and extend the effort into our summer "super-start" programs. As a result we have been able to reduce the referral rate (those who are moved from general classes to special ed) from 7 to less than 3.5 percent in two years, a 50 percent reduction. That's not only important to the kids, it's important to the budget. Special ed classes cost almost three times as much as regular classes: a $16,000-a-year per-pupil expenditure.

• Incidents of violence and crime (including assault, robbery, use of "controlled substances," weapons possession, and sex offenses) have decreased overall, but not enough to make any of us in administration happy. Serious incidents peaked in the mid-'80s (5,233 in 1983–84) and were down to 3,843 in '91. That's still unacceptable. We have taken significant measures — those special subway cars, for example — but mainly await funding for a number of others we've sought, including additional safety officers, more conflict resolution and guidance classes, etc., etc. What we are pushing for more than anything else is a dozen more "alternative schools" where the incorrigibles — the kid who can't stay out of trouble, the kid who beats up a teacher or waves a gun in somebody's face — can be grouped (but *not* expelled or bounced from school to school) for more specialized, intensified counseling and training. Alternative schools work. We don't have enough.

As for those other "unique" initiatives that may or may not be original but we're pushing hard anyway, most are covered elsewhere in this book, but to sum up:

We have our first satellite school in operation — a school "at the workplace" for the convenience and peace of mind of working parents. We have more at the ready.

We pushed through the "warranties" on our high school graduates, guaranteeing employers who have signed onto the program that we will retrain — at night or on the weekends — those who prove to be academically or functionally deficient, providing they are allowed to stay on the job.

We are on schedule to have every school in the system School-Based Managed by 1995. To emphasize the difference the SBM schools make, we took an unprecedented step near the end of the '92 school year: we released the itemized school budgets of all thirty-two districts so that spending could be publicly scrutinized, results compared on a regular basis — and administrators and principals held accountable for their fiscal decisions.

We have taken the first steps toward extending the school day an hour and the school year by twenty-five days, first in middle schools and ultimately for the whole system, to help catch up educationally with our international competition. Don't let anyone kid you about this one. The whole country needs a longer school year.

We introduced the system's first "one-stop" school, Intermediate School 218 in Washington Heights, in a cooperative venture with the Children's Aid Society. The concept is one I am particularly excited about: a "community school" as the hub of the neighborhood. IS 218 will be open fifteen hours a day, six days a week, fifty-two weeks a year, for use not only by its eleven hundred students, but by parents and neighbors interested in adult studies, or needing medical or dental treatment or drug counseling, or just wanting to come around for the cultural and athletic events. My hope is that we'll have hundreds of such schools/centers before long.

We completed a plan, partially financed by the Aaron Diamond

Foundation, to create some thirty New Visions schools, embracing another pet prejudice of mine: school enrollment size as a key element in academic and social success. Each school will handle only five to seven hundred students at a time and will be financed through a melding of public funds and private grants. I am convinced that smaller enrollments (and smaller classroom sizes) are the answer for our high schools, where the sheer weight of numbers and anonymity exacerbate behavioral problems. We'll find out.

We have bolstered all facets of our community reach-out and coop ventures so that we now have an annual grant and gifting pipeline that provides more than $15 million a year. Numerous special services and programs, financed through consortiums with the business world and featuring concentrated teaching efforts, have already led to high schools being oriented completely toward specific fields. In New York, we now have schools of transportation, aviation, finance, tourism, and environmental studies (the latest).

We have put proposals in motion to reinforce our early childhood intervention strategies, to more quickly identify kids who are lagging so that they can be brought up to speed before getting too far along, and are expanding the curricula and the school year for middle school students to better prepare them for tougher new high school requirements for graduation. We have put together a broader plan for comprehensive computer technology to be used to teach basic skills in the earliest grades. Computers as learning tools have proven to be eminently cost-effective. Kids who achieve computer literacy early are way ahead of the game.

We launched a strategy to take math and science requirements from a two-year minimum to a three-year sequential curriculum by 1996, totally displacing dead-end consumer math (all those crip courses that teach kids how to make change behind the counter at McDonald's but little else) with academic math (algebra, geometry, trig-analyt, etc.) and upgrading all sciences to the laboratory level. That means that not only will our math scores rise, but we'll be sending graduates into the work force better prepared for a high-tech world. A big reason we have fallen so far behind in math and the sciences is the failure to update curricula and require courses that count. The rest of the industrialized world passed us by on this one years ago.

We introduced a pilot program that, if implemented, will lead to parents "grading" their children's schools systemwide, with their findings publicized *at the schools*, and the schools obliged to make improvements based on the findings. Getting parents involved is one reason I first pushed for this in Miami, but I also think it is more important than ever that schools — meaning the principals, teachers, and staff — be more responsive to the parents' concerns about how they're performing. Some of the targets I'd expect to get called down (and acted on): discourteous staffers, unresponsive teachers, unclean facilities, and disorderly classes.

We introduced a step-by-step strategy to restore the cultural programs that had been decimated by the budget cuts of the '70s, returning arts and music to the curriculum and creating a Chancellor's Art and Cultural Council to generate private funding.

We initiated a Library Power Project to restore or install libraries in every school, and got initial financial help from the DeWitt Wallace/ Reader's Digest Fund.

And on and on.

Beyond those things, I have a growing number of entries on my "gotta-try" list. Again, I don't claim originality. Some of the ideas have been batted around for years and make for lively breakfast-table talk at Great City Schools conventions, so I'm not sure whether my thinking has enhanced them or not. I do know they make sense and deserve a shot, not just in New York but across the country.

For sure we should already be into national testing and national standards (providing they do not lead to a rigid national curriculum). National tests, given at grades 3, 5, 8, and 11, would tell us where we are — wher*ever* we are — on a consistent basis. They would be infinitely more manageable (and decipherable) than the hodgepodge of examinations we give now. When everybody's in the same testing mode, there would be truer reporting on progress and no need for conversions or interpolations or educated guesses to make valid comparisons.

You hear arguments about the danger of teachers teaching "for the tests," but there's a flip side to that: is it so bad to be taught specific things that you're "supposed" to know? The real problem with a national test is in its language — making it as meaningful and fair to the daughter of the welfare mother in Hell's Kitchen as it is to the movie mogul's son in Beverly Hills. That has to be worked out, but I think it can be.

National standards are a little touchier. I think, for sure, we should have a standard that says, "All students who have completed the eighth grade should be able to perform at the following levels . . ." But I *don't* believe the standard should say, "In the eighth grade, every child must

use such-and-such a textbook for algebra 1." We should have the
standard to go by, but be given the freedom to reach it the best ways our
individual school districts can come up with. I know from experience
that some people will find better methods of doing things, and they
should be given a free hand to do so. My kids in New York, for example,
have a math game they're using that has proven very effective. If they
were limited by a national curriculum, I might not be able to sanction
that game.

Gradeless schools, like those piloted in some districts around the
country, deserve a trial run. In such a school students advance by
mastering subject matter instead of by grades, thereby minimizing the
psychological damage of being "held back" and at the same time end-
ing the farce of graduating without educating. I'd like to see the idea
tried in a variety of carefully chosen schools nationwide over a period
of years and then weigh the findings and make a judgment. What could
be the harm in at least trying as long as the students come out knowing
the material? In a gradeless school, that's the whole idea.

Opponents argue that in a classroom where kids are progressing at
different speeds — some fast, some slow, some "average" — chaos
would surely reign as harried teachers tried to cope. Years ago this
would have been a valid argument. But today we have the technology to
assist individual instruction: the computer at the student's desk, piped
in to the teacher's desk and on to the mainframe downtown to access his
records and progress. The same computer can also stop him from
advancing in a subject until he answers the questions correctly.

The logic that makes this so attractive is awesomely simple: the
student who does not know "unit 1" should not be allowed to go on to
"unit 2." That's exactly what most schools do today: pass their failures
on toward more failure. In subjects where learning is a progression of
building blocks — math, science, foreign languages, reading, writing
skills — it can be disastrous to advance a student to the next level if he
hasn't mastered the foundation or the row of blocks he's on. When you
do that, you risk having the pile collapse and producing that stereotypi-
cal high school senior who doesn't know four-times-five and reads with
his lips moving and his finger under the words.

One program, called "basic school," was started with kids in what
would be K through 3. Some "first-grade" students read at third-grade
level, and some in "third grade" read at "first-grade" level, but they
don't know that. They know they're moving along at their own rate of
speed. The teacher serves as facilitator.

Can the program be expanded into a K through 12 classroom environment? Cologne, Germany, has such a model that seems to be working, and although we're not close to going that far yet, it's something to think about. It would require more teachers and more paraprofessionals, but you could also use volunteers who *aren't* licensed teachers because much of the work would be assisting ("facilitating"), not teaching, and that would be a bonus, not a detriment. One of the things we've been trying to do for years is get more adults into the classrooms.

What else to try? I think within the context of the "community schools" idea, many things. It's time to think in terms of a whole new format, one that will eliminate forever the old "factory" model and replace it with the school of the twenty-first century. A school that would be open all day long, from early in the morning to late at night, not just for straight academics but as a place to interact in a positive way with the community at large and be a focal point for all kinds of innovations, including after-school activities for kids with working parents.

In short, a place not only for learning but a place for being.

Such a school is the antithesis of the model we now work with — that throwback to a time when the students' background was almost entirely Eurocentric and the school year was tied to the growing season, with time off in the summer for the harvest.

I'm not saying that kids should go to school full-time twelve months a year. Not at all. There has to be time off and vacation breaks. But almost every educator I know agrees that the customary 180-day school year is way too short. Even if you add thirty days of summer school that some students attend (in Miami, less than 50 percent; in New York, less than 20 percent), that's still only 210 days, which means that the schools are dark more than a third of every year, a terrible waste. In the information age, with high-tech advances putting unbelievable demands on the flexibility of curricula, American students simply need more classroom time. Their Japanese counterparts go 240 days-plus a year; Germans 220 or 230.

Our school year could easily run that extra month. A school day could go two or three more hours. There is no particular magic, either, in an 8:30-to-3 schedule. In many countries, the school day lasts until 5 o'clock. Japanese students attend school five full days a week and a half day on Saturday. Where there's a shortage of space, it would be easy for a school whose doors virtually never closed to revert to shifts, with some students coming in early and others after lunch, even as a way to accommodate outside jobs.

Would the kids like it? Probably not, at first. But there are ways to make an expanded schedule palatable and to make the school itself more "agreeable," including adopting elements of the "community school" concept. It would cost, of course. Additional utilities, custodial services, materials and supplies. Teachers would have to get paid more.

But every sampling I've seen tells me there's a national attitude for an expanded school day and year. Urban parents argue all the time for more after-school activities — more sports coaching, tutorials, and peer teaching; more drug counseling and outreach programs to deal with drugs; more crime-prevention programs and neighborhood-watch programs to interact with the police for making schools safer; more cooperative scheduling with the business community to help kids get jobs: more user-friendly programs geared to the community's ethos — its culture and life-style.

In New York I'm already pushing for funding to make that part of the next level of School-Based Management: creating schools that would be like cities in themselves, locked in partnership with all the appropriate local agencies to become places where serendipitous things are happening all the time. At these "super-schools," certain "teachers" might teach only an hour a day, but one would be a John Updike, giving insight into writing, or a William Simon, giving insight into government or finance. And kids who are truly interested in government would be given a chance to intern at city hall. And the best of the performing arts would be available on a regular basis in the auditorium. Such schools would be limited only by their enterprise and imagination.

In turn, I see the kids in these schools reaching out to the neighborhood with their own helping hands. One of my aims from the start for our NYC high schoolers has been to get them involved in community service, even as a requirement for graduation. To have them "give something back." I even got a $300,000 grant from the Surdna Foundation for a three-year pilot program to that end. The state of Maryland put together such a plan, requiring seventy-five hours of service work between the sixth grade and high school graduation as a way of combating what one Washington columnist called the "social illiteracy" of our young people. It deserves to be replicated, at least on a trial basis.

Would a greater community involvement do anything to curb the violence and fear that now sap the life from so many inner-city schools?

I think so, if you commit it to a constant vigil against the symptoms and influences. But no one thing will cure that particular sickness. No matter where the school is, to curb hostile, aberrational behavior you have to start at the source: with a code of conduct that the kids will know is ironclad, and the teachers will know *has* to be enforced, and then remind them of it over and over again.

Some teachers tend to start off "too nice," and when it comes time to tighten the reins, they can't do it. I learned early that in schools where discipline is a problem you have to come on tougher than you think necessary and then relax when and where you can. The first day of school you have to say, "This is the way it's going to be: here's my on-time policy, my homework policy, my seating policy. If you're tardy, you'll have to explain; if you're five minutes late, you'll have to stay after school." Assertive discipline has to be clear, consistent, and fair. Kids like structuring. They relate to it.

Second, you have to put in place at the school the kind of physical environment that is conducive to good conduct. Easier said than done? Sure, but that's one area where a community school would have a big advantage, being more attuned to its surroundings and under a closer neighborhood watch. A lot of things that happen aren't caused by the kids. We see it all the time. A young thug comes through an outside door, as one did recently at a school near Gracie Mansion, invades a classroom, and slashes a teacher's face. That kind of thing reflects the individual, not the school, and we have to find better ways not only to secure ourselves from it physically but to interact so that safe schools will be just as important to the people outside as they are to those inside. A point of pride.

But under no circumstances can you permit antisocial behavior and chronic trouble-making to disrupt a school. When kids do that, you have to say they have forfeited their right to be there. You have to move them out, not into the street, but into an alternative school (we have thirty-five in New York) where there are behavior-modification classes and counseling to deal with specific problems. One of the more effective of these programs is The Door, opened with private funding in Greenwich Village and used by the public school system since 1990. Its teachers are trained to work with the worst cases of maladjustment.

I went into one class at The Door where there were eleven kids and every one was on crack cocaine. From the outside, it sounded like a free-for-all, but when you went in you saw that they were "resolving" their inner turmoil in open discussion. I went into another class where counselors were working with the assimilation problems of immigrant kids, and another where Village artists were teaching kids who had been caught defacing buildings with graffiti how to rechannel their talent.

Meanwhile, we face an ongoing problem with how our schools are perceived through all this. I'm not pleased with the armed-camp aura you get when you walk into so many of our problem schools: guards and metal detectors everywhere, and walkie-talkies buzzing from floor to floor. Is this a school under control? Is this a *school?* For the time being, however, that's the hard reality of "coping." We had one site that had six hundred weapons "incidents" (assaults, confiscations, robberies) one year. In the fourteen schools where we beefed up security and put in metal detectors, the number went down 37 percent.

But the long-term answer to the violence is more than guards and metal detectors and padlocked doors and suspensions and expulsions. It's changing the atmosphere, and the attitude, of a place. I am committed in New York to putting together whole teams of qualified teachers and counselors to descend on troubled schools en masse to make that happen. Every school has its own special problems, of course. One might be in the throes of racial unrest, another might be into a perpetual student-faculty conflict. But what I found as a teacher and a principal in the inner city of Miami I'm finding in New York and everywhere else: you don't isolate a school from the community it serves if you want to turn it around. You make it a part, and let your "neighbors" help you make happen what all neighborhoods really want: their schools to be better.

The thrust of my thinking along these lines, obviously, is that the more willing we all are to give of ourselves, the better our schools will be. You'd be surprised how easy that position is to sell (once you realize that people *want* to buy it!). One of the things that blew my mind when I took the New York chancellorship was how quickly the cognoscenti rallied to the cause. Besides approximately $30 million in cold, hard cash from donations and in-kind services over the first two years, we got something I hadn't expected: an extraordinary willingness on the part of wealthy individuals to pitch in. The city's movers and shakers, stepping forward like a volunteer army, to contribute things you couldn't put a price tag on.

How do you measure, for example, the value of having Reuben Mark of Colgate-Palmolive providing his helicopter to get us up to Albany for lobbying purposes — and then lobbying for us. Or Ron

Lauder, the millionaire who ran for mayor, bringing in representatives from businesses all over the city to get them involved in the schools. Or Gay Talese, the New York writer, and Kitty Carlisle-Hart, the actress-author, and Tony Randall, the actor, pulling together a series of writing and performing workshops for teachers and students. They got three hundred writers and actors to take part, a terrific, exciting resource.

Eugene Lang started his "I Have a Dream" program in New York some years ago when he went back to his old elementary school in East Harlem to speak and wound up personally guaranteeing every kid in the sixth grade a college education if they finished high school. The son of Hungarian immigrants, Lang made his fortune spreading REFAC Technological Development Corporation around the world. When he asked the kids at PS 121 (the school Burt Lancaster attended) if they were planning on college, he was stunned to hear so many say they didn't have a chance. He gave them one.

Other New Yorkers joined in. Felix Rohatyn, the investment banker and chairman of Municipal Assistance Corporation, and his wife, Liz, adopted a class. The Steinberg brothers of Reliance Corporation adopted two classes and later created the Reliance Awards to honor teachers, principals, volunteers, and partners — at $10,000 a pop. Lang took the program to prominent people in other cities. In Washington, D.C., the Graham family, which owns the *Post*, and Jack Kent Cooke, who owns the Redskins, became "Dreamers." At last count, the program had 141 projects going in forty U.S. cities, reaching ten thousand disadvantaged students.

Joe and Carol Reich and Pfizer Pharmaceuticals took it to another level in New York City. Reich (pronounced, appropriately, "rich") was one of Eugene Lang's disciples. I met Reich after Lang had presented me the I Have a Dream Foundation's Genie award in Washington. Reich said he'd been mulling over something we'd been saying about early intervention being critical in turning inner-city kids around. He thought the sixth grade might be "too late" to get started. He said he wanted to take a group from the *first* grade. And not just one class but an *entire school*. He pledged $500,000 for initial funding and got Pfizer to donate a building in the Williamsburg section of Brooklyn, big enough for a K-through-8 elementary school. Pfizer agreed to lease the building for $1 a year and to make $500,000 worth of on-site improvements. You can't minimize the impact of such a gift.

What common thread ties all these people together? A love for New York City is part of it, sure. But greater than their loving it, I think, is their common desire to make it a better place and their determination that at the beating heart of any kind of revitalization is education. And education, of course, begins with the schools.

The economic psychology at work in this scenario is played out over and over again in cities throughout the country. When a city is hurting, its schools hurt — and vice versa. When a school system carries the stigma of being subpar, businesses have a harder time attracting quality people. The first thing management types ask about an area is "What are the schools like?" While good schools can raise the expectations (and the property values) of a neighborhood, chronically deteriorating schools lower them and often result in businesses pulling out. And when they do, it's not only the jobs that go, but the tax revenues. The decay quickens. It all ties together.

Where do parents fit into this? Against the weight of so many bewildering changes, and under the impact of so many political and fiscal pressures, they would seem farther out of the loop than ever. But I think not.

I submit to you that the role of parents in the public schools of America has been dramatically changed — but has never been more important.

Yes, the traditional "PTA Mom" is still needed: being a room mother, serving on fund-raising committees, helping out at the Valentine's Day dance, bringing in "PTA Pop" for Career Day. But there is a need now for a deeper, broader parental involvement, and it is an absolute must that the school systems of the country open their arms to let parents in, even to sharing the decision-making process (as we do at SBM schools). Not just because parents are more sophisticated than before and have a right to know, which they are and do, but because so many terribly complicated things are happening to our schools, and happening so fast, that they *need* to be part of it.

And I mean part of everything involving school operations: on advisory and ad hoc committees, in budgetary and curriculum discussions, in staffing decisions. Institutional school people get nervous when you say things like that — about putting parents into positions where they've never been. But we're not talking about friends of the court or the casually interested; we're talking about the fathers and mothers of the children who are being affected by all this. And I should also add that parents ought to be *demanding* such an involvement, and getting involved where they don't have to demand anything.

They should be lining up with reform-minded superintendents and chancellors, helping them get agendas through. They should be assisting school boards and helping to lobby legislatures. They should be a force at the ready for any crisis that comes along. In New York, we're trying to put all the parent organizations — there's a bunch of them — under one flag, the Citywide Parents Coalition, so that it can be a more effective lobbying and pressure group. The time is long past when institutions should be allowed to co-opt parents, rendering them mute and harmless and riding at the back of the bus.

Clearly we are at a juncture in the history of education in America where a greater involvement all around is crucial. We see the value of that brought home over and over in SBM schools — faculty and parents and students combining to forge change and the *spirit* of change. I had to smile. One SBM high school in the south Bronx is in a pocket of Hispanic (mostly Mexican) and Asian immigrants and has a mostly white faculty. To bridge the differences and promote harmony, the school's SBM cadre came up with an idea that charmed the whole community: they hired the students to teach the teachers Spanish. It worked so well that they're now going to do the same thing with the Vietnamese students. Serendipitous indeed.

Of course, if cooperative effort and harmonious intent were as prevalent in America as talk is about them, education's troubles would be over. But they're not. They're not because too often we are served by an entrenched bureaucracy that simply won't let go, and *dis*served by an incompetence in high places that relentlessly turns giving hands and goodwill away. The Reichs are a prime example. They went through torture trying to give us the school in Williamsburg in 1991, pitting their generosity and noble intentions against what Carol Reich called the "glueland" of District 14, and I feel compelled to pause here to tell that story because it makes the point so well.

As bad luck would have it, District 14 was run by a divided school board dominated by rabbis and headed up by a tough-talking superintendent the locals referred to as "John Wayne." This was the same superintendent who had put up a wall at one school to separate Hasidic children from others when it was ruled that they had to get bilingual training.

The Reichs were treated as if they were trying to steal a school instead of donate one. Negotiations begot more negotiations — or no negotiations. Finally, when the wheels began to turn, they were confronted by a slew of division heads and their staffs, raising objections about security, the size of classrooms, the size and number of windows, the height of the urinals, and all manner of potential "health hazards." Carol Reich said the real problem was that age-old deal-killer, "It's never been done."

In desperation, they came to me. I put Stan Litow on it, and we turned the project into an experimental "chancellor's school," independent of the local board. We put together what amounted to an SBM team of parents, teachers, and trustees, and moved to establish the Pfizer site as a bilingual satellite of a nearby high school. Instruction would be provided in both Spanish and English so that every student would come out bilingual, with classes beginning in September 1992 for kindergarten and first grade and the school to expand a grade a year into a model K–8.

But you learn not to hold your breath in New York. It had taken two years for the Reichs' gift horse just to get to the starting gate.

The one fact of life that is common to any reform that I know of is that in such circumstances you have to have the kind of impetus that makes the statement "We're going to keep banging away at this no matter how many barriers you throw up." And, with all due consideration for leaders everywhere, you have to have a catalyst in the captain's chair who is willing to stay on course no matter how discouraging it gets.

But no one person is the "system." I couldn't do what we do without people around me who are similarly dedicated. The climate for taking a chance, for taking risks, for going the extra mile is created by the man or woman with the baton, but it works because good people join in. Change is a process. Most people resist change, particularly dramatic change. Most people will take the path of least resistance, being comfortable with the status quo. But once you've got reform working, they can't stop it. They can slow it down, but they can't stop it.

We're at a point in New York now where reform sometimes gets staggered and shoved back for no good reason, the way the Reichs were in trying to give us a school, but we can never go all the way back. It's like what happened to the Soviet Union. The door opens, and you can't really shut it again. They couldn't rebuild the Berlin Wall now with *two* Russian armies.

But that isn't just a New York condition, it's a national condition, with the schools of America in the vortex of this thing called reform, for reasons both frightening and profound. As an educator, I'm especially sensitive to it. People see the crises we now face — the economic instability, the international tensions, the *national* malaise — and invariably look to the schools for a fix. "Education is the answer," they say, and point a finger at the schools and add, "Do it." They say this almost blithely, like it was an article of faith, without giving it a second thought.

A lot of my colleagues respond: "No way. We can't do everything."

But I say that all those politicians and commentators and columnists who lay this burden on us with such superficial conviction are dead right.

Given the resources, I think we *can* do all that's asked of us, and quickly. Why do I believe that? Because we've done it before, in a way. When sputnik put us on the defensive after the Korean War, we found our sciences lagging, and we looked to our schools. The federal government took us on as if it were a new war and pumped in the fuel. Schools were paid an unprecedented deference in terms of priority giving. Teachers were retrained across the country (even me, for a year at Penn State, paid for by a grant). Math teachers, biology teachers, physics teachers — they flocked back to school to bring American education back to the top. The lessons garnered were pounded home in high school classrooms from Seattle to Sarasota.

And it worked. In no time, we regained the lead in the space age.

You could argue that we're right back at that crucial make-or-break point in education in this country, except I have to think it's a whole lot more serious than a race to the moon. We've lost ground in every economic area, and at home we are especially traumatized.

The state labor department found in a study of the recent recession, when the ranks of the unemployed in New York City soared to more than 10 percent, that many jobs were left open because employers couldn't find skilled people to perform them. Positions went begging in everything from computer technology to pipe fitting. Thomas Nardone of the U.S. Bureau of Labor Statistics told *Newsday*: "You go out to talk to employers and you find they're not talking about a lack of bodies, they're talking about a lack of qualified people."

Make no mistake about it. Public education in America *can* be renewed. I know, I've been there, I'm there now. But there are limits to how much we can do *without* the resources, and as a closing, sobering thought, let me remind you that all change and all innovation — and any hope of achieving those goals President Bush so hopefully put up as a target for the year 2000 — must be weighed against one crushing factor: the unremitting crisis in school financing and the failure to see that crisis for the killer that it is.

Schools everywhere, and in New York City in particular as the case in point, are under siege for one abiding reason: they are grossly under-funded, and it is the shame of the nation.

In New York we have done what we have done against an oppressive tide of budget cuts: $250 million in fiscal year 1991, $475 million in '92. We have had to sacrifice in the process more than forty-five hundred veteran (and relatively high-paid) teachers and more than two hundred principals to early-retirement plans so that we could still afford to have *somebody* in the classroom. But instruction suffered, and class sizes ballooned, adding to the burden of the teachers we had left, and supplies and maintenance needs went unanswered, and almost on a regular basis I found myself threatening suit against somebody — the city for funds that weren't delivered, the state for the fair share we don't get — just to get us through another budget period.

So I add as a fleeting call for reason an innovation or two that ought to top the list of things worth trying:

A "Marshall Plan" for schools nationwide to fund reform, not just to bring our schools back to parity with the schools of our free world competitors, but back in line with our own historic respect for the redeeming power of education.

Such a plan should include whatever new tax initiatives and fair-share formulas we can come up with that might be agreed on, together with a wholesale restructuring of where the money goes and why. I would target those moneys first toward the inner-city schools, to break the pattern of despair and failure at those lowest and most volatile levels. It is positively scandalous that the vaunted Head Start program, clearly a must for bringing the poor and deprived back into the educational mainstream, reaches so few children. There are scores of other programs that go begging, and no relief is in sight.

But, ah, where to go for the *big* money? I have or have heard a hundred ideas, but let me just give you one as a closer: a national sales tax, specifically and unequivocally earmarked for education. Not a big tax, either. Say one percent.

But, money going *only* to education.

Money from the federal government, which up to now has only talked a good game. The $9 billion the feds budget for the schools is a cruel joke compared with the multibillions it spends for all the mistakes it makes (the savings and loan bailout) and the adventures it takes (the war in the Gulf).

So if I had the ear of the President and the vote of the Congress, I'd come right out and say it: "We're going to war against the deficiencies in our schools. Our illiteracy, our wholesale decline in performance, our inability to keep up internationally. And we're going to do it by the least painful means we can think of: we're going to levy a federal sales tax of one cent on the dollar."

And I would guarantee, at the threat of some awful, life-altering penalty for anyone who dares try to divert it, that the money will not be supplanted in any way by politics, the way it always happens when there's an outlay tagged "exclusively" for education. A one percent sales tax would generate $53 billion if it were treated as a value-added tax (excluding food, housing, and medical care) and come wonderfully close to funding every plan I've mentioned up till now. And it is my experience that the American people would buy the idea in a minute.

The American people will sacrifice for education, first out of a deep-rooted appreciation for its saving power, but also out of a love for their children — and other people's children as well. In Miami they sacrificed in a big way, and in New York they're sacrificing now (and will have to again). I think they'd buy it just as quickly everywhere else, given the proper promotion.

It's an idea. And I'd say that the one thing you must *always* do with a good idea is to try it. You'll hate yourself in the morning if you don't, and with any luck you might make education in America a little better if you do. It seems to work that way for me.

Index

Aaron Diamond Foundation, 240, 255
Abdur-Rahman, Amina, 214
Abraham Lincoln Club, 29, 49
absenteeism, 2, 69
Academy of Finance, New York, 22
Academy of Medicine, New York, 244
accountability, 148, 206, 221, 235
ACT-UP, 230
adult education programs, 66, 91
affirmative action, 241
after-school activities, 259, 260
AIDS, 4, 10, 244–245, 246, 248. *See also* condom availability plan
AIDS Advisory Committee, New York, 247
Air Force, U.S., 27, 29, 44, 45–52, 173
alcohol, 2, 39
Alexander, Lamar, 6, 81–82
Allgood, Cleophus, 97
all-male/all female academies. *See* single-sex schools
American Bankers Insurance Group, 17, 161, 162, 176
American Can Company, 176
American Civil Liberties Union, 81, 241, 248
Annunciation Boys School, 26, 31, 36, 37
Arnold, Burt, 185
athletic programs, 88, 103
Atlas, Helaine, 202, 203
Attendance Boundary Committees (ABCs), 116–118, 119, 120, 121, 122, 130, 138

Baker, Gwendolyn, 235, 237, 238, 241, 243, 244, 245
Baltimore, MD, 82
Bank Street College, 218

Barber, Rudy, 101
Barnes, Solomon, 122–123, 126
Barnwell, Matthew, 201–202, 216
Barry College, 121
"basic school" programs, 258–259
beacon schools, 10
Becker, Larry, 209, 214
Beckner, Wayne, 185
behavior-modification programs, 261–262
Bell, Paul, 139, 141, 166–167
Bell, Terrel, 5
Berger, Joseph, 242
Bermudez, Bobo, 33
Betanzos, Amalia, 235
bilingual education, 11–12, 147, 254, 265–266
Bishop DuBois High School, 27, 31, 37, 38, 39, 63
black(s), 80–81, 133
   militancy, 86, 131–132, 218
   teachers, administrators, 79–80, 130
B'nai B'rith Award, 140
Board of Education, New York City, 188, 189, 195
   affirmative action and, 241
   budget, 239
   /chancellor relations, 244, 251–252
   condom issue and, 242, 244, 245–248
   reform of, 212–213, 234, 235–242, 249–250
   SBM and, 251
   selection of principals, 240
Board of Examiners, New York, 14, 197, 198, 201, 206, 224–230
Booker T. Washington High School, 116
Boston, MA, 11

boundary change issue, 115, 117, 118,
    119, 121, 129
Bower, Mattie, 116
Boys & Girls High School, 38, 81, 220
Braddock, Holmes, 115, 119, 129, 138,
    171, 178, 194, 238
Brandt, Nora, 155
Britton, Leonard, 90, 108, 112–113, 115,
    122, 125, 127, 128, 130, 136, 139,
    172, 177
    appoints J.F. deputy, 137–138, 150
    opposes SBM program, 134–135
Bromir, Alex, 152, 185
Buckley, Father, 27, 37
Bush, George, 3, 5, 7–8, 267
Bush, Jeb, 12
business community, 79
    /school relations, 21, 22, 60, 109, 113,
        130, 133, 160, 168, 256, 263–264
    See also satellite schools
busing, 72–73, 74, 121
    in Miami schools, 85, 86, 89, 115–116,
        117–118

California, 2, 3, 11, 74, 107
career-awareness programs, 58–59, 60
Carlisle-Hart, Kitty, 263
Carr, Frank, 201
Carson, Sonny, 218
Carter, Jimmy, 125
Castor, Betty, 224
Catholic church, 15, 36, 182, 246, 247. *See
    also* parochial schools
Cavicchia, Gida, 222, 224
Cejas, Paul, 130, 137, 138, 139, 140, 171
Central High School, 98–99, 102
    J.F. as principal, 71, 93–94, 102, 109,
        185, 219
    security, 99–100, 103–104
    violence and conduct problems, 86, 93–
        95, 96, 97, 99, 104
Cerra, Tom, 152, 170, 174
certification, alternative, 175
Chancellor's Art and Cultural Council, 257
Chancellor's School, 22
chancellor's school project, 266
Chandler-Goddard, Barbara, 204, 216
Chapman Elementary School, 156–157
Chapter I program, 17, 110, 113, 123, 124
Chasen, Audrey, 75
Chicago, IL, 2, 71, 76, 215, 253
child care, 16–17
"Children of the Rainbow" curriculum,
    239
Children's Aid Society, 255
Chiles, Nick, 244
choice in education, 8, 9–10, 59–60, 240

Citrus Grove Junior High School, 142
Citywide Parents Coalition, 265
civil rights, 81, 156, 240, 248
Clapp, Gene (Choo-Choo), 101
Clark, Joe, 220
Classroom Teachers Association, 64, 91
cocaine, 5, 19, 42, 261
Coconut Grove Elementary School, 143
Coleman, John, 43, 44
College Assistance Program (CAP), 178
college education, 58
Columbia University, 26, 31, 52–53
Commerce High School, 27, 39, 40, 42,
    43, 45, 69
community
    service programs, 178, 260
    /school relations, 22, 89, 98, 259, 260–
        261, 262, 264
    schools, 74, 113, 255, 259, 260
    violence and, 76–77
    See also business community
competition, 8, 133
compulsory education, 56–57, 71
Computer Assistance School Allocation
    System (CASAS), 150
computer technology, 59, 60, 256, 258
condom availability plan, 4, 15, 242, 244,
    245–248, 251
conduct codes, 98, 261
Coney, Jim, 214
conflict resolution, 2–3, 34, 110, 133
Cooke, Jack Kent, 263
cooperative learning models, 67–68
Coral Gables High School, 65
Coral Park High School, 62, 63–64, 65,
    66, 67–68, 83, 90–91, 93
Coral Reef Elementary School, 117
Corridor Plan, 168
Council of Great City Schools, 6, 188
Council of Supervisors and Administrators
    (CSA), 219
    building tenure issue and, 220–224
Craig, Barry, 194
crime-watch programs, 169
Cuomo, Mario, 18–19, 190–191, 224,
    228–229, 247
curricula, 2–3, 4, 239, 256–257
    cluster programs, 67–68
    flexibility of, 259–260
    multicultural, 80, 235, 253–254
    national, 257, 258
    public vs. private schools, 38
Cutler, Brent, 202–203

Dade Academy of the Teaching Arts, 179
Dade County Parks and Recreation
    Department, 55

Dade County Public School System, 12,
107
  bond issue, 12, 14, 22, 116, 140, 163,
    181–183, 195
  budgets, 10, 11, 150–151, 156
  directors, 145–146, 152
  dropout rate, 102, 157, 162
  funding, 10, 13, 229
  J.F. as assistant superintendent, 109, 171
  J.F. as superintendent, 104, 139, 141–
    146, 185, 187
  integration, 68–69, 70
  salaries, 23, 61, 66, 90–91, 92, 104, 145,
    160, 177, 186, 187
  strategic plan, 114–115
  superintendents, 165–166, 215
  teacher exchange program, 68–71
  transportation department, 136–137
  violence and drug problems, 97, 108,
    131–132
Dade County School Administrators
  Association, 91
Dade County School Board, 154, 167, 189,
  194
Dade Partners program, 113, 130, 138,
  160
Daily, Bishop Thomas, 246
Dallas, TX, 1
DeChurch, Joe, 127, 128, 129
Department of Community Affairs, 109
Department of Education, New York, 244,
  248
Department of Education, U.S., 10
desegregation, 72, 86, 115, 116, 121
Detroit, MI, 71, 81–82
DeWitt Wallace/Reader's Digest Fund, 257
Dinkins, David, 24, 105, 193, 196, 228,
  233, 234
  Board of Education and, 237, 243, 249
  condom issue and, 19, 247
  school funding and, 190–191, 236
  school security and, 76
discipline
  assertive, 261
  corporal punishment, 38–39, 101–102
  of principals and administrators, 129–
    130
  public school vs. private school, 38–39
Donovan, James, 225–227
Door, The, 261–262
Doral Industrial Park, 162
Downing, Frank, 66
dress codes, 36–38
Drew Elementary School, 155, 177–178
Dreyfuss, Gerald, 134, 135, 150, 151, 152,
  166
dropout prevention programs, 60

dropouts/dropout rates
  black, 80, 81
  ethnic, 12
  foreign, 57
  inner-city school, 69
  Miami, 102, 157, 162
  night school for, 155
  New York, 14, 190, 253
  U.S., 36
drug testing, 235
drug(s), 2, 5, 40–42
  awareness programs, 34
  deaths, 41
  gangs and, 34
  in inner-city schools, 69
  J.F.'s use of, 34, 39–40, 42–43, 46
  legalization, 39, 42
  pre-employment testing, 21
  substance abuse programs, 3–4, 42
Duran, Bobby, 33
dysfunctional families, 5

Eastern District High School, 216, 217,
  218
Edison High School, 119, 120
Edison Project, 9
Edouard, Luc, 205
England, 7, 57
Essential Schools, 149
extortion, 2, 19

F.C. Martin School, 117
Feinberg, Rosie, 177
Feldman, Lawrence, 156
Feldman, Sandra, 168, 230
Fernandez, Angela (J.F.'s mother), 25, 28,
  29, 35–36, 45, 55, 140
Fernandez, Angie, 29, 36, 55–56
Fernandez, Joe (J.F.'s father), 25, 28, 29,
  35–36, 45, 49, 55, 140
Fernandez, Kami, 56, 61
Fernandez, Keith, 31, 54, 56, 61, 83
Fernandez, Kevin, 56, 61, 83
Fernandez, Kristin, 56, 61, 83
Fernandez, Lily (née Pons), 35, 41, 44, 61,
  83
  dates, marries J.F., 25, 33, 45, 47, 51, 52
  life with J.F. in Miami, 24, 54, 104–105,
    187, 192, 195
  life with J.F. in New York, 52, 54
Fienberg-Fisher Elementary School, 180
Finley, Sonny, 33
Finnerty, John, 55, 56
Florida, 107, 145. *See also* Dade County
  listings, Miami *listings*
Florida Atlantic University, 66
Florida International University, 184

Franse, Stephen, 235
Frates, Bill, 124, 125
Fuller, Fred, 64
funding, 13, 22, 256
  caps, 116
  construction, 8–9
  federal, 6–7, 9, 10–11, 179, 268
  foundation grants, 179, 267
  local, 7
  private, 256, 257
  state, 7, 9, 179, 228, 229, 254
Future Educators of America, 179

gangs, 2, 27, 32–34
Gary, Howard, 182
Genn, Coleman, 201, 203, 209, 235
George Washington High School, 190
Germany, 7, 57, 103, 259
GI Bill of Rights, 52, 54, 55, 57
Gill Commission, 235
Goodman, Roy, 227
government, federal, 42, 233
  school funding, 6–7, 9, 10–11, 179, 268
government, local, 7
government, state, school funding, 7, 9,
    179, 228, 229, 254
grade configuration changes, 121
gradeless schools, 258
graffiti, 142–143, 144, 198, 199, 231, 262
Grant, Corina, 205
Green, Richard, 177, 191, 192, 201
Green, William, 201–202, 216
Greer, Tee, 141, 167
Gresser, Carol, 237, 245, 247, 248
Griep, Marvin, 85, 88, 92
Gross, Sonny, 116
guns and weapons, 2, 3, 35, 76. *See also*
    security; violence

Hall, Joe, 90, 91
Hammer, M.C., 126
Harlem/Spanish Harlem, 26–27, 35, 56,
    186
Head Start, 7, 231, 268
health programs, 3
Hellenbrand, Lenny, 214
Herbert, Bob, 221
Hernandez, Sonya, 180
heroin, 34, 39, 40, 42–43, 46
Hialeah High School, 155, 157
Hialeah–Miami Lakes High School, 71,
    85–87, 88, 89
Hinds, Dick, 170, 174
Hines, Vinny, 87, 88
HIV-AIDS Advisory Council, New York,
    244, 245
Hochstein, Robert, 191

Holland, Spencer H., 82
Homestead Air Force Base, 66
Horace Mann Junior High School, 120–
    121, 155
Hufstedler, Shirley, 125

IBM, 22, 168, 203
I Have a Dream Foundation, 263
Illinois, 73, 74
illiteracy, 254
immigrants/refugees, 11–12, 107, 133,
    254
  in Miami schools, 11, 107–108, 158,
    162–163
Impellizzeri, Irene, 235, 237, 245, 248
inner-city living, 32, 35, 77–78
inner-city schools, 7, 9, 39, 69, 95–96, 268
  single-sex, 81–82, 240
  violence, 69, 71, 75–77, 80, 103, 260–
    261
integration
  faculty, 68–69, 70
  school, 71–72, 73, 74, 89, 207
interdisciplinary teaching, 68
Interface, 213
Intermediate School 218, 255
International Union of Operating
    Engineers (I.U.O.E.), 199, 200
interracial dating, 86

Japan, 7, 36, 47, 48, 259
Johnson, Felton (Buddy), 203
Jones, Dick, 56
Jones, Johnny, 85, 86, 91, 92, 104
  desegregation plan, 115–116
  scandal surrounding, 108, 122–127,
    129, 131, 137, 184–185
  as superintendent of Dade County
    schools, 109–111, 112–114, 170
Jones, Mattie, 125

Killian High School, 155
kindergarten, 72, 89
King, Rodney, 131
Kingsborough City College, 17
Koch, Ed, 20, 105, 193, 195, 198, 234, 236
Korea, 49–51
Kostyra, Connie, 196, 217, 228
Kowski, Father, 38–39
Krop, Mickey, 137, 171, 194, 195
Kunstler, William, 206

labor relations, 128, 174–175. *See also*
    Council of Supervisors and
    Administrators (CSA); United
    Teachers of Dade County
Landon, Kirk, 161

Lang, Eugene, 178, 263
language programs, 155, 156–157. *See also* bilingual education
latchkey children, 16, 234
Lauder, Ron, 262–263
Lawrence, Matt, 100–101, 103, 104
lawsuits, 208, 218–219, 228–229
    condom issue and, 247, 248
leadership, 5, 77, 129, 165, 166, 197, 214–215
Leadership Experience Opportunity (LEO), 173, 179
LeMay, Curtis, 51–52
Lennar Builders, 162
Levy, Sidney Meyer, 53–54
Library Power Project, 257
Lilly, Levander, 204, 205
Litow, Stan, 192–193, 195, 196, 212, 213, 242, 266
Little River Elementary School, 158–160
Los Angeles, CA, 71, 76, 131, 215, 253

McAliley, Janet, 115, 137, 154, 171, 172
McAllister, Red, 124
MacArthur North High School, 96
MacArthur South High School, 122
McCall, H. Carl, 16, 243–244
McCann, Gene, 31, 39, 41
McCarthy hearings, 49
magnet schools, 73, 102, 120, 155
Majors, Father, 98
Manhattanville Neighborhood Center, 43
marijuana, 39–40
Marino, Ralph, 227
Mark, Reuben, 262
Matthews, Westina, 237, 242, 245
Medgar Evers College, 82, 240
media, 97, 131
    Miami, 184, 194
    New York, 184, 194, 211, 213, 221, 222, 230, 231–232, 248
Miami Beach protests, 116
Miami-Dade Community College, 161
Miami High School, 66, 91
Miami International Airport, 161
Miami school system. *See* Dade County Public School System
Miami Shores Elementary School, 119–120
Michigan, 74
Mickens, Frank, 38, 220
Miller, Mel, 198, 226
Miller, Phyllis, 90
Milwaukee, WI, 82, 240
Mitchell Air Force Base, 51–52
modular scheduling, 68
Montessori schools, 119

Moore, Ian, 75
Moore, Steve, 101
Moralez, Al, 29, 54
Moralez, Hugo, 29
murder and killing, 35, 75, 76, 80, 82–83

NAACP, 77
Nardone, Thomas, 267
National Defense Loans, 57
National Organization for Women, 81
National Science Foundation, 57, 83
National School Boards Association, 73, 249
National Teachers Examinations, 225
national testing and standards, 257–258
Nation at Risk, A, 5, 132–133
Nautilus Junior High School, 155
neighborhoods. *See* community
New Jersey, 74
Newmeyer, Jim, 64, 65, 66–67, 93
New Visions schools, 190, 256
New York, NY, 4, 5, 11, 13, 75, 77, 223, 233
New York City Public School System, 5, 21, 209–210
    academic statistics, 189–190
    attendance, 253
    budget, 10, 19–20, 21, 230
    building tenure policy, 14, 197–198, 201–202, 206, 219, 220–224
    corruption, 189, 199–206, 235
    custodians, 198–200
    decentralization, 169, 188, 200–201, 206, 207
    districts/district boards, 200, 201, 203–204, 205, 207, 209
    dropout rates, 14, 190, 253
    funding, 10, 18, 169, 190–191, 228–230, 236, 253, 254, 267–268
    health curriculum, 244
    J.F. as chancellor, 187, 188–189, 193, 207–208, 212, 235–236
    monitoring strategy, 207–208
    personnel policy, 213–217, 219
    politics, 188
    racial divisions, 203
    reforms, 14, 17, 227, 266–267
    salaries, 160, 175, 198–199, 225
    strategic plan, 214, 235
    tenure policy. *See* building tenure policy
    violence, 71, 75–76, 78–79, 235, 254–255
New York City teachers union. *See* United Federation of Teachers (UFT)
New York state, 73
night school, 155, 157

North Miami Elementary School, 183
Northwestern High School, 69–71
Novas, Joe, 87, 88
Nynex Corporation, 21

O'Brien, Gavin, 91, 92, 93, 108, 109, 112, 174
O'Connor, John Cardinal, 246
Office of Legislative and Labor Relations, Miami, 91
Office of Special Investigations (OSI), 47, 48
Olkes, Alan, 137
"one-stop" schools, 255
Overtown, Miami, 107, 115–116, 131

Page, Ralph, 123
Palermo, George, 202, 203
Palmetto Elementary School, 155, 156
Palmetto High School, 84–85
parent(s)
    advisory boards, 98
    community report cards for, 178
    grading of schools by, 256–257
    involvement in SBM schools, 149, 155, 252
    involvement in schools, 9, 38, 109, 119, 120, 133, 256–257, 264–265
    volunteer work, 9
Paret, Gerard M., 205
parochial schools, 8, 36–39, 81, 248
Peace Corps, 175–176
Pennsylvania State University, 57, 83–84, 267
Perales, Danny, 65
Peterson, Lillian, 92
Petrides, Michael, 237–238, 240, 242–244, 246–247, 248
Petruziello, Frank, 152, 166
Pfizer Pharmaceuticals, 263
Philadelphia, PA, 215
Pinecrest Elementary School, 163–164
Pine Villa Elementary School, 119, 156
police
    at riots, 99, 132
    in schools, 35, 76, 77, 205
    See also security
Pons, Billy, 41, 52
poverty, 5, 19, 35, 59, 103, 190
pregnancy, 2, 81
preschool, 7
principals, 129–130, 172, 180–181, 219–221
    SBM role of, 163, 164, 165, 167, 181
    See also New York City Public School System: building tenure policy
private schools, 8, 9, 37, 38, 155, 182

Professional Development Center, 218
professionalization of teachers and principals, 23, 151, 160, 173, 175, 180
program enhancement, 121, 172
Project Achieve, 253
PS 41, 230–231
PS 121, 263
public schools. *See* Dade County Public School System; New York City Public School System

Queens School of Aviation, 59–60

Ramos, Ernesto, 111–112
Randall, Tony, 263
Rand Corporation, 157, 158
Range, Athalie, 128, 182
rape, 2, 75
reach-out programs, 256
reading programs, 155–156
reform of education, 13, 14–15, 18, 22, 135, 162, 167–168, 187, 191, 206
    funding for, 268
    J.F.'s strategy for, 116, 251, 252–262
Regan, James, 235
Reich, Carol, 263, 265–266
Reich, Joe, 263, 265–266
Reinemund, Steve, 62–63, 65
Reliance Awards, 263
religious education, 4. *See also* parochial schools
Renick, Bob, 171
Renuart, William, 166, 167
retraining programs, 218, 219, 267
Reyes, Luis, 237, 240, 245
Rhodes School, 43
riots, 27, 86, 99, 131, 132. *See also* violence
Rivera, Sonia, 216, 217, 218, 219, 221–222
Riviera Junior High School, 64
Robert E. Lee Junior High School, 116
Rockefeller Foundation, 160
Rohatyn, Felix, 263
Rohatyn, Liz, 263
Rojas, Waldemar (Bill), 216, 217
Ryan, Tom, 214

Saccente, Joe, 213, 214
Sacks, Burt, 17, 213
Sadowsky, Edward, 235
Saez, Carmelo, 203
salaries
    Dade County, 23, 61, 66, 90–91, 92, 104, 145, 160, 177, 186, 187
    differentiated staff basis for, 175
    incentive pay, 64

merit pay, 175
New York City Public School System, 160, 175, 198–199, 225
SBM schools, 155, 175
Salerno, Fred, 241
Salerno Commission, 229–230
Sampson Air Force Base, 45, 47–48
Sanders, Ted, 6
satellite schools, 136, 147
Miami, 16, 17, 160–162, 176
New York, 17, 255
Saturday classes, 155
Schmidt, Benno C., Jr., 9
Schwartz, Gerald, 116
scholarships, 9
School-Based Management (SBM) (general discussion), 14, 135–136, 148, 222
cadre management teams, 149
decentralization strategy, 206
decision-making process, 11, 264
parent involvement in, 149
principals and, 163, 164, 165, 167, 181
principles and forms, 148, 149–150
School-Based Management, Miami, 14, 134, 138, 141, 146, 147, 150–167, 168, 192
budgets, 134, 150–151, 156, 174
cadre management teams, 152, 154, 155, 163, 164–165
decision-making process, 151
dress codes, 38, 155
evaluation of programs, 57–58
funding, 152
number of participating schools, 153–154
principals' roles, 163, 164, 165, 167
salaries, 155, 175
superintendents and, 165–166
teachers union and, 151, 153, 156, 174–175
School-Based Management, New York, 14, 15, 22, 147, 168–169, 192, 196, 230, 260, 265
Board of Education and, 251
budgets, 169
dropout rate and, 253
number of participating schools, 153, 154, 168, 252–253, 255
parental involvement in, 252
start-up, 233
School Mathematics Study Group, Columbia University, 53
Scott Air Force Base, 46, 47
Seavers, Major, 47–48
security, 76, 87, 261, 262
Segarra, Ninfa, 237, 238, 242, 243–244, 245, 248

segregation, 82
sex discrimination, 82
sex education, 230
abstinence/celibacy counseling, 4, 246, 248
AIDS programs, 248
condom availability plan, 4, 15, 242, 244, 245–248, 251
Shadowlawn Elementary School, 143
Shanker, Albert, 135, 158
Sharkey, Phil, 162
Singer, Donald, 221–222, 224
single-sex schools, 80–82, 240–241
Sinkler, Tyrone, 75
Sizer, Ted, 149
Smith, Harry, 185
Sobol, Tom, 18, 124–125, 154
social programs, 3, 4, 133
Sofia University, 47, 48
South Miami Junior High School, 155
special education programs, 8, 217, 235, 254
sports. *See* athletic programs
Stavisky-Goodman statute, 20
Stein, Andrew, 204
substance abuse programs, 3–4, 42
suicide, 2, 57
summer school, 190, 254, 259
Sumpter, Khalil, 75
Superintendent's Awards Dinner, 178
Superintendent's Council, 178
Superintendent's Scholarship Ball, 178
Surdna Foundation, 260

Talese, Gay, 263
taxes, 7, 9–10
Teacher Assessment Development System (TADS), 175
teacher exchange program, 68–71
Teacher Recruitment Incentive Program, 176
Tekerman, Barbara, 143
Tekerman, Joe, 64–65, 172, 173, 196, 213, 222, 231
as J.F.'s executive assistant, 10, 64, 136, 137, 141, 142, 144, 170, 185, 192–194
SBM and, 152, 166
tenure. *See* New York City Public School System: building tenure policy
Textile High School, 43
theme schools, 59–60
Thomas Jefferson High School, 75, 76, 82–83
Thornton, Johnny, 31, 41, 187
Tisch, Laurence, 232

Tokyo University, 47, 57
Tolbert, Ken, 103
Tornillo, Pat, 139, 158, 172, 193
    as executive vice-president of United
        Teachers of Dade County, 134, 135,
        151, 152, 158, 159, 161, 171, 174–
        175
training programs, 176–177
tuition vouchers, 8, 9
Turner, Bill, 90, 171, 194

Ujaama Institute, 82, 240–241
unemployment, 78, 80, 267
unions. *See* Council of Supervisors and
    Administrators (CSA); International
    Union of Operating Engineers
    (I.U.O.E.); United Teachers of Dade
    County (U.T.D.C.)
United Federation of Teachers (UFT), 168,
    188, 230
United Parents Association, 246
United Teachers of Dade County
    (U.T.D.C.), 64
    contracts, 92, 93, 134–135, 145, 194
    J.F.'s activities in, 90, 92–93
    SBM and, 151, 152, 153, 156, 174–175
    strike (1969), 90–91, 108
University of Miami, 97, 176
    J.F. as student, 54–55, 56, 62, 64,
        65

Vasquez, Felix, 204–205
Velella, Guy, 228
Veritas, Sister, 31, 36

violence, 2, 5, 19, 74–75, 77, 126
    inner-city school, 69, 71, 75–77, 80, 103,
        260–261
Visiedo, Octavio, 13, 167
Vlasto, Jim, 172, 196, 213, 233

Wagner, Dan, 93
Wagner, Robert F., Jr., 192, 193, 212, 220,
    234, 235, 237, 251
warranty of students, 21–22, 241, 255
Washington, DC, 215
welfare, 17, 35
Wells, Earl, 128, 129
Welty, Angie, 114–115, 124, 127, 140–
    141, 167, 170, 214
Wesley, Bob, 65, 67–68
Wheatley, Bonnie, 163–164
Wheatley, Russ, 88, 163
Whigham, Ed, 85, 90, 91, 92, 93, 101,
    104, 108, 150
    reforms at Central High School and,
        102
Whitney, Edward, 203
Whittle Communications, 9–10
William Jennings Bryan Elementary
    School, 155
Williams, Prof, 116
Williams, Ted, 49
Willner, Robin, 214
Wolinsky, Annie B., 201, 202, 203, 216
Wright, Linus, 108

Zephirin, Henriot, 205–206
Zerlin, Fred, 59–60

3

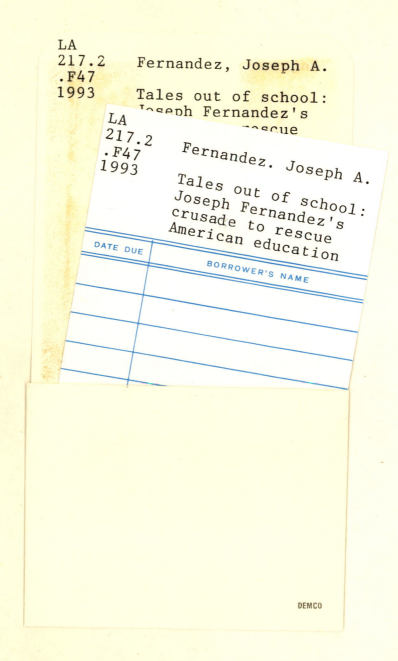